Music from the True Vine

MUSIC
FROM THE
TRUE
VINE

Mike Seeger's Life & Musical Journey

Bill C. Malone

UNIVERSITY OF NORTH CAROLINA PRESS   CHAPEL HILL

Designed by Kimberly Bryant and set in Whitman with Gotham types by
Tseng Information Systems, Inc. Manufactured in the United States of America

The paper in this book meets the guidelines for permanence and durability
of the Committee on Production Guidelines for Book Longevity of the Council on
Library Resources. The University of North Carolina Press has been a member
of the Green Press Initiative since 2003.

Library of Congress Cataloging-in-Publication Data
Malone, Bill C.
Music from the true vine : Mike Seeger's life and musical journey / Bill C. Malone.
p. cm.
Includes bibliographical references and index.
ISBN 978-0-8078-3510-4 (cloth : alk. paper)
1. Seeger, Mike, 1933–2009. 2. Folk musicians — United States — Biography. I. Title.
ML420.S4447M36 2011
782.42162′130092 — dc22
[B]
2011015090

15 14 13 12 11   5 4 3 2 1

I wish to dedicate this book

to my wife, Bobbie, for her critical support and unfailing love,

and to the memory of Willie Benson, my old friend and musical partner

from the Austin days of long ago. How I wish I could pick and

sing with him just one more time!

Contents

Illustrations

Acknowledgments

Although my research debts are indicated in the note on sources and in the chapter notes, I feel the need to acknowledge more clearly those who have made exceptional contributions to my work. Judith Tick not only wrote the marvelous biography of Ruth Crawford Seeger that informed much of my understanding of the Seeger family, but she also made available much of the research that underlay her own writing. Richard Straw of Radford College let me hear and see his interviews of the members of the New Lost City Ramblers (including both Tom Paley and Tracy Schwarz) and of Hazel Dickens and Ralph Rinzler. Michael Scully in Austin, Texas, loaned me cassette copies of discussions that he had with Mike Seeger, John Cohen, and Tracy Schwarz. Kate Hughes Rinzler consented to an interview and sent me a copy of "A Source of Wonder," her unfinished manuscript of the biography of her husband, Ralph. Roland White told me about his days at the Ash Grove in Los Angeles and gave me a book that he and Diane Bouska wrote on Clarence White. Tom Martin-Erickson, who was host of the *Simply Folk* program on Wisconsin Public Radio, recorded and provided a copy of the concert that Mike Seeger did at the Sugar Maple Traditional Music Festival in Madison. Bill Clifton provided much counsel and loaned me some memorable photographs and a disc copy of an interview of Mike that he did for *Folk Voice* in October 1960. Roger Abrahams clarified many of the details concerning his friendship with Ralph Rinzler as well as his recollections of the early stages of the folk music revival.

Several people read one or more chapters of my manuscript: Ray Allen, Ronald D. Cohen, John Cohen, Henry Sapoznik, Bobbie Malone, and Alexia Smith. Ray Allen also sent me a manuscript version of his invaluable book *Gone to the Country: The New Lost City Ramblers and the Folk Music Revival*.

Charmaine Harbort of Madison, Wisconsin, painstakingly transcribed the reminiscences that Mike Seeger recorded on mini discs. Hazel Dickens and Archie Green were good friends and patient counselors over many years of my life. Archie's advice began in about 1965, when he read the manuscript of my first book on country music. My relationship with Hazel was much briefer, but she was a faithful correspondent and confidant and is one of my favorite singers and songwriters. Regrettably, neither she nor Archie lived to see the completion of this book.

Alexia and Mike Seeger, of course, were abundantly generous in their support of this project. They were gracious hosts in their home in Lexington, Virginia, and were constantly on call through e-mail and telephone conversations. I hope that this book lives up to their expectations.

Music from the True Vine

Introduction

"Who is Mike Seeger?"

I was asked that question far too often after mentioning that I was writing his biography. And a second question frequently followed: "Is he related to Pete Seeger?" Trying not to show my irritation, I generally responded with, "Yes, he's his half brother, but he's a much more talented musician than Pete." (That statement shouldn't shock anyone, for Pete himself said that Mike was "the best musician in the family."[1]) But realizing that my answer was unsatisfactory—largely because it was both defensive and incomplete—I then noted Mike's commanding presence in the folk revival of the last fifty-plus years and quickly tried to sum up his remarkable achievements as a collector, documenter, and popularizer of the music of the southern working class.

It is difficult to provide an adequate conversational, sound-bite assessment of Mike, though, when most people are very aware of the almost iconic status that his brother Pete occupies in American popular culture. The name Pete Seeger conjures up images of noble causes and heroic action, of the charismatic singer leading massive and adoring crowds in the performances of "We Shall Overcome" or "Which Side Are You On?" Mike, on the other hand, always went about his work quietly and mostly below the radar of public recognition.

People who have seen *Pete Seeger: The Power of Song*,[2] the video documentary of Pete's life and career, cannot be blamed for not knowing about the fraternal link between Pete and Mike. Mike's name is never mentioned in the documentary, and we are given only a fleeting glimpse of him playing in an old-time string band. But anyone who got caught up in the folk music revival of the late fifties and early sixties will be well aware of Mike Seeger and his music and of his membership in the influential trio called the New Lost City Ramblers. The Ramblers brought something new and vital to the folk music scene and, singly and collectively, changed the ways in which the music was performed and defined. Perhaps most important, they made us aware of the older and too often unsung musicians who had created or preserved the music in the first place. In the renewed flowering of old-time music that has come since the seventies, Mike Seeger remained a powerful and patriarchal presence among the young musicians who kept the flame of tradition alive while using it to fuel new stylistic departures.

It may seem surprising, if not ironic, that I have written a biography of Mike Seeger. My writings for the past forty or so years have been concerned almost solely with mainstream country music, with only an occasional nod at what might be described as the music of the folk revival. I've never had any reservations about Mike's musical brilliance, nor any doubts about the profound impact that he has had on the preservation and popularization of traditional southern rural music. Nevertheless, I was once sure that I didn't like him. He seemed distant at best, or mildly arrogant at worst. Beyond that, I must confess that I was also skeptical of his intent and motivations. I was interested in his music, largely because I thought it was *mine*, but I believed that he and his pals in the New Lost City Ramblers were interlopers: they were dabbling in old-time music because they saw it as exotic or as a welcome relief from the urban culture that seemed stifling to many city youth in the late fifties and early sixties.

In my thinking, Mike and the New Lost City Ramblers were pretenders, New York boys who, never having lived in the South or on a farm, could not accurately sing or play traditional rural music. I, on the other hand, was a southern country boy who had grown up with the music. I was born and reared on a cotton tenant farm in East Texas about twenty miles west of Tyler. The first music that entered my consciousness was the sentimental parlor songs and gospel hymns sung by my Pentecostal mother. That music was soon joined after 1939 by the hillbilly songs that came to us from Tyler, Dallas, Fort Worth, Shreveport, Tulsa, and Nashville through the broadcasts heard over the Philco battery-powered radio that Daddy had bought that year. Roy Acuff, Uncle Dave Macon, Sam and Kirk McGee, and Ernest Tubb were only a few of the entertainers that we heard each Saturday night on the Grand Ole Opry. I was even lucky enough to see Uncle Dave in a tent show in Tyler in about 1949. Other childhood favorites included Cowboy Slim Rinehart and the Carter Family, whom we heard each weekday night over broadcasts from XERF and other stations on the Mexican border.

When I first went to the University of Texas in Austin in 1954—the beginning of what proved to be an extended eight-year stay stretching through my undergraduate and Ph.D. degrees—I was a passionate fan and amateur singer of country music. The music, it seemed to me, was artistically healthy; that is, it was clearly linked to its southern working-class roots. And it was economically sound, for it could be heard everywhere on juke boxes and radio stations. I liked to tell people that the music in the early fifties was both "good" and "country." Elvis Presley, in my opinion, changed all that. He emerged that same year and appeared in concert in Austin the next year. When I saw him at the old coliseum, I was shocked both by his performance and by the adoration given to him by the young people in the audience (they were about the same age that I was, of course, but I was there to see the opening act, Hank Snow). I was upset at what appeared to be a threat to traditional country music. I lacked the perspective to understand that Elvis and the rockabillies constituted a logical outgrowth and extension of traditional southern working-class music, both black and white.

Elvis was the harbinger and principal agent of the sea change that swept over American music in the next several years—a revolution wrought by restless and relatively prosperous youth here and around the world. Country music was dramatically reshaped and, in my opinion, adversely affected by these changes. In the eight years between 1954 and 1962, when I began my first full-time job as a professor of history at Southwest Texas State College (now Texas State University) in San Marcos, country music went through a multitude of changes, at first declining as an economic entity and then having its identity blurred by the efforts of Chet Atkins and other producers to make it palatable to urban middle-class listeners. They removed the steel guitars and fiddles, emphasized singers with smooth voices, added background vocal choruses, and shunned songs with a hard or working-class edge. At times I frankly worried about the music's future and questioned whether it would survive.

But in popular culture, eight years is a long time. By the end of the fifties and the beginning of the sixties, country music began to experience a renewed and vigorous growth. The genre saw the emergence of a new generation of singers and musicians that included Loretta Lynn, Merle Haggard, Buck Owens, the Country Gentlemen, and other artists who were respectful of the music's roots and talented enough to take them to new and exciting dimensions. This phase of neotraditionalism came in the context of a national reawakening of interest in old songs and styles now described as the "urban folk music revival." It was epitomized by the Kingston Trio and other youthful acts who played acoustic string instruments and performed traditional or tradition-based songs for urban audiences who gloried in the novelty of the music or reveled in the opportunity to vicariously "get back to nature" and the simple life. The musicians tapped into a recurring theme in American life: the search for a refreshing rural alternative to the dominant pop sounds of the city. The fascination with folk music in the fifties was one of several revivals that have occurred in the United States, but it was clearly linked to that of the late thirties and early forties.[3] Many of the young musicians who played in New York's Washington Square or in college folk music sessions (often called "hootenannies") had been introduced to folk music through the recordings or concerts of Leadbelly, Woody Guthrie, and Pete Seeger.

I was ambivalent about the folk revival. I liked many of the songs that I heard, and I bought some of the recordings made by the Kingston Trio, Burl Ives, and other urban-based musicians and even sang a few of the songs that they featured. But on the whole, I thought that their styles of presentation were either fraudulent or contrived. They weren't "real" like the music made by my hillbilly heroes. Along with a few of my friends—graduate-school buddies Stan Alexander, Willie Benson, and Ed Mellon—I sang each week at a bar called Threadgill's in north Austin. The place was owned by a genial fellow named Kenneth Threadgill, who tended bar but was always ready to host a jam session and sing and yodel his trademark Jimmie Rodgers's songs. The songs that the rest of us did came from the repertories of people like Roy Acuff, Hank Williams, Ernest Tubb, the Carter Family, and Bill Monroe and his bluegrass brethren.

One day, while browsing in the Austin Public Library, I had also discovered the Harry Smith collection, the famous three-box set of LPs issued in 1952 that was made up of hillbilly, blues, Cajun, gospel, and other roots-style songs taken from 78-rpm records made in the twenties and thirties. I encountered exciting musicians such as Buell Kazee, Frank Hutchison, Dick Justice, Dock Boggs, and Charlie Poole, all of whom were new to me. Best of all, I found songs by artists who had long been cherished by my family: the Carter Family and Uncle Dave Macon. Here they were, in a collection produced by a New York company called Folkways and described as "folk music"! It seemed to me that the collection validated the music of my childhood and, by implication, my culture as well. Songs from the Harry Smith anthology became part of the mix we performed at Threadgill's, and all of it provided context and sources for the research that I had begun to undertake in the early sixties for a doctoral dissertation on the history of country music. In my mind, I was studying a slice of my own family's culture, the music of working-class southerners.

I was well into my research, then, when I first met Mike Seeger and heard and saw the New Lost City Ramblers. Sponsored by the University of Texas Folk Music Club, they gave a concert on March 30, 1962, at the Student Union. During their brief stay in Austin, two of the Ramblers, Tom Paley and John Cohen, went out to Threadgill's and sang a few songs with the rest of us. Although I didn't actually meet them at the time, I did manage a brief conversation with Paley and asked him what he thought about Ernest Tubb. He didn't say much, but he did at least mention that he found Tubb's guitar style to be "sometimes interesting." Looking back, I guess I was testing Tom on the breadth of musical material used by the Ramblers, and without saying so explicitly, I was also chiding them for their preoccupation with the southern mountains and their neglect of other regions of the South and nation that were rich with music.

I voiced the same concern a day or two later when I met Mike Seeger at a party given by Roger Abrahams, the University of Texas folklorist who acted as the faculty sponsor of the folk music club. Already miffed by the omission of Jimmie Rodgers from the Harry Smith collection, as well as from the repertoire of the New Lost City Ramblers, I asked Mike what he thought about another one of my heroes, Hank Williams. His obvious disdain for the question and refusal to say anything of substance about Williams confirmed my belief that he and most of the folklore establishment had romanticized the Appalachian South and ignored the rest of the region. These folkies seemed unwilling to recognize or explore the ways in which tradition had been readapted and reshaped in other less-romanticized parts of the nation.

Now, many years later, I can confess that although I was initially skeptical of Mike Seeger's motivations and sometimes made sport of him and the other New York boys, I borrowed heavily from the music that he made and produced. First of all, he was hardly a New York boy. He was born in New York City but spent most of his life in the Upper South. Despite the criticisms or reservations I may have expressed to my friends about Mike Seeger and the New Lost City Ramblers, I bought all of their LPs, listened to them avidly, read with meticulous attention their discographical notes, and purchased their songbook and memorized its contents. To this day, I can still sing many songs, like "The Baltimore Fire," "Everyday Dirt," "No Depression in Heaven," and "Franklin D. Roosevelt's Back Again," that came directly from the New Lost City Ramblers; and others, such as "All the Good Times Are Past and Gone" and "When First unto This Country," that came from *Mountain Music Bluegrass Style* or other albums that Mike Seeger produced on his own. I learned biographical and musical details about the old-time performers and their music that I had not seen elsewhere. Along with material absorbed from my earlier immersion in the Harry Smith collection, I learned the identities of many hillbilly performers for the first time. While I can now refer to "Franklin D. Roosevelt's Back Again" as a song originally written and performed by Billy Cox, I should admit in all honesty that I learned this fact from the liner notes of a New Lost City Ramblers record. My scholarship as a whole was profoundly influenced and enhanced by their pioneering work.

So the question remains: who is Mike Seeger? He was a brilliant musician who devoted well over fifty years of his life to the preservation and commemoration of the music and culture of white and black southerners—what he affectionately termed the Music from the True Vine. Not nearly as well known as his brother Pete, who wielded his voice and banjo to promote the cause of the voiceless and downtrodden, Mike did something that ultimately may prove to be more important: he searched out and found the very people from whom the folk revival borrowed its songs and made us aware of their identities. Archie Green, his friend and lifelong champion, said that Mike was "potentially more radical" than Pete because he "unconsciously opted for pluralism in his work" and came "closer to the reality of the folk" than did his brother.[4] In the pages that follow, it will become clear that Mike's commitment to old-time music was a lifelong enterprise, and that through his multifaceted contributions as a musician, documentarian, and scholar, he preserved the old music and lent dignity to the people who had originally produced it.

As I got to know Mike Seeger, I learned that he was far from being an interloper. His engagement with old-time music had begun as early as mine. We were both Depression-born children whose interests in the people's music were similarly shaped by that great economic watershed. While I was listening, as a child, to the Carter Family and other musicians on our Philco battery radio, Mike was absorbing the music of similar old-time performers, either from the recordings that his father and his father's assistants had collected for the Library of Congress archives or from the few commercial records that his parents possessed.

This book really began to take shape in the years after 2003, when I became acquainted with Mike Seeger primarily through the intercession of Gary McDowell, who was then the head of the American studies program at the University of London. Mike and I participated in a celebration of the Carter Family at the University of London in 2003, and the following year, I returned to London to give a scholarly paper on country music as a working-class expression during a tribute to the New Lost City Ramblers. Over the years, as I began to do serious research on Mike and his remarkable family, I started questioning my initial assessment of him as being aloof or emotionally distant. Of course, by then I had matured considerably (as had he) and had come to realize that my own shyness and biases had contributed greatly to whatever distance lay between us. The Mike Seeger I came to know was a man of kindness, generosity, and patience—qualities often used to describe him by his contemporaries in the old-time movement and by the young people who acknowledged or sought his guidance as a teacher. In this book, I hope to acknowledge Mike Seeger's contributions and show how he and the folk revival made people everywhere aware of America's great treasury of roots music. Above all, I hope to explain why successive generations of traditional-music fans and musicians have looked to Mike Seeger as their mentor and inspiration, and why he should be revered as a champion and guardian of American roots-music culture.

1

The Seeger Heritage

When Mike Seeger began contemplating a musical career in the early 1950s, he despaired about whether such a goal was possible. He certainly would have been acutely aware of, and probably burdened by, the Seeger name and the prominence that his family enjoyed in the realm of American folk music. His parents, Charles and Ruth, had won fame and distinction in the 1920s among avant-garde classical musicians (an admittedly small group); driven by the radical consciousness of the Depression years, however, they had moved far away from the fascination with musical dissonance that had once enthralled them and had become ardent champions of traditional rural music. Working closely with the equally famous John and Alan Lomax, Charles and Ruth had redefined the whole concept of folk music that had prevailed since the days of Francis James Child and Cecil Sharp in the late nineteenth and early twentieth centuries. To the Seegers and Lomaxes, folk songs were not some rarefied body of artifacts gathering dust in libraries and ancient books but were instead living and changing forms of art that had always embodied the experiences and dreams of working men and women. Thanks in no small part to the pioneering work done by these crusading scholars—and launched largely by revolutions in technology and the science of recording, as well as by the emergence of an infrastructure of promoters, clubs, festivals, and music journals— traditional music in the 1950s was beginning to enjoy the fruits of a burgeoning national exposure.[1]

Mike's older half brother, Pete, had played a crucial role in that cultural flowering with his unique blend of charisma, missionary zeal, and strong musicianship. First as a disciple and colleague of Woody Guthrie and later as a member of the Almanac Singers and the Weavers, Pete had become a universally recognized figure in American popular culture as a folksinging champion of racial justice and human rights.

We cannot know with certainty how this consciousness of family visibility and distinction affected the young Mike Seeger. Mike always expressed his admiration for his brother Pete and was clearly influenced by him. That's where he got his love for the banjo. But he always knew that people were comparing the two of them. And wherever he went, he often got the question, "How's Pete doing?" Archie Green, the prominent folklorist, was not alone in believing that "Mike somehow knew intuitively that he had to make it in a new area or a different area. To achieve himself he had to do something that neither Charles nor Pete could do."[2] He was no less enthralled by traditional music than was his family, and he was, in his own way, just as passionate in his desire to share that regard and affection with the world. But as an independent spirit, Mike found it imperative to carve out a career in music that would set him apart from the exploits and multiple legacies of his illustrious family. In ways that he could not have then realized, Mike absorbed the ideals of his family—their passion for music and their desire to introduce it to a larger public. While he ignored the classical tradition of his parents and the musical theory that his mother tried to introduce to him, he did not reject the sense of mission and the political consciousness that they bequeathed to him. He instead turned them in different and more sublimated directions.

The first American Seeger, Karl Ludwig, brought an ardent love for this country and an identification with its professed goals when he came to the United States in 1787 from what is now Germany. Karl Ludwig had studied to be a veterinarian at the Karlschule of the Duke of Wurtemburg in Stuttgart, but he became obsessed with America after reading a copy of the U.S. Constitution that had been peddled on the streets. Like many immigrants, he was inspired by "the idea of America," and he resolved to make his home in this faraway western land that offered freedom to all human beings. Karl sailed first to Charleston, South Carolina. Although his feelings have not been recorded, he could not have been sympathetic to the institution of slavery that he found in that city. At any rate, he returned to Europe for a few years; in the early 1800s, he again sailed to the United States, this time settling down in the more compatible area of Northampton, Massachusetts. Although he remained a committed Jeffersonian Democrat, his second marriage to Sally Parsons brought him into the ranks of the New England aristocracy. Mike was heir on both sides of his family to a long line of teachers, preachers, physicians, and abolitionists. The Seegers, then, were American to the core and could boast of their profound commitment and service to the nation. According to Charles Seeger's principal biographer, Ann Pescatello, "Charles recognized a certain superiority in the Seeger view of the world" and was conscious of the mixture of familial and Harvard snobbishness that sometimes surfaced in his own attitudes. Charles grew up aware that his family believed that there were three kinds of people: Seegers, friends of the Seegers, and people who were not either of these.[3]

Charles Louis Seeger was born in Mexico City on December 14, 1886, as one of three children (two boys and a girl) born to still another Charles Louis Seeger and his wife, Elsie Adams Seeger. The elder Charles Louis was a journalist and importer/exporter from Springfield, Massachusetts, who had been lured to Mexico by President Porfirio Diaz, who was eager to attract American business and capital. Mike's grandmother, Elsie Adams, was a New England blueblood, a strait-laced, rigid woman with trivial tastes. Peggy Seeger recalls that Elsie read only Victorian romance novels and could recite them almost word for word. In the years between the birth of Mike's father and 1913, the family acquired sufficient wealth to move repeatedly between New York and Mexico, with the elder Charles working first for the *Mexican Financier* and then as an importer and exporter of products that included the first automobiles brought into Mexico. The family spent many of these years in Manhattan and Staten Island but did not resume permanent residence in the United States until the Mexican Revolution of 1910 ended their Latin dreams. After a two-year stay in Europe, where Charles worked as a vice president for the United States Rubber Company, the family retired to a home called Fairlea in Patterson, New York. The younger Charles, however, who had spent many of his boyhood summers in Mexico, never lost his affection for Mexican culture. Eventually, he turned this interest into a professional relationship through his work in the 1940s at the music division of the Pan-American Union, an organization that worked for harmonious and mutually beneficial relations between the United States and Latin American nations.

Although Charles's father was a successful businessman, he was passionately devoted to the arts — or what his grandson Pete later described as "Culture" with a capital C. "Folk" music, that which had not been written down and transmitted in the proper cultivated fashion, held no interest for him. His love of music, which he demonstrated as an amateur organist and pianist, and his patronage of all forms of art certainly influenced his children. His only daughter, Elizabeth (Elsie), became an educator and writer and was perhaps best known as a student and patron of Indian and Chinese history and art. She was also remembered as a great storyteller. She taught from 1922 to 1957 at the Dalton School in New York City and, dissatisfied with the world history texts available to children, wrote a Newbery Award–winning book titled *The History of China*.[4] Charles's youngest son, Alan, was a minor poet who was best known for the World War I poem that prophesied his death. Alan had a romantic daredevil streak, and he liked to live life on the edge. He was thoroughly imbued with the Teddy Roosevelt sense of honor and obsession with "manly" principles. Dismayed at his country's tardiness in entering the war against Germany, Alan joined the French Foreign Legion, dying in action during World War I on July 4, 1916, at Belloy-en-Santerre in France. His poem "I Have a Rendezvous with Death" defined his legacy.[5]

In supreme ironic contrast, Alan's brother Charles was an outspoken critic of the war. Charles's public opposition to American involvement in the conflict drew the censure of administrators at the University of California, Berkeley, where he served as chair of the Department of Music, and in 1918 he was forced out of his job. Charles had initially set out on a career path that was expected of him. He went to Harvard, where he graduated magna cum laude in music in 1908. Charles eschewed, though, the business and professional interests of his forebears and instead pursued a career in music as a performer, composer, and theoretician. Pescatello describes this decision as a youthful act of rebellion that arose from "a dichotomy in his personality." That is, Charles remained loyal to the "structure and ideals" of his family but nevertheless resisted doing what was expected,[6] an independence that years later surfaced in the behavior of his son Mike. From 1910 to 1911, Charles worked in Europe as a guest conductor with the Cologne Opera. On December 22, 1911, he married Constance de Clyver Edson, a violinist, who bore him three sons: John, Charles, and Peter.

From 1912 to 1918, Charles taught at Berkeley while also composing and presenting concerts as a pianist (he and Constance made at least one tour during this period, playing piano and violin). When Charles first arrived at Berkeley, music classes were held in the YMCA, the foyer of the Hearst Mining Building, and other assorted sites, and the entire department was treated largely as a service auxiliary for agriculture, mining, industry, and forestry students. Becoming its second head in 1916, Charles made the music department a first-rate and independent entity with a four-year curriculum and its own library, and he introduced America's first course in musicology (the scientific and systematic study of music). Recognizing the need for a contextual understanding of music and its relationship to society, Charles sat in on sociology, history, anthropology, political theory, and philosophy courses at Berkeley. He also ventured beyond the areas conventionally explored by music departments of his time. He made some tentative explorations into what became known as ethnomusicology and heard his first field recordings in 1916, items selected from the 1,200 wax cylinders composed of folklore from California Indians and housed in Berkeley's anthropology department. He was already exhibiting a catholicity of taste that presaged his future interest in folk music. In his first music history class, for example, he included a performance of folk songs in seventeen languages and rejected the idea that classical music, which had allegedly evolved from lower and more "primitive" forms, was the only music worthy of serious study.[7]

The famous "Seeger radicalism" also began to manifest itself during Charles's stay at Berkeley. He exhibited an interest in socialism, expressed sympathy for the militant labor union the Industrial Workers of the World, and became preoccupied with the mistreatment suffered by migrant workers in California. Accompanying the Berkeley economist Carlton Parker to the hop fields and fruit ranches of Northern California, Seeger often saw young children in the fields doing the same brutal work that their parents were doing. It was his resistance to American involvement in the Great War, however, that provoked the wrath of the administration at Berkeley. Inspired in large part by the death of his brother Alan in 1916, Charles spoke out openly in the Berkeley area against the war. Encountering hostility toward his position—particularly from the ardently anti-German Englishman Charles Gayley, dean of faculties—Charles decided to give up his post at the university. It is unclear whether the university formally told Charles not to return or whether the decision was totally his own. On its website, the Berkeley music department now states merely that Seeger took a sabbatical and never returned.[8] Charles's son Pete suggests that his father was either fired or was asked to take a sabbatical and then told not to come back. At any rate, the incident indicates that Mike, who registered as a conscientious objector during the Korean War, shared his father's commitment to pacifism.[9]

While Charles's idealism was praiseworthy, his wife and two very small children still had to eat. Consequently, on their way back east in 1918, Charles and Constance periodically gave concerts on organ and violin, respectively. A third son, Peter, was born in New York City in 1919, and the young family moved to Fairlea, the family farm in Patterson. Charles's concert dreams grew increasingly expansive. He constructed a large canvas-topped trailer with a built-in portable stage, and together the family set out to dispense classical music at stops along the Atlantic Seaboard. Camping in the woods with three small children, cooking over a campfire, and boiling the family's clothes in a wash pot must have been daunting experiences for Constance, who was city born and aesthetically oriented. Pete Seeger, only a baby at the time, later spoke about the experience, saying: "My poor mother with her violinist fingers, having to wash diapers in an iron kettle night after night. It didn't work." Charles's latent folk music consciousness was awakened, however, sometime in 1921 near Pinehurst, North Carolina, when a local fiddler and pianist, after hearing a couple of sonatas by the Seegers, treated them to a spirited rendition of some of their favorite country songs. Charles finally realized, he told Pete, that "these people had a lot of good music of their own." Charles's grand scheme of taking classical music to the masses ran aground in Richmond, Virginia, where the cumbersome and heavy trailer collapsed because of its fragile rubber wheels.[10] He and Constance soon found refuge in academia. In August 1921 Frank Damrosch, brother of the famous symphony conductor Walter Damrosch, asked Charles and Constance to join the faculty of the Institute of Musical Arts (now the Juilliard School of Music) in New York. Throughout the 1920s, they lived in a variety of apartments in New York City, but they spent most of their summers in Patterson with Charles's parents. In the meantime, their marriage disintegrated, with Constance walking out temporarily in 1927 and permanently in 1929.

By the time Charles began his stay at the Institute of Musical Arts, composition and musical theory, not performance, had become his chief preoccupations. As a composer, Charles was already pushing the boundaries of melody and harmony and experimenting with what he called "dissonant counterpoint." He sought to create a new kind of music by essentially substituting dissonant intervals where consonance had once prevailed. (William R. Ferris describes the practice as "a concept that describes how musical lines that are very different from each other sound harmonious when they are played together" and argues that it was actually not new in Charles Seeger's time.[11]) Charles was at the forefront of a small contingent of composers, such as Henry Cowell (who had been his star pupil at Berkeley) and Ruth Crawford, who strived to break free from European constraints and conventions and create a truly indigenous American musical art.[12] In both his high art and folk phases, Charles was fired by the idea of Americanism—declaring American uniqueness and accomplishment—and by radical sympathies.

Charles Seeger's most famous disciple, Ruth Crawford, became his second wife. She grew up in a family that was no less American than the Seegers but lacked their "first family" pedigree. The Crawfords were respectable and sturdy midwesterners who valued hard work, music, and culture. Ruth was born in East Liverpool, Ohio, on July 3, 1901.[13] Her father, Clark Crawford, was a Methodist minister who, under the rules of that church, moved quite often, taking his family to such cities as Akron, Ohio; St. Louis; and Muncie, Indiana. He died in 1914 while they were living in Jacksonville, Florida. Ruth's mother, Clara, loved music and was determined that her daughter receive a good musical education.

Ruth had been studying piano since the age of eleven, and in 1921 she enrolled at the American Conservatory of Music in Chicago with the intention of continuing her piano studies (she also taught there and at Elmhurst College). She soon became consumed with composition, working first with Adolph Weidig and then with Djane Lavoie Herz, who in turn introduced her to Henry Cowell. Ruth was already experimenting with radical dissonance, or what she liked to describe as "modern music." By 1924 she was deep into experimentation with the bold innovations made by Alexander Scriabin, Edgard Varese, Dane Rudhyar, and Carl Ruggles. Between 1924, when she earned her BA, and 1929, she composed about half of her total classical music output. By the time she left Chicago in 1929, Ruth had already drawn the chief outlines of her musical career. Her interests and her work had carried her into the rarified dimensions of avant-garde classical music, including the mystical theorizing espoused by Scriabin.

But the seeds of Ruth's later immersion in folk music were also planted during these years. Through her friend Alfred J. Frankenstein, she met Carl Sandburg and virtually became a member of the great iconic poet's family. Ruth taught piano to Sandburg's two children, and she sometimes attended informal folk music sessions at his home in Elmhurst, where she listened to the poet sing and strum his guitar and talk about the ballads he had collected. Along with fifteen other composers, she contributed a few piano accompaniments for Sandburg's famous book *The American Songbag* (1927),[14] including "Those Gambler's Blues," "Lonesome Road," "There Was an Old Soldier," and "Ten Thousand Miles from Home." Although her arrangements were overly burdened with "brooding Romantic harmonies"[15] that carried the marks of her classical training, the songs were Ruth's first introductions to indigenous American folk music. When she ventured once again into this domain ten years later as a transcriber for John and Alan Lomax's *Our Singing Country*, she was prepared to sacrifice romance for "authenticity."

In the summer of 1929, Ruth studied at the MacDowell Colony in Peterborough, New Hampshire, a secluded retreat designed for artists, writers, and composers. Later that year, at the urging of Henry Cowell, she moved to New York to study with Charles Seeger. This first encounter with her future husband was not entirely auspicious. Charles, for his part, was uncertain that women could be successful composers and thought that artistic involvement with them was possibly a waste of time. Ruth remembered him as "tall, aristocratic, ultra-refined, and a bit cold." But when she witnessed the passion that he exhibited for music, she revised her opinion. Confiding in her diary sometime in the winter of 1930, she wrote: "[A]nyone who can be as excited as Charlie was last week over a counterpoint lesson . . . anyone who can be so emotionally upset that he can't eat and his hands are trembling and his whole evening is a flare of sparks, they call him cold?"[16] In any event, she was determined to put to rest any reservations that he might have about her abilities. Blossoming under his tutelage, she soon could declare, "I feel now a confidence which I never felt before, that music could still continue in the midst of life."[17] Ruth matured rapidly as a composer of dissonant pieces, and the musical bond forged with Charles quickly evolved into an ardent friendship that seamlessly ripened into love. She could not have known at that stage of her life that, while music would indeed continue to be her life's work, it would be expressed in forms far removed from classical composition.

In 1930 Ruth became the first woman to receive a Guggenheim Fellowship in musical composition. On an automobile trip to Quebec, from whence Ruth was to embark on her Atlantic journey to Europe, Charles openly declared his love for her. The family believes that the moment occurred while the two were walking across a bridge in Arlington, Vermont, in sight of composer Carl Ruggles's home.[18] Studying in Paris and Berlin, Ruth made uncompromising use of dissonance and contrapuntal ostinati in her compositions, which included the Diaphonic Suites 1–4 and Three Chants for Women's Chorus. Her request for a Guggenheim musical extension, however, was rejected in November 1931. Back in New York, she tearfully expressed her despondency to Charles. He consoled her and told her not to worry; they would marry and have beautiful children together. Charles had been estranged from Constance since at least 1927, and he and Ruth had often traveled together and had spent some time at his parents' house in Patterson. After she returned from Europe, Ruth moved into Charles's small apartment at 204 West 13th Street in Greenwich Village.

Charles and Ruth lived together for several months while waiting for his divorce from Constance to become final. After spending the obligatory six weeks of residence in Winnemucca, Nevada, they were married there on October 3, 1932. Ruth's active period as a composer (1926–32) came to an end with the marriage, apparently with the consent of both parties. While Charles believed in strong women, he thought that they should play a traditional role within a family and balance their extracurricular activities accordingly. Ruth certainly had occasional self-doubts about the life she had chosen,[19] but on the whole she seems not to have overtly questioned or challenged her newly assumed role. Except for a few scattered creations, such as "Risselty Rosselty" in 1939, she did not compose seriously again until 1952, the year before she died. Ruth did have, however, the "beautiful children" that Charles had promised. Michael arrived on August 15, 1933; Margaret (Peggy) on June 17, 1935; Barbara on May 4, 1937; and Penelope (Penny) on December 24, 1943. In addition to motherhood, Ruth took on new professional tasks as a piano teacher, an arranger/transcriber of folk songs, and a compiler of folk songbooks for children—endeavors that were deeply allied with the work of her husband and consonant with his ideas of marital roles. These decisions clearly came at great cost to Ruth's art, a sacrifice that her children now regretfully realize: Peggy and Barbara speak with deep sadness about not having known about their mother's early accomplishments as a composer until her death in 1953.

The politics of the Seegers and the nation moved left during the 1930s. Among intellectuals and artists, hard times inspired a rediscovery of "the people" and of grassroots America. In every realm of the era's artistic expression—from the visual arts to music—one finds a preoccupation with working people and rural roots, a presumption that they embodied the real soul of America. The definition and perception of folk music itself was changing under the impact of economic crisis, moving away from the work of Francis James Child—the late nineteenth-century Harvard scholar whose magisterial collection of English and Scottish folk songs had stressed their literary qualities and origins[20]—and toward the idea of the folk song as an emotional resource through which working people defined themselves and voiced their most vital concerns.

As the Seegers moved to the left, they also reassessed their musical priorities. Ideology played a role in redirecting their art, but so did their personal economic distress—the difficulty of surviving with a growing family. Charles lost his job at Juilliard in 1932, primarily, it seems, because the school's famous director, Walter Damrosch, was skeptical of Charles's growing political involvement. Peggy Seeger believes, too, that Constance used her influence to prevent Charles's retention at the school. Although Charles continued to teach for a short time at the New School for Social Research in New York City, the period was one of genteel poverty for the Seegers, and they lived in a series of residences—first at Charles's small apartment on 13th Street in Greenwich Village and later at the home of Charles's parents in Patterson. He sometimes did farm work during these bleak years to raise a little extra money, and Ruth often gave piano lessons. On occasion, though, Charles actually had to borrow money from his older sons. Fortunately for his family, Charles was not solely an ethereal musician; he was also able to avoid or reduce most household expenses because he possessed excellent woodworking and mechanical skills.

Politically and musically, Charles and Ruth moved toward the conviction that theories of classical dissonance were too rarified for a society whose workers were struggling for survival. They began to grope toward a musical perspective that would accommodate and promote social justice for working people. In the winter of 1931–32, largely through the suggestion of Henry Cowell, Ruth and Charles became active members of the Composers' Collective, an offshoot of the Pierre DeGeyter Club (which, in turn, was a wing of the Workers Music League). In 1871 DeGeyter had written the music for "The Internationale," first used by a communard in Paris. Inspired in part by the Russian communist experience but also by the philosophy of Hanns Eisler (the German Marxist composer who believed that music should be put to the service of radical social change), the members of the Composers' Collective set out to introduce classical music to the workers and to write pieces that would reflect proletarian interests. Meeting in various lofts and apartments around the city, composers like Seeger, Cowell, Elie Siegmeister, Mark Blitzstein, and Norman Cazden sat in a semicircle around a piano and tried out their socially conscious songs on each other.[21] Busy with the children, Ruth participated infrequently in the Collective's meetings, but she did venture into the realm of political music with "Sacco, Vanzetti" and "Chinaman, Laundryman," musical settings for two poems written earlier by Chinese author H. T. Tsiang. In the meantime, Charles wrote music columns for the communist newspaper the *Daily Worker* under the name Carl Sands. His son Pete, who was making an even more decisive turn toward the left, now speaks of the efforts of the Composers' Collective as "ludicrous." Charles himself later declared that "everything we composed was forward-looking, progressive as hell, but completely unconnected with life, just as we were in the Collective."[22] Folk music scholar Benjamin Filene concludes that the Collective made no effort to assess popular taste but instead acted under the presumption that "music for a revolution should be musically revolutionary."[23] Their songs consequently were designed to challenge listeners' rhythmic and harmonic expectations. Most workers, though, clearly were not interested in classical music, particularly the avant-garde, modernist pieces composed and presented by the Collective.

The Collective viewed both folk and popular music of the Tin Pan Alley variety with equal disdain. The latter, they believed, was clearly a product of capitalist market forces. Charles and Ruth and other socially conscious musicians, on the other hand, soon moved toward an embrace of folk music. While the Seegers generally held a very catholic view of folk music, they definitely equated such music with rural life and the South, two entities that heretofore had been deemed hopelessly reactionary by left-wing ideologues. Through the Popular Front after 1935, when communists began trying to "Americanize" their movement through alliances with native reform elements, the American Left in general moved toward an embrace of vernacular music as the voice of common people.

It should be made clear, however, that the infatuation with folk music during the Depression years did not belong solely to communists and other radicals. The noncommunist Left exhibited a similar interest. Franklin and Eleanor Roosevelt even began to patronize folk music. Eleanor made a well-publicized trip in 1933 to the White Top Mountain Folk Festival in Virginia. President Roosevelt was photographed with a hillbilly string band at Warm Springs, Georgia, and after 1934 he and Eleanor sponsored a series of concerts by such musicians at the White House. By that time, Charles Seeger had completed his conversion to folk music, and by the end of the decade, he was participating in the planning of musical events for the Roosevelt administration. One such concert, held at the White House on June 8, 1939, featured the Coon Creek Girls and Bascom Lamar Lunsford's square dance troupe and was presented in honor of the visiting King and Queen of England.[24]

Given the context of hard times, avant-garde music seemed selfish and insular. In the winter of 1930–31, the artist Thomas Hart Benton introduced Ruth and Charles to a dimension of folk music usually ignored by the classically trained elite: commercial hillbilly music. Benton, who played the harmonica, and a few of his art students (including the revolutionary painter Jackson Pollock, who labored away on the Jew's harp) organized a string band, the Harmonica Rascals, that sometimes played at Saturday night gatherings in Benton's apartment and at exhibitions in Greenwich Village. One night in January 1931, at the dedication of Benton's *America Today* murals at the New School for Social Research, Charles joined them, playing the guitar (he had learned to play the instrument at Harvard as part of a mandolin-banjo-guitar club). He later remembered that the group played such songs as "Cindy," "Ida Red," and "My Horses Ain't Hungry." Pete Seeger also recalled that his introduction to the great ballad "John Henry" came when Benton played the song on his harmonica at one of these parties.[25] Benton also introduced Charles and Ruth to his large hillbilly record collection and expressed surprise that they were unaware of such music. This collection included an artist and a recording that were destined to play crucial roles in Mike Seeger's awakening musical consciousness: Dock Boggs and his starkly gripping version of the mountain murder ballad "Pretty Polly."[26]

At about the same time, the Seegers became aware of two seminal books of folklore scholarship that contributed vitally to their absorption in southern rural music: John and Alan Lomax's *American Ballads and Folk Songs* and George Pullen Jackson's *White Spirituals in the Southern Uplands.*[27] Charles and Ruth, of course, were destined to have an ongoing working relationship with the Lomaxes. Jackson's book, on the other hand, introduced them to austere southern shape-note hymns and suggested an interrelationship between rural music and medieval music forms. Most significant, the Seegers learned that these hymns and the methods by which they were taught and preserved were still very much alive in the rural South.

The other event that signaled and reaffirmed Charles's conversion to rural folk music was the arrival in New York in 1931 of the Kentucky ballad singer Aunt Molly Jackson. The former wife of a Kentucky coal miner and radical union activist and the half sister of two now-famous ballad singers, Jim Garland and Sarah Ogan, Aunt Molly came to New York after being blacklisted in Kentucky because of her union militance and radical song-writing. Alan Lomax took Aunt Molly to a meeting of the Composers' Collective. They were unimpressed by her "outmoded" style,[28] but Charles became a permanent convert to "traditional" music and, along with New York University professor Mary Elizabeth Barnicle, a strong promoter of Aunt Molly's music.[29] He gave up on the Collective, abandoned the idea that classical composers could write music *for* the workers, and became increasingly absorbed in the collecting of music made and preserved *by* the rural folk. He later confided to one of his interviewers that "the music must serve. You must use the music that the people have in them already."[30]

In November 1935, with his family practically destitute, Charles became part of the huge community of intellectuals converging on the nation's capitol during the Depression years. This became, as one historian has noted, the Seegers' path to the discovery of "unmusical America."[31] The artist Charles Pollock (student of Thomas Hart Benton and brother of Jackson) had recommended Charles for a position in the newly created Resettlement Administration (RA), established by executive order in April 1935.[32] Soon after Charles accepted the position, he, Ruth, Mike, Peggy, and Margaret Valiant (one of Ruth's musician friends, whom she had met on her return trip from Europe) drove to Washington, D.C., where Charles began work as a technical adviser in the Special Skills Division of the RA. Eventually replaced by the Farm Security Administration, the RA was burdened with the responsibility for a variety of programs, all designed to provide immediate relief for struggling farmers and to relocate many of them (along with unemployed city workers) to new and more productive agricultural communities. Historian Paul Conkin describes the RA as "a repository for a multitude of New Deal programs" and notes that some of its resettlement projects had begun earlier under the auspices of the Federal Emergency Relief Administration and other government agencies.[33]

The RA can be viewed as an example of the "Back to the Land" impulse of the 1930s and an expression of the belief that a new and better America could be built through a revitalization of its rural base. In hindsight, however, the RA's goals seem daunting, if not impossible. Conservative legislators saw the agency's objectives as, at best, temporary attempts to alleviate distress or, at worst, communist-style threats to replace private property and individual freedom with government-planned and -directed communities. The RA also encountered much difficulty in its efforts to bring widely scattered and intensely individualistic farmers together from diverse areas while at the same time preserving a sense of unity and common purpose among them.

By design, the Special Skills Division of the organization strived to promote a consciousness of community that the RA hoped would prevail among the resettled farmers. Music, folklore, plays, handicrafts, art, and similar enterprises were seen as resources that might "defuse social tension" and promote harmonious relationships and a feeling of common identity within the government-created communities.[34] Blessed with very talented and musically trained assistants, such as Herbert Haufrecht, Margaret Valiant, and Sidney Robertson (who married Henry Cowell in 1941), Charles Seeger set out to collect music that could be used in the resettlement communities.[35] While such music would serve the immediate purposes of bolstering the morale of farmers and introducing RA workers to the true idiom of the people, its presence on sound recordings would also ensure its preservation for posterity. Resettlement workers were instructed to look for music that would be true to the people's interests and reflect their heritage—an idea far removed from the working principles of the Composers' Collective. Charles told his assistants to collect everything that the people possessed, an implicit recognition that the "folk" and their preferences were as important as the music they liked. He explicitly wanted the researchers to avoid a narrow approach that reflected their own aesthetic or ideological interests to the detriment of those of the people. Charles also proposed to send an undetermined number of musicians to most of the resettlement communities to serve as folk music facilitators, unearthing old-time songs that the residents knew, writing new songs based on traditional materials, and encouraging people to sing songs from their folk traditions instead of commercial music (although it was never clear how one was supposed to tell the difference between the two—or if there even was a difference—since radios had been available in rural America for at least fifteen years and Victrolas or other recording machines for even longer).[36]

The history of the Resettlement Administration's experience with music has not been fully documented. We know that both Margaret Valiant and Sidney Robertson tried hard to understand the social contexts of the music they collected and to share the lives of the poor farmers and workers with whom they dealt.[37] But we do not know how the other professional musicians in the project related to the people from whom they collected songs, nor how they responded to styles of music that were dramatically different from those they had studied in their colleges and conservatories. Charles Seeger left a rather bleak assessment many years later when he spoke of a 90 percent failure among the RA musicians and described them as "politically and culturally naïve" people who were unable to slough off their own musical prejudices.[38] We similarly cannot be certain of how the residents of the resettlement communities responded to the cultural intervention of the government workers. On balance, they seemed to have welcomed government displays of social service but sometimes felt that an emphasis on music was a misplaced priority.[39]

The music collected under the auspices of the Resettlement Administration, however, has become part of the national inheritance. Profiting from the introduction in the early 1930s of portable electric recording machines (earlier field recordings had been made on wax-cylinder phonographs), RA workers compiled about 159 disc recordings of various kinds of ethnic music, mostly on a Presto sound recorder that made channels in aluminum discs. Although this device was described as "portable," it was actually quite heavy and cumbersome, and in backwoods areas where electricity was unavailable, it required the use of a generator or car battery for power.[40] Implanted on aluminum discs coated with an acetate lacquer, songs could be recorded immediately and then played back to informants. The records were designed for immediate use by the RA but were eventually deposited in the Library of Congress Archive of American Folk Song, along with the illustrated song sheets[41] that had been used in community sing-alongs and other RA music programs.

Without realizing it, Seeger and his RA colleagues were helping to build the sound track for the emerging folk music revival. During the next thirty-plus years, urban singers of folk songs dipped repeatedly into the enormous song bag of traditional material that had been collected by government workers or by other collectors who had become active during the Depression years. Evidence of this music's movement into urban popular culture via radio broadcasts and recordings had become clear by the beginning of the 1940s. For example, one of Charles's researchers in South Carolina collected a version of the venerable white spiritual "The Wayfaring Stranger," which was then printed on an RA song sheet. Alan Lomax became aware of the song and taught it to one of his favorite ballad singers, Burl Ives. Ives's performances of the song on his CBS radio show became so widely popular that he became known as the Wayfaring Stranger.[42]

While Charles exhibited impressive liberality as a folk song collector and scholar, he nevertheless remained wary of some of the ways in which folk material was disseminated. He realized that folk songs were dynamic and ever changing, but he was suspicious of commercial utilization of such music. Charles was hostile to the radio, for example, and would not permit one into his home during Mike's childhood — although many of the songs collected by RA and Library of Congress researchers had first been heard, or had won renewed circulation, on radio broadcasts or commercial recordings. With a perspective somewhat similar to that held by Mike in later years, Charles felt that he was rescuing those folk songs that had somehow survived the commercial revolution of the 1920s and 1930s. He attended folk festivals, and while he was generally receptive to the music that he heard at Bascom Lamar Lunsford's Mountain Dance and Folk Festival in Asheville, North Carolina (where Pete in 1935 heard Aunt Samantha Bumgarner and fell in love with the five-string banjo), he remained skeptical of the motives that often underlay the promotion and preservation of such affairs. The chief chronicler of Virginia's White Top Mountain Festival, David Whisnant, notes that Seeger spoke of "sinister" and "reactionary" ideas that undergirded that festival. Presumably, he was offended by the "Anglo Saxon" racist views of John Powell, the classically trained codirector of the festival. Seeger rejected the snobbery and cultural interventionism that he found at White Top in 1936, calling it a "feast of paradox" where the "holy folk" were idealized and submitted to controls and rules that kept them from performing the music they may have preferred.[43]

Charles certainly did not romanticize the folk, and, as indicated by the advice given to his assistants that they record "everything" that the people possessed, he strived to present a complete picture of folk song performance and preference in America. Radio stations and commercial recording companies had "launched folk music into the public sector" back in the early 1920s, but such music did not assume "a position in the nation's official culture" until Seeger, the Lomaxes, Ben Botkin (of the Federal Writers' Project), and other "New Deal folklorists" attached to it the stamp of academic and government approval.[44] Through their lead, folklorists had taken a bold step beyond the realm once defined and occupied by Francis James Child and Cecil Sharp. Significantly, they were no longer preserving the remnants of a dying or primitive culture; they were instead document-ing cultures in transition.

It is fortunate that much of the RA's folk song labors were preserved on recordings and song sheets, because the organization itself was short-lived. It was a casualty of the recession of 1937, when congressional conservatives seized the opportunity to withhold appropriations from an agency that they viewed as radical. The Department of Agriculture assumed the RA's functions through the new Farm Security Administration. Faced with a reduced staff and a diminished budget, Charles left the Special Skills Division and went to work as deputy director for the Federal Music Project of the Works Progress Administration. He hoped not only to collect and preserve folk songs but also to encourage their performance. He never intended to lock these songs up in an archive where they could never again be used. Between 1935 and 1941, when he left the Federal Music Project, Charles and his assistants added over 1,000 discs to the Library of Congress. They also contributed to the three-volume *Check-List of Recorded Songs in the English Language* for the Archive of American Folk Song.[45]

In the meantime, Ruth had also made her own enormous contributions to the documentation and appreciation of American folk music. She had accompanied Charles on a few occasions to resettlement communities, but her most valuable contributions came as a transcriber of folk songs. In 1937 she began transcribing tunes for John and Alan Lomax's influential song collections. Her first collaboration with them came through the preparation of *Our Singing Country*, which was published in November 1941, over four years from its inception. Ruth transcribed about 300 songs, from which the final 190 were selected. Charles may not have always brought his work home with him, but the Seeger kids were acutely aware of Ruth's work as she repeatedly played the Lomax disc recordings. Listening to the music through earphones, she slowed the recordings down, moved the needle back repeatedly and listened again and again to phrases and portions of phrases, striving faithfully to transcribe every nuance of the song's style.[46]

This classically trained musician took traditional rural music seriously, and in striving to show how rural musicians moved from note to note, she revealed the complexities that drove the performances of seemingly simple songs. Bess Lomax Hawes, the daughter of John Lomax who often acted as a courier between her father and Ruth, later noted that Ruth tackled a fiddle tune "with the same precision, determination, and awe that she would have devoted to a brilliantly realized cadenza from a Mozart violin concerto."[47] Indeed, Ruth felt so strongly about these matters that she wrote a very long essay on folk style designed as a preface for *Our Singing Country*. Already frustrated by what they considered to be the interminable nature of Ruth's labors, the Lomaxes and the Macmillan publishing company rejected the essay because of its length, but she managed to make her most salient points in a greatly abbreviated version.[48] Ruth argued in her preface that "no one who has studied these or similar recordings can deny that the song and its singing are indissolubly connected—that the character of a song depends to a great extent on the *manner* of *its singing*."[49] Her emphasis on performance and the style in which a song or tune was presented, as well as her painstaking efforts to document this experience, were insights that strongly colored the work of her talented son Mike.[50]

Together and separately, then, Charles and Ruth made immense contributions to the preservation, documentation, and public awareness of American folk music. Along with the Lomaxes, they compiled the repertory that fueled the singing of at least a couple of generations of urban folk revival musicians. Charles and Ruth recognized the humanity that lay behind the songs, and they felt a sense of mission to present this music to the American public. It is fitting that the greatest influence exerted by these songs may have been on the little boy who sat quietly on the living room floor of the Seeger home, replicating in many ways his mother's passion for precision by listening to these recordings again and again on the variable speed recorder that she used in her sound transcriptions.

2

Folk Music and Politics

Growing up in the Seeger Household

Although Mike Seeger spent most of his youth and early adulthood in the Washington, D.C., area, he lived his first thirty months in New York. He was born in the Sloane Hospital for Women in New York City and, except for brief interludes at Fairlea, his paternal grandparents' home in Patterson (Putnam County), lived the rest of his New York years at 111 East 87th Street in Manhattan. Mike understandably had few memories of these early years, but he gained some glimpses in stories, family recollections, and photographs (including one of the famous four-wheel trailer that Charles and Constance had used in 1921 during their abortive touring concert season). After 1921 the trailer was seldom used, except for occasional camping excursions and when Charles worked on Mr. Hammell's blueberry farm during the hard times of the early 1930s. Charles, Ruth, and Mike apparently lived in the trailer briefly during the summer of 1933.[1]

During his stays at Fairlea in the summers of 1933 through 1935, Mike lived with his parents in an apartment in his grandfather's spacious remodeled barn. Divided by a garage, the barn had been outfitted with a comfortable apartment for Charles's sister, Aunt Elsie, and a variety of other spaces used as a kitchen, a workroom, a carpentry shop, and sleeping accommodations.[2] These early New York years were times of severe privation for the Seeger family. Judith Tick refers to this period as "the nadir of their poverty." Charles had lost his job at Juilliard because of his former wife's resistance, and Ruth was restricted to home with two small babies. Ruth joined her husband at the farm in August, and the small but growing family lived for awhile in the trailer. Pete later recalled to Judith Tick that Ruth was sometimes "frantic, trying to take care of two babies with no running

Baby Mike playing with Charles Seeger in Central Park, New York City, 1934.
(Photo courtesy of Alexia Smith)

water." He went on to observe that the Seeger wives had a problem: "Their husbands would ask them to do more than human beings could do."[3] Pete may have been referring to his father's two wives, but he, and later Mike, also expected the mothers of their children to live on little and perform heroically. Charles, for his part, struggled to support his growing family with earnings obtained from part-time teaching and odd summer jobs performed on farms near his father's house in Upstate New York.

The move to Washington promised security and prosperity, but relocation there certainly did not bring immediate relief. Before settling down in 1938 in Silver Spring, Maryland, the Seegers lived in a succession of houses and apartments in the Washington area. They stayed first in a suburban brick house on Pershing Drive in Arlington, Virginia, and spent the summer of 1936 in a very wooded place near Turkey Run, Virginia, that Mike described as "just kind of camping out between leases." They lived from late 1936 into 1938 in a tiny row house at 2441 P Street NW in a racially integrated section of Georgetown. Mike's first memories are associated with the Georgetown residence, and in particular the night in May 1937 when his mother hurriedly gathered items from the top of a bureau on her way to the hospital to give birth to Barbara.[4]

In 1938 the Seegers rented a house at 10001 Dallas Avenue in Silver Spring, a suburb of Washington that at the time still had the flavor of a small southern town. Mike always remembered this home on the edge of the city with great affection.[5] It was a big rambling house with a peaked roof, heated with a basement coal furnace and surrounded by an expansive yard that was adjacent to open fields of woods and blackberry patches. It was almost like living in the country. One of Mike's "indelible childhood memories," in fact, was of a neighbor, a burly ex-Texan who worked as a carpenter and fireman but also raised chickens that ran freely in his backyard. Mike sometimes watched with a mixture of fascination and horror as the man wrung the neck of one of his chickens, which then flopped around the yard uncontrollably until it died.[6] The house was sparsely furnished, and Charles, who was an expert carpenter and craftsman, built some of the furniture. The Seegers lived in the Silver Spring house until 1944. Ruth's maternal duties, musical transcription work (done for books by the Lomaxes, George Korson, and Ben Botkin), and children's songbook compilations often necessitated household assistance. Mike recalled one housekeeper in particular, an unmarried African American lady named Mamie Hairston who worked for the family for about fifteen years. He described her as a very good woman (a "first-century Christian," according to Charles) who took care of the kids and made them sassafras tea and other treats.

Residence in Silver Spring came during a very busy and productive period for the Seegers, a time when many important people came in and out of their lives. Mike said that the Seegers were "oddballs" in their neighborhood and did not mix very much with their neighbors. He was too young to be aware of Depression issues, politics, or radicalism, but he recalled, or at least had heard stories about, some of the visitors who came to the house, including Elie Siegmeister, John Jacob Niles, John Lomax, Alan Lomax, Bess Lomax Hawes, Lee Hays, Huddie "Leadbelly" Ledbetter, Sidney Robertson, and Henry Cowell. Peggy recalled that "exciting people were always dropping in" and even spoke of "assorted refugees from Hitler's Germany" who occasionally showed up at the Seeger home.[7] John Lomax and Henry Cowell provided Mike with his fondest memories. Lomax permitted Mike and Peggy to ride on the running board of his big automobile as it rolled down the long driveway of their home.[8] Cowell, who married Sidney Robertson in 1941, gave the kids piggyback rides and, to their great amusement, sometimes played jigs on the piano with his fists and elbows. Mike recalled that his mother had serious misgivings about Cowell's seeming eccentricity; she was fearful that he might jar the family piano out of tune. Cowell, though, was famous for the experiments he had made in the 1920s when he played tune clusters on the piano by using his elbows or by actually reaching inside the instrument to pluck directly on the strings. He sometimes held down the keys and then strummed the strings like an Autoharp.[9]

Music was a constant in Mike's young life. He experienced it in the songs that the family played and sang, in the piano lessons given by "Dio" (the childhood name that Mike gave to his mother after he heard his father call her "dear" with his New England accent), and on the recordings to which they listened. The Seegers held family singings once or twice a week, sitting on the couch or in a few surrounding chairs with Charles and Ruth playing four-handed piano or Charles picking the guitar and Ruth chording the Autoharp as it lay in her lap. Until Uncle Carl Crawford gave Mike a radio in 1945, the only "instruments" allowed at family sessions were a piano, a guitar, an Autoharp, and a slow-speed phonograph for song transcription.

Ruth frequently gave piano lessons and spent hundreds of hours after 1937 transcribing tunes for the Lomaxes and other compilers of folk songs. Folk music was a refreshing and liberating experience for Ruth, as she discovered the wonderful sounds that could be made by people who had no formal musical training. When Barbara began attending the Silver Spring Cooperative Nursery School in 1941, Ruth entered a new dimension of musical service as a volunteer teacher, or "music mom."[10] She used the school as a laboratory for teaching folk music to children and became convinced that the available songs for children were trivial and uninspiring. She later said that she was "disturbed by the sweetness and lack of backbone in nursery songs."[11] Borrowing mostly from songs transcribed from Library of Congress field recordings and from *Our Singing Country* and other sources, Ruth compiled three songbooks: *American Folk Songs for Children* (1948), *Animal Folk Songs for Children* (1950), and *American Folk Songs for Christmas* (1953). Early versions of the first songbook, a collection of fifteen or twenty songs held in a loose-leaf binder with cardboard covers, were initially assembled on the floor of the big family living room in front of the fireplace, with Mike and his sisters painstakingly duplicating each page in a jellylike dye solution and helping with the binding.[12] Ultimately, pub-

The Seeger family playing music. From left: Ruth Crawford Seeger, Mike Seeger,
Peggy Seeger, and Charles Seeger. (Photo courtesy of Alexia Smith)

lished versions of Ruth's arrangements of folk songs went into schoolrooms
throughout America.[13]

During this period of great productivity, while also working on *Our Singing Country* and attending to the needs of three small children, Ruth could
not drive a car, had no washing machine, and went about her work on a
"cranky portable typewriter." In December 1943, at the age of forty-two,
Ruth gave birth to a third daughter, Penelope (Penny). She once described
her life as a four-ring circus, giving piano lessons, writing books, being a
wife, and raising four children. The kids learned not to disturb their mother
if she was busy with her transcribing work. Barbara and Penny, the youngest daughters, may have been the most severely affected by their mother's
preoccupations. She was generally asleep when they left for school and too
busy to greet them when they returned home in the afternoon. Penny recalled that when they got home from school, they often found a note on
their mother's door saying "Do not disturb. I'm working." Dio did not enjoy

house cleaning and usually relied on housekeepers or the kids to keep the house in a reasonably clean condition. She was a health-conscious "subsistence cook" who typically provided her family with "simply cooked meats and animal innards," vegetables, fruits, and breads. Mike recalled that she made soups and hashes "out of almost anything." Her liver-paste lunches with crumbly whole-wheat bread were delicacies that he learned to appreciate only after he became an adult. Encouraged to be as self-sufficient as possible, the kids learned how to make their own breakfasts. When they got home from school, they found lists of duties that each had to perform.[14]

The Seeger children grew up largely unsupervised, except for the day-to-day care received from their housekeepers and the principled examples provided by their hard-working parents. Peggy says that she and her siblings were raised in an easy, joyful way with relaxed discipline. Her father, she believes, was reacting against his own Victorian and regimented childhood. He read Boccaccio and the Bible to the kids on Sundays. While Peggy could assert that she and her siblings were "talked to, not at," Mike recalled that he and his father seldom talked to each other—a relationship that did not really change, he said, until his father was in his sixties. Charles definitely made distinctions among his children. Peggy, who was clearly his favorite, admitted that her father sometimes seemed to dislike her sister Barbara, who, in appearance and temperament, may have too closely resembled the Crawford side of the family.[15]

Ruth enjoyed being a mother and was fond of devising games for the kids that would be both entertaining and instructive, a penchant that carried over into her work as a music educator. Peggy's observation that Ruth related well to small children but was unable to understand them as they became teenagers is a criticism that many parents have received.[16] Ruth's dedicated and meticulous work, which only became more intense after the family moved to a bigger and more expensive house in 1944, deprived her of the time that might have been spent more productively with her children. While Charles and Ruth's love for their children was obvious, their commitment to their work always came first. The burdens of work also led to some decisions concerning child rearing that, viewed in retrospect, seem problematic if not downright harmful. For example, during one eight-week period in the summer of 1939 when Ruth's work was particularly intense, six-year-old Mike was sent to Florida to stay with his aunt and uncle at their beach home in Jacksonville. He traveled by plane to Florida with his Uncle Carl and seems to have enjoyed romping on the beach with his cousins, fishing, being towed along the sand behind the family's old Nash car, and experiencing a tropical storm. This was the first time that he had ever been with his uncle, whom he recalled as being warm, fatherly, and self-assured.[17] When Uncle Carl enrolled him in a local school, however, Mike rebelled and immediately exhibited symptoms of depression. He was sent back home, by himself, on the Silver Meteor train, dependent on the stewardesses to make his trip comfortable and safe. During his Florida stay, Mike had received occasional letters from Peggy and his mother. In a letter dictated to her mother, Peggy had implored her brother to come home soon. Ruth's letter of October 14 (also signed by Charles) was filled with expressions of love and careful words of advice: be nice to the stewardess, go to the toilet before you go to sleep, and take a piece of paper to lift the toilet seat. She said she hoped to send him some paper seat covers before he boarded the train.[18]

Mike rejected all formal music instruction urged by his mother. Yet, recalling his parents' reverence for music and their missionary zeal to introduce it to the world, he insisted that they trained him better than they knew. When he was five or six, his mom tried to get him started on the piano, but he hated to play scales and quickly abandoned piano lessons. He rejected with similar disdain the clarinet lessons he received at the age of eleven. Peggy, on the other hand, embraced lessons and readily absorbed musical theory. By the age of six, she was playing both piano and guitar. At eleven, she could transcribe musical notation and took great delight in taking a song such as "The Irish Washerwoman" through the circle of fifths in every key. Peggy fondly appreciates the way her mother "just opened me up as a musician."[19]

Although Mike remained indifferent to classical theory, he fell in love with the traditional music that by then was consuming his parents' lives. Sitting in the large central living room where Ruth did some of her transcriptions, he and Peggy joined in with the family songfests, singing from mimeographed song sheets and from the Lomax songbooks. An early photograph shows Mike, at about age five and in short pants, listening with absorbed interest as his dad and mom played the guitar and dulcimer. They sang songs like "Get Along Home, Cindy" (learned from Thomas Hart Benton) to get the kids to go to bed.[20] Sometimes when their parents played music in the big living room, the kids would dance a circle around the couch and family desk. By the time he was five years old, Mike could sing a whaling song and many of the verses of the venerable ballad "Barbara

Allen" (which Charles documented on a home recording). He also started strumming the Autoharp when he was about eleven years old, with no intimation that he would one day be acknowledged as one of the masters of the instrument.

Mike was fascinated, above all, by the music he heard on the recordings that his family owned or had borrowed. This collection included about 200 aluminum discs of Library of Congress field recordings and a small assortment of commercial 78-rpm records. Mike has said, "I'm thankful we didn't have a radio. Our parents didn't want us to be influenced by commercial media." (The 78-rpm phonograph records, of course, were indeed "commercial.") When he was about seven, his parents gave him "the great honor" of being permitted to use the variable-speed record player that Ruth used in her tune-transcription work. Mike sat on the floor with it, sharpened the cactus needles on a little rotating sharpener, and played the records over and over. In this way, he completely absorbed the music that permanently captured his life.

The Seeger record collection contained an intriguing and diverse mixture of styles, encompassing, as one might expect, classical and operatic pieces but also a generous admixture of everything from the boogie-woogie classics of Meade Lux Lewis and Albert Ammons to the blues of Roosevelt Sykes and Sonny Boy Williamson. The hillbilly and country blues performers, however—such as Jimmie Strothers; Leadbelly; Emma Dusenberry (who Sidney Robertson Cowell had "discovered" in Arkansas); the Ward Family of Galax, Virginia; Gid Tanner's Skillet Lickers (particularly with their version of "Fiddlers Contest in Georgia"); and Dock Boggs (with his compelling version of "Pretty Polly")—made the most enduring impressions on Mike's developing musical consciousness. To Mike, these were disembodied voices and instrumental sounds, however, and he would have had no particular reason to associate them with a specific region, culture, or way of life. In 1941, when he was eight years old, he did accompany his father to the big fiddle contest in Galax and actually heard the Bogtrotters, an old-time band that he later revered. But at the time, he was more captivated by the social and carnival-like atmosphere of the scene than by the music. He did not yet associate old-time music with southern working-class culture. Instead, he understood it as a staple of his own family's life and his growing-up years.

Big brother Pete's occasional visits were also exciting and life-shaping events for Mike. Ruth liked Charles's older boys and thought that Pete would be a good influence on her kids. For the rest of her life, she and Pete enjoyed a comfortable and mutually beneficial work relationship, learning much from each other and sharing songs and musical ideas. When Pete visited, she permitted the kids to stay home from school, feeling that they could learn as much from him as from a classroom. They jumped up and down and cried: "Pete's here! Pete's here!"[21] Peggy remembers Pete as "our tall, exotic half-brother, with his long long-necked banjo and his big, big feet stomping at the end of his long, long legs. . . . He'd sit and talk and sing and we'd stay up late and toast marshmallows and bawl out the choruses and try and lay our hands over the strings and detune the pegs while he played." Pete had flirted with jazz during a brief stay at Harvard, but, consumed with a growing passion for social justice and the conviction that he should actively battle on its behalf, he had dropped out of the university in 1938.[22] He chose folk music as his chief arena of social activism and the five-string banjo as his major weapon. Pete had heard and liked Aunt Molly Jackson's singing back in 1931, but his real epiphany came in 1935 when his dad took him to Bascom Lamar Lunsford's festival in Asheville, North Carolina. Lunsford was a country lawyer, fiddler, and banjo player who had founded his festival in 1927 as part of a larger celebration called the Rhododendron Festival. He had also recorded both commercially and for the Library of Congress.[23] When the sixteen-year-old Pete heard Lunsford and Aunt Samantha Bumgarner play the five-string banjo, he fell in love with the instrument. A little later, he learned even more about the versatile stylistic capabilities of the banjo when he heard a record by Uncle Dave Macon, the Tennessee musician who had long been a star of the Grand Ole Opry. In mid-1939 Pete worked with the Vagabond Puppeteers, a group of four college students who performed protest songs and radical skits for farmers and small-town people throughout New York State.[24] In that same year, he took a job at the Archive of American Folk Song at the Library of Congress working as Alan Lomax's assistant and listening to hundreds of commercial records in order to assess their suitability as folk song sources. Whenever he got a hankering for a home-cooked meal, he would bike out to the Seeger home in nearby Silver Spring and spend some time with the family.

Pete continued to combine traditional music with radical politics after he met Woody Guthrie in New York on March 3, 1940, at the famous "Grapes of Wrath" benefit for migrant workers. He soon thereafter went through a "bum" stage, hitting the road with the Oklahoma balladeer in a romantic quest to get close to "the people." Pete was a captivating presence, his charismatic style of performance made more striking because of his long legs and long-necked banjo. To his growing public audience, he conveyed the aura of a wanderer and itinerant balladeer, but to his younger brother and sisters, he was simply a beloved big brother. When Pete went into military service in 1943, he sent letters to his younger siblings addressed with such terms as "the Three Little Angels" and "the Associated Son and Daughters of Charles Seeger, Silver Spring Chapter." Once, after Mike and Peggy baked a batch of cookies and mailed them to Pete at Keesler Field in Biloxi, Mississippi, Pete responded with a charming set of self-drawn cartoons with captions. The pictures showed Pete receiving the cookies and ruefully "sharing" them with his barracks mates.[25] Such memories conjure up the best of the Silver Spring years. Recalling and summing up that time, Mike said, "I absorbed a lot in those years—the family life, the singing, the visitors and their talk, my parents' passionate belief in musical values. It's given me a strong foundation in life, and I'm thankful."[26]

But Mike's world changed significantly, both physically and emotionally, when he was about eleven years old. During the summer of 1944, he was sent to a farm in Norwich, Connecticut, that was run by an ex–Brooklyn Dodger. The former athlete, whose name Mike did not recall, was apparently a back-to-the-lander who worked with city kids to acquaint them with the virtues of hard work and rural life. When Mike came home from a short season of haying and bringing in the cows, he found that his family had moved out of the big, rambling, comfortable house in Silver Spring, where he had felt free to run loose. He returned instead to a three-story Victorian structure—a "splendid white clapboard, three-story house on a substantial corner lot"[27]—at 7 West Kirke Street in Chevy Chase, Maryland.

The purchase of the new house—the first one that the family had ever owned—marked the growing economic security of the Seeger family, and it was also partly designed to locate Ruth closer to Washington so that she could enlarge her potential pool of piano students. Charles now worked at the Pan-American Union and often felt the need to entertain visiting dignitaries from abroad. He had even ordered calling cards from Tiffany's, as well as a call bell under the dining room table to summon the hired help. Ironically, the expensive house imposed a greater burden on Ruth. Typically working a thirteen- or fourteen-hour day on Saturdays, she now felt obligated to take on even more students in order to contribute to the house's cost and upkeep.[28]

The move to Chevy Chase also deeply upset Mike. In the new neighborhood, he found few kids to play with and became more of a loner—more concerned about being an "oddball," which was one of his favorite self-descriptions. In his first few years in the new environment, he had very little life outside the family, and even the sense of family togetherness was reduced because Ruth had to work so hard. Furthermore, the new house had no big central living room like the old one had, a space where music, work, and family bonding could be combined. The behavioral difficulties that Mike experienced in school during this time, along with his problems with reading, may have been caused by undiagnosed learning disabilities. (He may have suffered from dyslexia and been afflicted with vision problems.) Many years later, when speculating about the causes of his early problems with reading, Mike remembered being tested as a child with some kind of instrument that resembled stereopticon-style glasses. This device, sometimes called a "flipper," was used in vision therapy as a means of measuring focus, eye tracking, and depth perception. Problems with his vision, along with the trauma of moving to the new house and neighborhood, only contributed further to Mike's difficulties in school.[29]

Aside from his feelings toward music, which as yet had no clear focus or direction, Mike's all-consuming passion during these years was cycling on both a bicycle and a unicycle. His interest began at the age of seven, when his dad gave him his first bike, an Iver Johnson model. Sometime during his early teen years, Mike learned that a local bus driver in Chevy Chase made and rode unicycles, so he commissioned the construction of one for himself. He delighted in riding his unicycle all through junior high and high school.

When he was about thirteen, Mike went to work at the Chevy Chase Bicycle Shop, first rebuilding old pedals for ten cents apiece and then repairing the bikes themselves. Although no one in the shop demonstrated any particular musical ability, employment there gave Mike his first day-to-day contact with working people, young men mostly in their early twenties who introduced him to a masculine competitive world far different from his experiences at home. Mike did not simply work on bikes, however; he also rode them in competition. While most of his races occurred locally and attracted very few competitors, he did participate occasionally in contests that featured state and national competition. Two such races were the 1949 Amateur Bicycle League of America junior competition in Kenosha, Wisconsin, where he placed ninth, and the same race the next year in San

Mike Seeger riding a
unicycle at the Lincoln
Memorial, Washington,
D.C., 1950.
(Photo courtesy of
Alexia Smith)

Diego, where he came in fifth. The California trip was a real adventure for the impressionable teenager. Carrying his partially disassembled bike in one hand and a traveling bag in the other, Mike traveled by train to Los Angeles, where his uncle Carl, now living in California, met him. He then journeyed on to San Diego, stayed in a YMCA dormitory, watched a midget automobile race on a dirt track, and then competed a day or two later in the bicycle race on the same track.

Mike continued to find formal schooling problematic. Poor reading skills, he believed, hindered his learning, and the large and almost anonymous classes in the public schools prevented the kind of personal attention that he sorely needed.[30] His parents were sometimes called in because of his failure to do the required work, or because of some undoubtedly defensive "wiseacre" remark he had made in class. Mike attended public schools in Silver Spring and Chevy Chase through the seventh grade, but he transferred in the eighth grade to Georgetown Day School, a private progressive school in Northwest Washington not far from American University. Founded in 1945 by Agnes Inglis "Aggie" O'Neil, a philanthropist and friend of Eleanor Roosevelt, the school stressed cultural diversity and was the first racially integrated school in Washington. Classes there were held in a brick mansion that had been built in 1809 by Nathan Loughborough, an early comptroller of the U.S. Treasury.[31] Because the school was beautifully situated on a wooded sixteen-acre plot, Mike had plenty of room to ride his bicycle and unicycle. Class responsibilities were structured in ways designed to maximize the freedom of students who utilized their time well and did their work promptly. When his work was finished, Mike spent his time either tutoring other students or just enjoying himself out in the schoolyard. He later recalled Georgetown Day as "the first school I ever enjoyed." Unfortunately, the school then had only eight grades, and so by the time he entered ninth grade in 1947, he was back in a public school— Leland Junior High in Chevy Chase, where he fell back into the pattern of being equally unsuccessful and unhappy.

From the tenth through the twelfth grade, Mike attended the Woodstock Country School in Vermont. This decision was in part a bow to family tradition. His father and older brothers had attended other boarding schools. Mike also surmised that he may have been sent north to get him away from the influence of the "late-twenties bachelors" who worked at the bike shop or who participated in the biking contests. A visit to a psychiatrist arranged by his parents further confirmed the decision that private school would be best for him. Woodstock was a liberal, co-ed, ninth-through-twelfth-grade boarding school with an enrollment of about 100 students.[32] Recalling his years at Woodstock, Mike remembered mostly the long and cold winters, but he described his overall experience as a good one for "oddballs" like himself. He got more attention than he had received in public school and felt that his idiosyncrasies were tolerated. He remembered the school as an environment of "freewheeling freedom and New England intellectualism."

Although Mike was not an outstanding student at Woodstock, either, he did profit from the friendship and counsel of Elizabeth "Buffy" Dunker (born Elizabeth Dennison), a music teacher who exuded the aura of a free spirit and became a confidant of many students, especially those who liked music. She came to Woodstock in 1946 and taught music there for twenty-three years before being named the school registrar.[33] True to form, Mike resisted formal music lessons at Woodstock and was erratic in his study habits, sometimes working hard on projects but too often sloughing off his academic assignments. Woodstock, on the whole, proved to be a productive and formative environment for Mike. He met his first two girlfriends there. Ruth, in a letter, suggested that Mike bring one of them—a Mary Lou—home during a school break. "We could give her one of the girl's rooms," she told him.[34] Through Jeremy Foster, one of his Woodstock classmates, Mike eventually met two of his future wives, Marjorie Ostrow and Alice Gerrard. Crucial components of his immediate future also began to take shape at Woodstock, including his decision to register as a conscientious objector and the happy realization that, in addition to his prowess as a cyclist, he could excel at music making.[35]

With the Korean War raging and the prospects of the draft staring him in the face, Mike began to consider the options for nonmilitary service. Unaware that his father had been a conscientious objector during World War I, Mike sought answers from his teachers at Woodstock. He found the vesper talks given by Mounir Sa'adah, a Christian Arab from Damascus, Syria, who taught history and philosophy and served as the local Universalist minister, to be particularly helpful.[36] More immediately, in his senior year in 1951, Mike won first place in the school talent contest by strumming his Autoharp and singing "Goodnight Irene," a song collected in 1934 by the Lomaxes from the great black folksinger Huddie "Leadbelly" Ledbetter and transformed into a national hit in 1950 by Pete Seeger and the Weavers. Although Mike downplayed his victory in the talent show—acknowledging that to make a chord on the Autoharp he merely had to press down a lettered key button—the experience was nevertheless a confidence booster and a hint that a musical career might be possible.

When Mike returned from Woodstock after his graduation in 1951, he was at loose ends. He had no desire to pursue higher education but made a half-hearted attempt at a college career in order to please his parents. He went to orientation at the University of Maryland in nearby College Park, but he was overwhelmed by the sea of people who surrounded him in the huge field house and was repulsed by the school's requirement of ROTC training. He did not continue with registration but instead enrolled at George Washington University, which did not require military training. By this time, however, Mike had become consumed by music, and his classroom performance gradually deteriorated. He dropped out of school in the middle of the spring semester of 1952. He said, "I felt a real sense of failure wasting my parents' money."

By this time, Mike's mother had come to terms with his rejection of classical music theory but nevertheless urged him to cultivate music of some sort. Since Mike showed no interest in the piano or the clarinet, which she'd also suggested, Ruth thought that perhaps a string instrument might suit him more. Like the piano, the family dulcimer held no intrigue, so Ruth and Mike visited a music store in Washington to look for a guitar. They left abruptly when the clerk showed them a model and announced that it was the brand that Burl Ives used on his radio shows. Since this incident happened a few months before Ives's appearance on May 20, 1952, before the Senate Internal Security Subcommittee, where he divulged the names of fellow musicians who had been communists or fellow travelers, politics seems to have played no role in Ruth's reaction.[37] Ruth instead was apparently offended by Ives's "commercialism."

For his part, Mike always ruefully recalled that the rejected guitar was a Martin with a mahogany top that he would have loved to have gotten his hands on. Ruth soon bought a guitar with nylon strings from another music store and paid for Mike to take lessons there. For about three months in 1951, he took "classical" guitar lessons from the great jazz guitarist Charlie Byrd. Mike still exhibited a reluctance to follow written instructions and notation, however, and instead "took liberties" with the tunes found in the book that Byrd recommended. Mike, in fact, was largely indifferent toward his training until the day he witnessed Byrd jamming with the country musician Zeb Turner (William Edward Grishaw), who at that time had regular radio gigs as a DJ and performer on WBAL in Baltimore and WEAM in Washington, D.C.[38] Permitting this unplanned and informal session to be Mike's lesson for the day, Byrd elicited an enthusiasm from his student that he had not earlier seen. The spontaneity, expertise, and confidence shown by the two professional musicians fascinated Mike. He readily admitted later that the brief period of instruction in Charlie Byrd's studio changed his life. He absorbed more than the few chord positions that he learned from Byrd and from Sophocles Pappas, the classical-oriented instructor and former student of Andres Segovia who took up the lessons when Byrd went on tour. Mike abandoned formal music instruction once and for all when Pappas instructed him to practice "I Gave My Love a Cherry" (a piece that Mike considered saccharine and soulless),[39] but he had learned that he could play an instrument. And he became confident that music could be a viable vocational option in his life.

Mike's lifelong love affair with the five-string banjo also began at this time. In January 1952, just as Mike's guitar lessons were winding down, his parents bought an S. S. Stewart model banjo that he and Peggy could share. Peggy actually learned more quickly than Mike and even gave instructions to her brother. The two of them waged a friendly but intense competition for the instrument, seizing every spare moment to practice their techniques. One time, when they were teenagers, they were both at home in bed because of sickness (Mike had shingles in one eye and Peggy had gout in her feet). Much to Peggy's consternation, Mike took the banjo into his room and was reluctant to relinquish it. She later remembered this childhood rivalry in a song that she wrote for Mike's memorial: "Two battling budding five-string-picking siblings fighting over one banjo / You told me 'Girls don't play the banjo.'"[40]

Big brother Pete, of course, was the major influence on his two younger siblings. Well before this time, Pete had become virtually a demigod in the folk music community, and young banjo players everywhere clamored to learn his style. A mimeographed copy of his instruction book *How to Play the 5-String Banjo* circulated widely. Mike could not decipher the frailing, or clawhammer, style from the book but learned its rudiments from Peggy or from Mike Vidor, one of her banjo-playing friends. Pete also invited young musicians, including his siblings Mike and Peggy, to come and work at his home near Beacon, New York, where, with the help of an instruction book he found in the New York Public Library, he was building a log cabin overlooking the Hudson River. Peggy later remembered the "New York city greenhorns and tenderfeet" who arrived "unprepared for Copperhead snakes, bears, mosquitoes, and crowds of biting insects." Pete installed loudspeakers all around the property so that his young work crew could hear music (mostly from Folkways records) while they worked.[41] Awakening his young disciples very early each morning to the sounds of his banjo and the impassioned strains of "Wake up, wake up, you lazy sleepers" (an adaptation of the old mountain ballad "Darling Cory"), Pete enlisted their aid in clearing the land, felling trees, scraping logs, and raising the foundations of his home. (Lee Hays, Pete's folksinger friend and a member of the Weavers, ruefully described these young musicians as "Seeger's slave gangs."[42]) In return for their labor, though, they earned the opportunity to sit in the presence of the master, learn his style of musicianship, and enjoy each other's fellowship.

Mike soaked up every morsel of banjo technique available from traditional recordings, from Pete, and from the budding musicians who came to Beacon. It was there that he first met John Cohen and Roger Sprung, New York musicians who had played often at the famous sessions at Washington Square.[43] Roger Sprung brought additional credentials to Mike's life as virtually the first northern musician to successfully play the bluegrass banjo style—the syncopated, three-finger method that was then being popularized by Earl Scruggs on the Grand Ole Opry.[44] Mike had already been introduced to the sounds of bluegrass music on recordings collected by Washington friend Richard Spottswood, and in fact he had seen Scruggs perform at a Maryland country music park, but Sprung provided an early flesh-and-blood exhibition of the three-finger style.

Mike's encounter with bluegrass music—and his revelatory realization that it was a modern commercial extension or outgrowth of the old-time music that he had loved during his childhood—came in the context of a thriving musical scene in Washington, D.C. In many ways a southern city, Washington already had its country and bluegrass enclaves. The city had long been a destination for both black and white rural southerners, who were drawn by perceived federal protections and the economic opportunities that existed there and in the surrounding neighborhoods of Virginia and Maryland. Commercial country music had actually existed in Washington since at least January 1926, when a string band from Galax—Al Hopkins and the Hillbillies—inaugurated a popular radio show on WRC. The "Father of Country Music," Jimmie Rodgers, lived in Washington for a few months in 1927 and 1928. He broadcast briefly on WTTF and did a series of four-a-night performances for a week at the Earle vaudeville theater.

Ernest Stoneman, another pioneer hillbilly musician, moved with his large family in 1932 to the area from Galax. He had made commercial recordings since 1924 (including the popular disaster ballad "The Titanic"). Relocating frequently in his search for steady employment as a carpenter or common laborer, Stoneman eventually wound up in Carmody Hills, Maryland. Stoneman found his lengthiest employment at the Washington Naval Gun Factory but continued to make music with his children at area clubs and radio stations. By the time Mike Seeger began his own musical forays in 1951, some of the Stoneman kids, who would eventually be known as the Blue Grass Champs, had become locally famous on area radio and television shows. Mike, of course, was destined one day to play a crucial role in the rediscovery and national exposure of their father, Ernest "Pop" Stoneman.[45]

During World War II, clubs and bars catering to military personnel and defense workers began to appear in great numbers in Washington and its suburbs. Recalling a D.C. club called the Camden Taverns, where he had played early in his musical career in the mid-1940s, the great country musician Roy Clark described it as a "fight-your-way in, play-a-little-music, fight-your-way-out type place." He estimated that at least 300 such bars thrived in the city during the war, filled to capacity each night with enthusiastic drinking and dancing patrons.[46] While these rough clubs may have provided employment for budding musicians, respectability and a degree of security were more attainable through performances in auditoriums and on radio and television shows. In this realm of commercial exposure, no one played a more profound role than transplanted Tennessee radio personality Connie B. Gay.

Gay gained his first experience in radio during the early 1940s as the host of the Farm Security Administration's *National Farm and Home Hour*. In 1946 he became affiliated with WARL in Arlington, Virginia, and introduced a midday country show called *Town and Country*, one of the first radio programs to use the term "country" to describe the music once known as hillbilly. Gay built a close business arrangement with the Grand Ole Opry in Nashville and began booking Opry acts in the Washington area. Two shows booked on October 31, 1947, at Constitution Hall and headlined by Eddy Arnold were both sold out and became the harbingers of many more successful concerts. With this kind of visible public support, Gay soon became one of the most active and successful promoters in the nation. His booking talents and radio exposure, exhibited on WGAY, not only introduced Nashville talent to Washington but also made it possible for such local talent as Roy Clark, Billy Grammer, Jimmy Dean, and Patsy Cline to become nationally known.[47]

Being too young and perhaps a bit too straitlaced to be a habitué of the local bars and honky-tonks, Mike Seeger missed out on much of this activity, and he seems to have paid much less attention to the shows promoted by Connie Gay than one might imagine. But Mike nevertheless began to be immersed in the broad arena of country music through a variety of venues and influences. He even began to listen to the once-prohibited radio. Radio Moscow and other international sites became available to him through a shortwave radio given to him by Aunt Elsie. When Uncle Carl gave him a table radio in 1945, Mike began listening to the country disk jockeys that broadcast from Virginia, Maryland, and the greater Washington area. He became part of a large and growing fraternity of mostly middle-class young people all over America who found common identity in their discoveries of roots-style music through radio broadcasts. The great acoustic guitarist and roots recording entrepreneur John Fahey spoke for many of these young people when he recalled his own experiences coming of age in the 1950s in nearby Takoma Park, Maryland. He spoke of the cultural isolation felt by many young men who grew up, as he had, in an affluent white family afflicted by ceaseless materialistic competition and dealing with the absence caused by working parents or divorce. He and his peers fought against loneliness and boredom by turning often to the music heard on local radio stations and then sharing with friends the excitement experienced from newly discovered songs. One day, while listening to the afternoon country show *Town and Country* on WARL, Fahey heard a recording that changed his life. The popular disk jockey Don Owens played Bill Monroe's version of the old Jimmie Rodgers song "Blue Yodel #7," recorded in October 1941. This was Fahey's introduction to the blues, and the experience led first to his search for the out-of-print recording and eventually to his absorption in black roots music in general. His search for recordings also introduced him to people with similar interests and to collectors such as Richard (Dick) Spottswood, who had a huge collection of the old records and abundant knowledge of the musicians who played on them.[48]

Mike Seeger also listened devotedly to the Don Owens show and to the music played by Curly Smith and other hillbilly announcers in the greater Washington area. Owens was a highly influential radio personality and musician who appeared on several radio stations, including one on the Mexi-

can border, before he was killed on April 21, 1963, in an automobile accident.[49] With casual, down-home banter, Owens and the other DJs provided
biographical and cultural contexts for the music they played and sometimes interviewed performers who dropped by their stations. Often musicians themselves, these disk jockeys could speak with authority about
the music, and in the days before the Top 40 concept became the norm
for American radio stations, they personally selected the records that they
played. The music heard on these shows was pure and unadulterated country, without any stylistic differentiation acknowledged. Mike, for example,
did not recall hearing the word "bluegrass" used to describe any particular style or artist. In the early 1950s, however, he gradually began to learn
about this exciting musical genre.

Sometime in late March 1952, Peggy told Mike about a schoolmate at
Bethesda/Chevy Chase High School who had informed her about the recent death (March 22) of the Grand Ole Opry pioneer Uncle Dave Macon.
This schoolmate was Dick Spottswood, who later explained that he needed
someone with whom to share his sorrow and reasoned that the sister of
Pete Seeger would surely be an understanding soul.[50] Peggy invited Spottswood to a picking and singing session at the Seeger home, and he and Mike
began sharing their enthusiasms for old-time music. Spottswood brought
a couple of hillbilly records, including a copy of the Stanley Brothers' rare
Rich-R-Tone recording of "Little Glass of Wine" and "Little Maggie."[51] Mike
described the recording as "the most incredible wonderful music"—his
initiation into the exciting world of bluegrass and, more significant, to the
transformative realization that old-time music still survived in a vibrant
and updated form. Later in the summer of 1952, Mike went to a country
music park near the town of Mount Airy in Montgomery County, Maryland,
where he heard a country band headed by the fiddler and disk jockey Curly
Smith and the dynamic bluegrass band of Lester Flatt and Earl Scruggs and
the Foggy Mountain Boys. Many years later, Mike recalled the event "as
near about to a religious experience as I've ever had"[52] and declared that
"the music was so powerful and the musicianship so dazzling."

Meeting Dick Spottswood brought Mike into the eccentric world of
record collectors, an association that also profoundly affected his life and
career. Although he was younger than Mike, Spottswood was already considered to be a world-class collector, assembling everything from hillbilly
and blues to ethnic recordings. He was closely allied with a loosely knit
fraternity of collectors. International in scope, they shared their passion

for the old 78-rpm recordings with each other through auctions and sales advertised chiefly in mimeographed periodicals such as *Disc Collector* and *Record Research*. The collectors often differed in their obsessions for the old music, ranging in their tastes from southeastern string-band music to blues, early jazz, cowboy, or western swing, but most of them (not including Spottswood) tended to agree that the only music worth collecting was that recorded prior to World War II. The Australian collector John Edwards, for example, referred to the years between 1922 and 1942 as "the Golden Age of Hillbilly Music." Joe Bussard, from Frederick, Maryland, and probably the most prolific collector of all, was willing to extend the date a few years forward. In Bussard's opinion, country music died on January 1, 1953, along with Hank Williams.[53]

Spottswood introduced Mike to still another Washington collector, Robert Travis, a technical writer for the Bureau of Standards. In 1953 Mike became a member of a small circle of enthusiasts who met periodically at Travis's basement apartment near Dupont Circle to listen to hillbilly, jazz, blues, ragtime, and other assorted styles of recorded music. Mike soaked it all in, asserting that the listening experiences there were "a big part of my music education." He was inspired, for example, to try to adapt the piano ragtime he heard to his guitar. Most important, he heard for the first time Harry Smith's famous *Anthology of American Folk Music*, released as three box sets (six LPs) only one year earlier by the Folkways label in New York. Drawn from Smith's enormous private collection, *Anthology* consisted of eighty-four carefully chosen, mint copies of original 78-rpm recordings of hillbilly, blues, cowboy, gospel, Cajun, and other commercial grassroots music released between 1927 and 1934. In his selections and accompanying notes, Smith made no reference to the race or ethnicity of the performers but instead presented the music as part of an interrelated whole that reflected the folk culture of the rural South. Smith's insight was far ahead of its time. When listeners first heard the anthology in the early fifties at the beginning of the folk music revival, the collection evoked a sense of mystery and the aura of a long-ago and faraway country—even though most of the musicians had been originally recorded only twenty or so years earlier.[54] And, unknown to Mike and the other young enthusiasts who gathered in Robert Travis's apartment, some of these musicians were still alive.

When Mike made his first visits to the apartment near Dupont Circle, his crucial contributions to the rediscovery and career revitalization of some of the musicians heard on the *Anthology of American Folk Music*—including

Dock Boggs, Ernest Stoneman, Eck Robertson, and Maybelle Carter—and to the overall popularization of the musical styles of the recordings were still several years away. His chief priority at that time was to learn old-time styles and songs and to perform them as often and as faithfully as he could. In addition to the guitar and banjo, Mike had added the mandolin to his complement of instruments and was busy trying to play the most difficult one of all: the fiddle. He took on the instrument after he repaired a broken and discarded one that a friend had found in a trash can behind her house. Mike's knowledge of and ability to play the fiddle set him apart from most other young folkies in the mid-to-late 1950s.

Despite Mike's growing instrumental eclecticism, the banjo was his chief obsession. He played the instrument constantly—in his room, at parties and occasional contests at country music parks, while riding his unicycle, and even while reading the *Washington Post* (playing banjo riffs over and over as he read the news). He remembered playing the banjo sometimes as much as twelve hours a day. The instrument, in fact, had played no small role in his flunking out at George Washington University. One of his best learning experiences, however, came when he started sitting in with square-dance musicians in downtown Washington. These were affairs organized by local promoter and square-dance caller Ralph Case and held weekly at a public school auditorium on 11th Street.[55] Mainly wanting to improve his sense of timing, Mike sat at the back of the stage with no microphone, playing his banjo unobtrusively while fiddler Blackie Morgan played such tunes as "Down Yonder" and "Alabama Jubilee" to the backing of an electric guitar strummed in sock rhythm style (a percussive, closed-chord technique). One night from a nearby room, he even heard the music of an exciting young bluegrass band—a group made up principally of the children of Ernest "Pop" Stoneman.

Mike's passion for old-time country music and his obsession to perform it with "authenticity" led almost inevitably to his efforts to capture on tape the performances of people like Blackie Morgan. His parents, of course, provided inspiration and precedent for such documentation, and he used their recording equipment in his "research." Mike's tapings appear to have been, at first, a measure of his desire for self-education, an effort to learn new songs and styles. But this motive was soon joined by the urge to preserve these sounds before they vanished along with the people who performed them. Only a few years down the road, Mike became famous at country music parks, folk festivals, and other concerts for his ever-present tape recorder.

Mike's first recording, though, occurred within the Seeger home itself during the Thanksgiving holiday of 1952. On Saturday evening, after her domestic work was completed, the Seegers' housekeeper, Elizabeth "Libba" Cotten, sat down for an informal recording session that Mike conducted. Libba (a name bestowed on her by Mike's youngest sister, Penny) had been hired as a maid in about 1945 after she'd come to the aid of Peggy, who had gotten lost on the fifth floor of Landsburgh's Department Store while her mother was buying dolls for her two younger daughters. A store employee at the time, Libba found the distraught child and took her to her mother. Ruth was so grateful that she soon hired Libba as her housekeeper.[56]

One day, Peggy heard Libba playing the family guitar—albeit in a quite unorthodox manner. When she relayed the news to Mike, he became anxious to share the information with Pete. Growing up near Chapel Hill, North Carolina, where she had been born in 1895, the left-handed Libba as a child had "borrowed" her brother's guitar and learned to play it upside down; that is, she did not restring the guitar but simply turned it around, fretting the instrument with her right hand and picking and strumming with her left. She played variations of the ragtime style heard in the Carolina piedmont, stroking the treble strings with her thumb and picking the bass strings with her fingers. Along with a repertory of traditional songs, both secular and gospel, she also played and sang one number that she had written when she was about eleven years old. This was "Freight Train," a song that eventually became known around the world.[57]

With Charles, Ruth, Pete, and the Seeger girls standing around as observers and Libba playing a steel-string Martin guitar borrowed from a visiting friend, Ed Badeaux, Mike used a recording unit that Charles had brought home from the office and a hand-held microphone to record Libba at the end of her long day's work.[58] Only one of these recordings has been released commercially—on *Close to Home*, the anthology of music that Mike recorded over the years—but the others are on deposit at the Library of Congress and in the Mike Seeger Collection at the University of North Carolina at Chapel Hill. Later in 1957, Mike visited Libba's home in downtown Washington several times with his recording equipment. These were the songs that Folkways released in 1958 on Libba's first LP, *Folksongs and Instrumentals with Guitar* (Folkways FG 3526).[59]

Mike also recorded Blackie Morgan in the Seeger home and a couple of African American musicians in their homes. During a visit to a Maryland horse stable owned by a friend, Bob Green, Mike was picking his ever-present five-string banjo when he encountered a black stable hand who exhibited curiosity about the instrument. After the man played a few chords on the banjo, Mike decided that he might be a worthy candidate for taping. He later searched for the man in Kengar, a black section of Kensington, Maryland, without success, but he did find and record a fiddler named William Adams.[60]

A tragic bombshell dropped into the midst of Mike's growing music obsession during the summer of 1953, when he learned that his mother was very sick. The intestinal cancer that had invaded her body required surgery and what Mike described as "primitive chemotherapy," and he took his mother into Washington each week for treatment. Determining that Ruth would be better taken care of at home and not in a hospital, Charles brought Peggy home from Radcliffe shortly after the beginning of her first semester at the school. Peggy in fact had gone away to college without knowing that her mother was ill. Uncle Carl also came over from California. Ruth tried to maintain her teaching schedule but finally had to abandon her commitments. Her illness assumes even greater poignancy when it is recalled that only a few months earlier, she had begun to resume her long-abandoned career as a classical composer and had written Suite for Wind Quintet, which won a competition held by the National Association for American Composers and Conductors. In a letter written to Carl and Charlotte Ruggles, Ruth had said, "I believe I'm going to work again." When Peggy saw her mother walk across the stage on December 2, 1952, to receive the award, she realized for the first time just how much Ruth had sacrificed to be a mother and a wife. In fact, it was only in the months following Ruth's death that Peggy and her siblings began to learn about the distinguished career that their mother had once enjoyed. Peggy said, "As a child and teenager, I do not remember her early life as a composer ever being a subject of family discussion."[61]

Ruth died on November 18, 1953, shortly after Mike and Peggy had sung and played at a book fair where Ruth's third children's book, American Folk Songs for Christmas, was being promoted. Ruth had been scheduled to make an appearance at the fair, but Mike and Peggy had agreed to stand in for her. When they left home that morning, Ruth had said to them: "Carry on." In the immediate aftermath of Ruth's death, though, no one in the Seeger family felt confident that they could easily survive the loss. Charles was particularly devastated. He soon began selling everything, including the house. Not much was left for him in Washington. The climate of McCarthyism was stifling dissent and creativity in the city, and Pete had brought further notoriety to the family through his blacklisted political activities. Charles had even counseled Mike and Peggy not to attend the Swarthmore Folk Festival earlier in 1953 because Pete was the headliner. Charles resigned from the Pan-American Union and moved to Boston with Barbara and Penny in order to be near Peggy at Radcliffe.

Peggy, however, did not remain in college for long. She believes that "apparently the money ran out after my mother died" because Ruth "was one of the two main breadwinners."[62] At the end of her second year, Peggy withdrew from the school and soon embarked for Holland on the SS *Maasdam* to stay with her Uncle Charles, who had lived and worked in Europe since 1950 as a radio astronomer. Soon after Peggy arrived in Holland, she traveled to Moscow to attend the World Youth Festival (this was enough to earn the revocation of her passport by the American government) and then continued through China, Poland, Germany, and France before settling down in England. Peggy had already begun to establish a reputation as a folksinger before she went abroad and had in fact recorded an LP while at Radcliffe titled *Folksongs of Courting and Complaint*. In England, she met her lifelong partner, the folksinger Ewan MacColl. She recalls the precise moment when she entered a basement apartment in Chelsea, London, and saw MacColl for the first time: March 25, 1956, at 10:30 in the morning. MacColl was similarly struck and memorialized his memory of the occasion by writing "The First Time Ever I Saw Your Face," which in 1971 became a hit recording in the United States for Roberta Flack. Peggy and Ewan became pillars of the British folk music revival, and Peggy did not return permanently to the United States until 1994, after Ewan's death.[63]

In March 1955 Charles married his childhood sweetheart, Margaret Adams Taylor (for whom Peggy had been named). He and Margaret moved with Barbara and Penny to Montecito near Santa Barbara, California, where Charles renewed his academic career at UCLA. There, he began his experiments with the Melograph, a device designed to measure and graph vocal sounds. The marriage to Margaret, however, did not endure, and they divorced in 1960. Charles maintained his prolific scholarship and academic productivity until his death in 1979.[64]

After Ruth's death and the scattering of his family, Mike lived on his own for three months in the third-floor apartment in the house in Chevy Chase.[65] He had to make some major decisions: Where to live? What to do about the draft? How to deal with his passion for music, especially considering the difficulties that Pete was having with his music and career? Mike recalled that, at that time, Pete was just "scuffling" to survive with a solo career.

The answers to these questions soon became apparent in Baltimore, with consequences that happily affected the nature and perception of American folk music.

3

Discovering Bluegrass

The Baltimore Years

The Baltimore period proved to be one of the pivotal phases of Mike Seeger's life. Between 1954 and 1958, he became immersed in the city's thriving bluegrass music scene and, with his introduction to Hazel Dickens and her family, became intimately involved for the first time with the working-class southerners who had made and preserved the music he loved. Profiting from his experiences playing and listening to bluegrass music in the clubs and house parties of Baltimore, Mike also made his first major contributions to the American folk music scene when he documented the emerging bluegrass phenomenon in two historic LPs made for the Folkways label.

The Korean War was raging when Mike turned eighteen in August 1951, and he was confronted immediately with the prospect of military service. Influenced by Woodstock Country School counselor and teacher Mounir Sa'adah, Mike had already made a decision to seek an alternative option. He had even toyed with the idea of refusing to register for the draft, but his father advised against such action. When Mike decided to seek conscientious objector status, he hadn't realized that he was following in his father's footsteps. Charles supported Mike's decision and wrote a lengthy letter on behalf of his son on November 23, 1952, citing the all-American credentials of the Seeger family and also recalling his own history of war resistance during his years at Berkeley.[1] While seeking guidance from the American Friends Service Committee, the Fellowship for Reconciliation, and other pacifist organizations, Mike explored a number of options for public service. His local draft board provided a list of approved choices for alternative service, but most of them, including religious groups such as the Church of the Brethren, offered little or no money. Charles tried to get him a job in the library of a conservatory of music in Cleveland, but Mike interviewed poorly. He also rejected a job at the Crownsville State Hospital in Maryland because the prospect of having to deal with mentally disturbed criminals was frightening to the impressionable young man. After initially rejecting Mike's petition for conscientious objector status, his local board finally relented and agreed that his service could be postponed during the last months of his mother's illness.

Mike chose to perform his alternative service at the Mount Wilson Tuberculosis Hospital near Pikeville, Maryland, a state-run facility about ten miles northwest of Baltimore.[2] That fateful decision ultimately permitted him to meet Hazel Dickens and her family and to become part of one of the most vigorous arenas of bluegrass music in the nation. Beginning in February 1954, Mike spent most of his two years at the hospital working as a kitchen orderly, cleaning the floors, washing dishes, sometimes helping to prepare meals (particularly at breakfast), and serving as a waiter in the cafeteria. He lived in a small ten-by-fifteen room in the hospital, and though he was discouraged from playing his banjo in his room, he made it known to the workers and patients there that he was a musician and that he welcomed the companionship of other people who played.

Though Mike had worked briefly at the Chevy Chase Bicycle Shop, his time at Mount Wilson provided him with his first long-term encounters with working-class people and their experiences. For one thing, Mike was now a wage earner himself, wearing not the blue collar of a factory worker but instead the white uniform of a hospital attendant. He worked forty hours a week for a dollar an hour at jobs that were menial, dirty, and boring. His room rent and other expenses were minimal, however, and he was able to finish paying for his automobile, a 1949 Chevrolet Carryall (a station wagon that seated eight people). Above all, as he later recalled, the Mount Wilson job provided him with "an education for meeting and working" with people "much less advantaged" than himself. Mike was young and small and obviously inexperienced in the ways of the world, but he seems never to have had any problems with bullying or intimidation from the other workers.

During his two years at Mount Wilson, Mike was usually confined to his tiny room at the tuberculosis hospital, but he did make occasional forays to Pete's cabin in Beacon, at least one to Washington Square in New York, and several to the country music parks in Maryland and Pennsylvania. Musicians at the hospital also started contacting Mike and responding to his inquiries about performance. At least a couple of his musical partners were Amish and Mennonite young men who had also chosen alternative service during the war. Fellow employees Ruth and Onza Cole, on the other hand, from northeastern Tennessee, were part of the large throng of southern migrants who had chosen Baltimore as their escape from rural poverty. They introduced Mike to the music of Molly O'Day, the soulful Kentucky singer who only a few years earlier had been one of the brightest stars on the Columbia label and the voice for whom Hank Williams had written some of his earliest songs. The three spent many happy hours singing from Onza's Molly O'Day songbook, in which Mike was delighted to find such chestnuts as "Barbara Allen" and "Poor Ellen Smith." Mike also shared social hours with some of his fellow workers away from the hospital and in their homes. One of his musical friends, a young man from West Virginia, provided Mike with one of his most vivid working-class learning experiences by taking him to a small storefront building out in the country, where a revival meeting was being held, and then to his home in a newly constructed tar-paper shack.

Mike's most important contact, though, came one day when someone recommended that he meet one of the patients upstairs who played music. This was Robert Dickens, one of the eleven children of Sarah and Hillary "H. N." Dickens (a Primitive Baptist preacher and supplier of timber for the coal mines). The entire Dickens family had sought refuge in Baltimore after fleeing the decline of the coal industry in their native Mercer County, West Virginia. Robert had lost part of his right index finger in an accident, but he nevertheless played the mandolin in an affecting hillbilly and prebluegrass ragtime style on such tunes as "Natural Bridge Blues" and "John Henry." One night, Robert invited Mike to come down to his parents' apartment on Eutaw Place in one of the little "Appalachian" enclaves of Baltimore. Robert's brother Arnold was there, and he became Mike's closest friend and musical companion among the Dickens boys. Father H. N., who had never let his Primitive Baptist affiliation interfere with his love for old-time country music, was persuaded to pick a few numbers, in drop-thumb style, on the five-string banjo. This was the first of Mike's many picking and singing sessions with the Dickens family and the beginning of his relationship with Hazel Dickens.[3]

At the time, Hazel was working at the Maryland Cup Factory and living with still another sister, Velvie, in Hampden. She came over one night to participate in the picking and singing with her family. Wary of Mike's intentions and uncertain of his commitment to and knowledge of the music, Hazel responded to the young "northern" visitor with considerable trepidation. At one point, while Arnold and Mike were playing, Hazel turned up the volume of a song that was on the radio and said to them, "*This* is the way it's supposed to sound." They smiled at her rudeness but kept on playing. Soon, however, her initial resistance broke down, and she began playing and singing with them. Before long, she brought out her songbooks and some examples of her songwriting. Mike recalls that some were "books of songs all written out" in longhand, and some contained clippings of song lyrics from *Country Song Roundup* magazine, the leading country music periodical of the day and a compendium of the current jukebox favorites.

Hazel was a shy young woman, sensitive and very conscious of the class prejudice and discrimination suffered by mountain folk in Baltimore. (She had once seen a sign on an apartment that was up for rent that said "No dogs or hillbillies allowed.") Hazel had worked at menial and factory jobs in the city since she was seventeen years old. She had only a seventh-grade education and was self-conscious about her clothes, her accent, and her lack of sophistication—or what she later described as her "lack of socialization." But she was extremely intelligent and had a powerful singing voice that exhibited (as it does now) the marks of her upbringing in the Primitive Baptist Church of Appalachia. That is, her voice carried a suggestion of the a cappella style favored by the church, with its bent and long-held notes and an indifference to formal rhythmic structures. Hazel embodied the traditional values and musical preferences that Mike loved, yet she was no relic. Her music was grounded in tradition, but it was immediate and real, and it voiced her aspirations for the working class as people like her struggled to cope with the pressures of modern urban life.

The relationship between Mike and Hazel proved to be crucial for both of them. Mike was a major catalyst in Hazel's artistic and emotional awakening, and she now insists, "Mike validated my culture." She responded positively to him as the first "outsider" who appreciated and understood her music. For Mike, the relationship with Hazel and the Dickens family could not have come at a more opportune time. The Dickenses became his surrogate family, filling the void left by the dissolution of his own family in the midfifties. With his mother gone and his family scattering to places all over the world, he needed the emotionally nurturing and caring environment that the Dickens family offered. Not only did Mike make periodic visits to their home, but he also began making music with Hazel and her brothers at local parties and jam sessions, in the Baltimore honky-tonks, and at the country music parks in Pennsylvania, Maryland, and Delaware.

Like the big and venerable fiddle contests, such as those held in Galax, Virginia, and Union Grove, North Carolina, the country music parks[4] provided crucial meeting grounds for city people who were just beginning to discover old-time country music and rural people who lived in the contiguous areas of Maryland, Delaware, Pennsylvania, Virginia, West Virginia, and North Carolina. Watermelon Park in Berryville, Virginia; Rainbow Park in Lancaster, Pennsylvania; Sunset Park in southern Chester County, Pennsylvania, near West Grove; and New River Ranch near Rising Sun, Maryland, were only a few of the rustic venues that featured country music on weekends.[5] At one time or another, virtually all of the leading country musicians of the time—Hank Williams, Roy Acuff, Ernest Tubb, Hank Snow, and many others—played in these country music parks. For Mike and the Dickens family, Sunset Park and New River Ranch, only a few miles apart, were the most accessible of these venues, within easy reach of Baltimore, Washington, Philadelphia, and other heavily populated urban centers.

Mike, Hazel, and her brothers occasionally packed lunches and rode together in Mike's big Chevrolet Carryall on a weekend trip to New River Ranch. As he demonstrated in all of his ventures, Mike was single-mindedly focused. For him, the trips were exclusively about music. Consequently, he was surprised when, on their first trip to the ranch, Robert Dickens asked him to stop to get a six-pack of beer. For Robert, like many of the good old boys who loved country music, drinking beer was an important social component of the music. Mike, though, was a teetotaler and a bit of a Puritan when it came to social behavior, and Robert's dalliance irked him because it delayed their arrival at the park.

New River Ranch opened in 1951 on the Sunday of Memorial Day weekend with a performance by Lester Flatt and Earl Scruggs and the Foggy Mountain Boys. For seven years, it was owned and operated by Bud and Ola Belle Reed and Ola Belle's brother Alex Campbell. Ola Belle and Alex were country musicians from North Carolina who had lived in Maryland since the mid-1930s.[6] Although a little stream ran in back of the stage, the name New River was inspired by a river back home in Ashe County, North Carolina, and by a band, the New River Boys and Girls, that the Campbells had organized there. Ola Belle was a powerful singer, banjo player, and songwriter whose "High on a Mountain," "I've Endured," and other songs have become standards in bluegrass music.[7] Since 1949 she and Alex had also been the hosts of a very popular radio show, *Campbell's Corner*, broadcasting from Havre de Grace, Maryland.

The open stage at New River Ranch was set at the foot of a hill with the stream about seventy-five feet behind it. The hill could accommodate about 1,000 people. Ads for car dealers and other businesses were posted at the back of the stage, and vendors of all kinds, including Gypsy fortune tellers, often populated the scene. Country musicians of varying stripes sometimes appeared at New River Ranch, but Mike and the Dickens family were thrilled most by the old-time and traditional music made by such entertainers as Marshall Louis "Grandpa" Jones, Bill Monroe, Don Reno and Red Smiley, and the Stanley Brothers.

By the mid-1950s, bluegrass music was becoming a refuge for fans who regretted the growing pop dilution of country music or for those who longed to identify with a style that seemed rooted in a simpler and more organic society. The music itself, though, was still taking shape and had not yet firmly assumed the name "bluegrass" as an identifying label. Most fans and musicians in the fifties, in fact, tended to call the music "hillbilly." The term "bluegrass" came from the name of Bill Monroe's band, the Blue Grass Boys, and (condensed to one word) became attached at some undesignated date to the music made by Monroe's imitators and disciples.[8] A growing number of people thought of bluegrass as the most vital and authentic style of country music then available. Since his earlier days in Washington, when he listened to Don Owens's radio shows and to records collected by Dick Spottswood, Mike had been convinced that bluegrass represented an updating of the old-time country string-band styles that he had loved since his childhood. Now, at New River Ranch, he was able to witness and document this music during one of its most important periods of transition and to introduce it to other people who might share his enthusiasm. Dick Spottswood said later that the performances at the country music parks had showed him and Mike that their "adopted music had survived on something besides scratchy 78s, and that it was a living, continuing tradition."[9]

Pete Kuykendall already knew and loved bluegrass music when he and Mike met at New River Ranch in the summer of 1955. Hailing from Arlington, Virginia, he shared Mike's suburban Washington, middle-class background, and he had also listened faithfully to Don Owens's radio shows and shared his musical enthusiasms with classmates (one of whom was future movie star Warren Beatty). Pete became highly skilled on the guitar, fiddle, and five-string banjo and a world-class collector of hillbilly records.

Learning that the two greatest masters of the bluegrass banjo style, Earl Scruggs and Don Reno, would perform on the same stage in July 1955, he came to the ranch and found Mike taping the show with his new Magnecord recording unit that he had purchased with his share of the royalties earned in 1955 from the sales of Ruth's Doubleday books. In the years that followed, Mike and Pete became constant partners in their patronage of bluegrass. Mike gained access to Kuykendall's huge record collection and in turn introduced Pete to his other avid collector friend, Dick Spottswood. Kuykendall later became the principal founder of *Bluegrass Unlimited*, the first and most important journal devoted to the genre.[10]

Mike became famous at New River Ranch and other performance venues for his ever-present tape recorder. After obtaining blanket permission from Bud Reed or Alex Campbell, the proprietors of New River Ranch, Mike then typically asked the individual performers if they would mind if he recorded their show. On May 1, 1955, Grandpa Jones became the first musician to permit Mike's audio documentation, followed by Bill Monroe exactly one week later. The proud Monroe was a hard man to approach, but he responded to Mike's request with a curt "I don't care." For this and other tapings, Mike typically stationed his tape recorder on the edge of the stage and then set up his one microphone next to the PA mike at the center of the stage. Monroe initially moved Mike's microphone to another location but made no further resistance when Mike resolutely moved it back to where he had first set it.[11]

Mike remembered this period as "a wonderful time" because the musicians were still creating the music, improvising their styles, and learning from each other. There at New River Ranch and other parks, they often performed new songs for the first time, played practical jokes on each other, and did flatfoot and other step dances onstage.[12] Some of the performers, including Ola Belle, even did an occasional song from the early Elvis Presley repertory (such as "That's All Right, Mama") because Elvis had made his exciting entrance into American music the previous year. Reno and Smiley harked back to the early days of country stage performances, and even to the era of minstrel entertainment, with their ribald brand of slapstick that often had the entertainers performing in drag or rube-comic costumes. For the most part, the musicians were easily approachable, and the entire atmosphere was comfortably "down-home." The Stanley Brothers, for example, occasionally evoked the early days of hillbilly barnstorming when they occupied the stage alone with banjo and guitar and sent the other members of their band, the Clinch Mountain Boys, into the audience to hawk their songbooks.

Mike was aware of the historic nature of the music being made at New River Ranch and was eager to share his experiences with his friends. One of these was Ralph Rinzler, a native of Passaic, New Jersey, and a student at Swarthmore College whose childhood affection for traditional music had been catalyzed in 1953 when he had heard Pete Seeger play at the Swarthmore Folk Festival.[13] As a consequence of this fateful event, he and a college classmate Roger Abrahams — who later became a folk musician and a distinguished folklorist — developed a love affair with the five-string banjo and a growing obsession with old-time country music. Although Mike was uncertain about when he had first visited Swarthmore, Rinzler, Abrahams, and others have insisted that Mike and Peggy came to Swarthmore in 1953 when Pete first appeared there. That particular festival attracted a large throng of students who came over from Oberlin and other colleges and universities. Many of the attendees, including Mike and Peggy, stayed outside of the concert hall when Pete wasn't playing and made music on their own. Rinzler became infatuated with the entire Seeger family but seemed particularly enamored of Peggy, with whom he pursued a musical and romantic relationship that endured long after she had relocated in England.[14]

Ralph virtually became a member of the Seeger family. He sometimes went to Beacon to help Pete build his cabin, became an occasional correspondent with Charles concerning folk music theory, and began sharing musical information and events with Mike. One of their most ambitious collaborations, and one that greatly enriched and enlarged their repertory of hillbilly material, was the taping in 1956 of hundreds of 78-rpm records from Harry Smith's unrecorded collection that had been deposited in the New York Public Library. Working as volunteers, Ralph catalogued over 1,000 records on three-by-five cards while Mike recorded his favorites on his reel-to-reel recording machine. When told to cease his recording, Mike then smuggled out scores of records in a suitcase — including many highly choice items from the Columbia and RCA Victor catalogues — which he then taped at Ralph's home in Passaic. The filched recordings were returned to the library the next day, but Mike had meanwhile gained knowledge of many songs that later became integral parts of his recording and performing ventures.[15]

While the old recordings revealed the spirit and beauty of bygone musical treasures, Mike knew that the sounds heard there still endured in bluegrass or in other modified or updated forms of old-time country music. He lost no time in encouraging Ralph to visit some of the special arenas where such music could be heard: the country music parks. Ralph may have first gone to the parks in 1954 to hear Bill Monroe or perhaps in 1955 to hear the Stanley Brothers. Mike kept logs of the music that he heard and recorded at the parks and elsewhere, but he was sometimes imprecise about dates.[16] Ralph later told Richard Straw that "it was Mike that taught us that the sound was still alive, that you could go to Sunset Park and hear the Stanley Brothers, and Ola Belle Reed would be there playing rapping banjo."[17] The most thrilling event for Ralph, however, came in May 1955 when Mike put in a hurried call to him saying that Charlie and Bill Monroe were scheduled to be reunited at the ranch. Promoter Don Owens from WARL in Arlington, Virginia, had organized this historic event by arranging for Charlie and Bill to come with their separate bands, the Kentucky Partners and the Blue Grass Boys, hoping that they would also combine for a musical set of their own.[18] The Monroe Brothers reunion was just too important to be missed by anyone absorbed in old-time music. Neither Mike nor Ralph realized, however, that the Opry old-timers Sam and Kirk McGee would also be at the park as part of Grandpa Jones's backup band. The duets performed by the Monroes between 1936 and 1938 had been central sources of the bluegrass repertory, and the McGees had performed and recorded even earlier in the 1920s with the legendary, but now deceased, Uncle Dave Macon.[19] Mike was then unaware of this historical McGee/Macon relationship. Ralph, on the other hand, had seen the names connected on an old phonograph record and was almost ecstatic as he witnessed this reenactment of old-time music history. When he heard the music of Sam and Kirk McGee, who had actually stood shoulder to shoulder with the legendary Uncle Dave Macon—one of the featured performers on the Harry Smith collection—Ralph realized that old-time music was still alive and assuming new and exciting forms.

Ralph was similarly impressed by the music of Bill Monroe and would one day play a major role in the commercial rejuvenation of this great Kentucky musician. But in the midfifties, Monroe was not easily approached. He was bitterly resentful of the neglect that his own contributions had received from writers and publicists and was aware of the enormous amount of publicity that Earl Scruggs was receiving. On one occasion, when Mike and Ralph asked Monroe a question about the early days of bluegrass, he quickly said, "Go ask Louise Scruggs" and abruptly walked away. He was referring, of course, to Earl Scruggs's wife,[20] who had become the principal guardian and historian of her husband's career and who had been skimpy in her acknowledgment of Monroe's contributions. (On the other hand, Monroe had not spoken to Flatt and Scruggs since they left his band in 1948.) Ralph had become convinced of Monroe's centrality in the making of the bluegrass style and was furious that his role was being forgotten. In a letter sent to Mike a few years after the concert at New River Ranch, Ralph waxed enthusiastically about Monroe: "The more I hear him the more certain I become that Bill Monroe is the backbone and vertebra of bluegrass music."[21] He became particularly incensed by a March 1962 article on bluegrass music in *Sing Out!* magazine in which jazz critic Pete Welding lauded Scruggs and scarcely mentioned Monroe.

With a dedication as passionate as that of Mike Seeger, Ralph set out to introduce Monroe and his music to the northern folk music audience. Working through Carter Stanley, who idolized Monroe, Ralph and Mike finally arranged a lengthy interview with the bluegrass giant. In early 1963, in his own contribution to *Sing Out!*, Ralph called Monroe the "Daddy of Bluegrass," offered an assessment of Monroe's vital contributions to American music, and described his role in the making of bluegrass music. In the months that followed, Ralph worked exhaustively to promote and reinvigorate Monroe's career. He persuaded the Decca company to rerelease many of Monroe's singles on LPs and then wrote extensive and detailed liner notes for them. He became Monroe's manager and his chief publicist, and he even played guitar for a brief period with the Blue Grass Boys. Through Ralph's timely intervention, Monroe's career completely turned around, and his personality gradually mellowed as he happily accepted the role of bluegrass patriarch.[22]

In the meantime, Mike had made his own vital contributions to the documentation of bluegrass, first as a musician and then as a record producer. Although Mike, Hazel, and her brothers often played at parties, sometimes at the Dickenses' home, and more often in someone's row-house apartment, they inevitably began thinking of other performance venues as their skills as a "band" improved. Robert Dickens would sometimes say, "Let's go put in a personal appearance." That meant playing in someplace like the Anchor Inn or some other rough club, usually in the corner of the bar and with a "kitty" for tips. Mike played informally with Hazel and her brothers but also in a variety of other groups, the most active of which was Bob Baker's Pike County Boys, which was composed of Baker, Mike, Hazel,

The members of Bob Baker and the Pike County Boys. Standing (from left):
Mike Seeger, Hazel Dickens, and Bob Shanklin; kneeling (from left): Dickie Rittler and
Bob Baker. (Photo courtesy of Alexia Smith)

Dickie Rittler, and Bob Shanklin. Baker was a good singer from southwestern Virginia who had a repertory of interesting songs, such as "Little Willie" and "Snow Dove" (a variant of "The Butcher's Boy"), that he had learned from his family. Baker played the guitar with a thumb pick and one finger pick in a style often favored by the first generation of bluegrass guitarists.[23]

The Baltimore bluegrass scene was very competitive,[24] and the Pike County Boys got very few paying jobs, usually playing only for tips. In fact, their only paying venue in Baltimore was a club called the Blue Jay on Broadway not far from the waterfront, where they earned about two or three dollars apiece per show. The audience consisted mainly of sailors, most of whom wanted to hear skiffle (the ragtime string-band style popularized in the midfifties by Lonnie Donegan in England) or the current songs heard on the jukeboxes. The Pike County Boys learned quickly that listeners wanted to hear a broad variety of current favorites. Hazel, for instance, was often asked to sing Kitty Wells's songs and other country-and-western hits.[25]

The audiences at such clubs were often indifferent at best and noisy and dangerous at worst. Conditions encountered in the bluegrass honky-tonks in Baltimore, Washington, Cincinnati, Dayton, Detroit, and other urban centers where working people sought musical entertainment refute the myths of bluegrass's pristine rural origins. Women—whether as employees, customers, or musicians—quickly discovered that these honky-tonks were basically male domains, suffused with quests for masculine dominance and competitiveness. The roots of Hazel's feminism—displayed in some of her greatest songs, such as "Don't Put Her Down, You Helped Put Her There"—grew from her experiences in Baltimore honky-tonks.[26] There she had to deal with the good old boys from back home who were uncomfortable with her presence in the bands and often sexually aggressive in their treatment of her. She acutely observed and was generally repulsed by their treatment of women. Hazel nevertheless felt that their boorish behavior sprang from more than a cultural inheritance of patriarchal dominance. Such behavior was also fed by working-class male insecurities concerning work, low pay, and industrial regimentation. Although she understood men's reactions and pretensions, she resented them nonetheless.

Mike's passion to make music also carried him into a cultural domain far more cerebral and refined than that of the honky-tonks. This was the realm of Baltimore's cultural bohemians—the artists, writers, and musicians of the city—whose interests in "folk" music generally reflected a romantic view of working people whom they had never really known and whose songs had been learned mostly from city singers of folk songs. Mike began to learn about this community through Andy Ramsey, to whom he had been introduced by the folksinger Jack Elliott. Ramsey, a bit of a bohemian himself, lived on Eager Street and was well acquainted with the local folk music crowd. Two of the prime movers in this community were local lawyer Myron Edelman and his partner, Lisa Kierra, who in the early fifties opened up their home, a former carriage house in downtown Baltimore, to folk music enthusiasts.[27] The fare heard and played there included traditional ballads and folk songs, Elizabethan madrigals, and items learned from such urban interpreters of folk songs as Richard Dyer-Bennett, Burl Ives, and the Weavers. Pete Kuykendall referred to the people who gathered at Edelman's as "bohacks"—that is, Bohemians who made hackneyed music. The scene encountered there, though, mirrored that found at similar gatherings throughout America in the late fifties. In New York's Washington Square, on college campuses, in folk music clubs and coffeehouses, and in similar music venues across the country, bluegrass and hillbilly music were gradually beginning to intrude into the traditional folk music settings. After Mike and Hazel began showing up at Edelman's house, the music there gradually began to take on a more pronounced bluegrass or old-timey character. As Mike phrased it, bluegrass "disrupted" the sessions at Edelman's.[28]

At about the time of the Edelman interlude, Alyse Taubman, whom Mike described as his first real romantic attachment, came into his life. Alyse was destined, in fact, to be a major influence in Hazel Dickens's life as well. When Mike and Alyse met, she was married to Willie Foshag, an aeronautical engineer whom Mike already knew through their mutual love for the Autoharp. Alyse was trying to learn the fiddle while she worked on a master's degree in social therapy. Alyse and Willie frequently attended the jams at Edelman's but also hosted their own country music sessions in their apartment at 1325 Eager Street, which also served as the site of informal discussions of art, politics, and literature.

Alyse was in rebellion against the lifestyle of her father, a prominent and wealthy Baltimore businessman who owned a chain of auto-supply stores. While Alyse and Willie did make one major concession to middle-class modernity—they owned a brand-new Volkswagen van—they lived modestly in a rented apartment, dressed in second-hand clothing, decorated their apartment with used furniture, and subsisted for a short time on the money that Willie earned when he was in the army. Her parents said rue-fully that Alyse was their principal gift to charity. Alyse had a compassion-ate respect for the poor and downtrodden and was deeply concerned with the plight of the Appalachian migrants who had thronged into Baltimore. Hazel Dickens and her brothers intrigued her not only because they were a family of southern migrants whom she hoped to help in their transitions to urban life, but also because they made the style of traditional music that she had come to love. Alyse became a close confidant of Hazel and did more than anyone else to further her socialization and adjustment to city life. For example, Alyse arranged for Hazel to meet an educational therapist who encouraged her to recognize her capabilities and to learn that "there's always another way to think."[29] Hazel remembers Alyse as being the most important mentor in her life and recalls the discussions heard in Alyse's apartment as invaluable introductions to a world that she had neither en-countered nor imagined. While Hazel remained too shy to participate in the discussions, she listened with absorption.

Mike was also shy, of course, but he seems never to have had any prob-lem attracting girlfriends (a few of them maintained contact with him right down to the time of his marriage in 1959). Alyse, however, proved to be special. His friendship with her began as a musical one, as she and Willie sometimes played their fiddle and Autoharp at the sessions at Edelman's. The relationship strengthened when Mike left the TB hospital and moved into a second-floor apartment in the same building where Alyse and Willie lived. After their marriage dissolved, Willie moved out of the building. Mike and Alyse became quite intimate and enjoyed a year's relationship that Mike says was the first "serious" one he had ever had. He enjoyed her companionship, and she traveled with him on at least a couple of his col-lecting ventures in the South in 1957 and 1958 while he was assembling his Arthur Smith and the McGee Brothers recordings and his famous blue-grass LPs. Mike felt that he was not quite ready for marriage, however, and when Alyse pressed him on the subject, he decided to end their rela-tionship.

Music was the only "relationship" that fully consumed Mike during this period. And he was on the verge of making his first great contribution to America's folk music scene. His knowledge of Baltimore's bluegrass music culture, combined with his crucial links to the northern folk music estab-lishment through his brother Pete, Moses "Moe" Asch, and Alan Lomax, provided some of the basic ingredients for the national popularization of bluegrass and for its entrance into the incipient urban folk music revival of the mid-1950s. New York City, of course, was the crucial nerve center and barometer of folk music in urban America. Folk music's prominence in the city had been energized there in the 1930s, when Aunt Molly Jackson, Leadbelly (Huddie Ledbetter), and other assorted refugees from the South inspired an interest in songs of the poor and downtrodden. One of the central moments in the unfolding of folk music history in New York— an event that some have described as the beginning of the urban folk music revival—came at the Forrest Theater on March 3, 1940, when Pete Seeger and Alan Lomax met the Oklahoma-born balladeer Woody Guthrie at a "Grapes of Wrath Evening" to benefit the "John Steinbeck Committee for Agricultural Workers." The event certainly galvanized Seeger's commitment to the musical crusade for social justice and reaffirmed the seemingly indissoluble link between folk music and radical politics.

Folk music in New York City remained largely politically leftist but a far cry from the vision of "workers' music" once promoted by the Composers' Collective. Rather than being songs written *for* working people by sophisticated composers, the music heard or performed at square dances, in settlement houses, on college campuses, at summer camps, at political rallies, and in coffeehouses was borrowed mostly from southern working folk. Sometime in 1946, George Margolin began taking his guitar down to Washington Square in Greenwich Village, where he sang for a small circle of friends. The event proved tempting for other musicians, and as their numbers grew, the city soon began insisting on permits for the afternoon singings that emerged there. Washington Square became the most crucial venue for folk music performance in New York, where small groups of musicians gathered around the big fountain for a few hours each Sunday.[30]

Most of the fledgling musicians were Jewish youths whose introduction to folk music often came as "red diaper babies" (children of communist or left-wing parents) at summer camps where Pete Seeger often performed.[31] Young banjo players usually imitated Pete, but they gradually became aware of the syncopated, three-finger style popularized by Earl Scruggs, and even Pete tried to adapt to it while providing some instruction about the style in his famous book *How to Play the 5-String Banjo*. Roger Sprung, a regular participant at Washington Square and dubbed by Dave Van Ronk as the "original citybilly," had first heard a Scruggs recording at Billy Faier's house in 1947, and he began popularizing the style in jam sessions at the square and with his band the Shanty Boys. Julian "Winnie" Winston, whose

Mike Seeger (on mandolin) with Roger Sprung (on banjo) and John Cohen (on guitar) at Washington Square, New York City, 1958. (Photo by Aaron Rennert of Photo-Sound Associates; courtesy of Ronald D. Cohen)

Mike Seeger (on mandolin) with Bob Yellin (on banjo) and Ralph Rinzler (on guitar) at Washington Square, New York City. (Photo by Aaron Rennert of Photo-Sound Associates; courtesy of Ronald D. Cohen)

introduction to the five-string banjo came as a summer camp disciple of Pete Seeger, recalled his "ah-ha" moment as a musician when he observed Sprung in 1955 playing the instrument at a concert in New York. The revelation came when he noticed that the shower of syncopated notes occurred because of what Sprung was doing with his right hand (that is, using three fingers to play alternating patterns on the strings).[32] Banjo players throughout New York City shared Winston's fascination in their efforts to recreate the sensational style that Scruggs had popularized. The time was ripe for a full-scale stylistic and historical survey of the style.

Sometime in 1956, Moe Asch, the owner of New York's Folkways Records, talked to Pete Seeger about the Scruggs style and suggested that it be memorialized in a recorded documentary. Aware of Mike's avid interest in both the performance and history of bluegrass, Pete recommended his little brother for the task. Asch wrote to Mike on September 13, 1956, and pledged $100 for expenses if Mike was willing to take on the project.[33] Mike welcomed the opportunity to document the emerging bluegrass genre and to show its relationship to old-time country music. Folkways LPs were poorly marketed and had only limited circulation (largely in libraries), but they were highly prized in New York or anywhere that folk musicians gathered. Along with the historic recordings of Leadbelly and Woody Guthrie, released on the earlier Asch label, the Folkways disks of the 1950s joined with Library of Congress recordings to provide the basic underpinnings for the folk revival's discovery of southern grassroots music. Only as recently as 1952, the label had issued the *Anthology of American Folk Music*, generally described as the Harry Smith collection. These recordings increased the circulation of, and lent legitimacy to, the old-time music that Mike Seeger was beginning to make his life's work.

Moe Asch was born in Poland in 1905, the son of Yiddish poet and novelist Sholem Asch.[34] The Asch family immigrated to the United States in 1914 but soon returned to Europe, where Moe had two experiences that shaped his life: he went to a technical school in Bingen, Germany, where he developed an interest in electronics; and in a local bookstore, he found a 1913 edition of John Lomax's *Cowboy Songs and Other Frontier Ballads* (originally published in 1910). The Lomax book and other western stories that his father provided inspired in Moe a romantic and lifelong interest in America's common people and their culture. He was back in the United States by the summer of 1925 working for RCA Victor, just in time to become part of the radical political scene that coalesced in New York City.

After a brief career as a sound engineer installing public-address systems in hotels, he moved into the field of recording, forming the Asch Recording Studios as a division of WEVD in New York (for which he recorded radio transcriptions and commercial Jewish music performances).

According to a story told by Asch, Albert Einstein actually had played an unwitting but central role in his decision to make the recording of folk music his life's career. In 1939 Moe and his father visited Einstein in New Jersey to record a statement from him about the need for civilized humanity to respond to the plight of Jews in Europe. After the scientist asked Moe about his business and aims in life, Moe told him about his intentions to record the authentic voices of the American people. Einstein applauded the idea and asserted that Americans did not appreciate the value of their own culture: "It will be a Polish Jew like you who will do the job." In May 1941 Asch recorded the powerful Louisiana-born black folk musician Huddie "Leadbelly" Ledbetter and began his epochal career as a documentarian of American folk music. Asch definitely did his part to document many of the long-neglected elements of American culture with the founding of such labels as Asch, Disc, and Folkways. He recorded a staggering array of sounds — everything from the croak of frogs to ethnic performances — and boasted that his recordings never went out of print.[35]

Equipped with the $100 promised by Asch and his own tape recorder and microphones, Mike set out on his quest to document the roots of the three-finger, or Scruggs, banjo style. Driving through the Upper South, he often slept in his car and subsisted on hamburgers and milk shakes. He did a good job of enlisting the cooperation of several highly skilled banjo players, including Larry Richardson, Smiley Hobbs, Joe Stuart, and a very young Roni Stoneman, daughter of Ernest. These musicians came mostly from the Baltimore and Washington areas and assisted Mike even though he could not pay them for their contributions. Mike also lent his support to the project with his own musicianship, playing guitar accompaniment on at least six tracks and taking the lead with his banjo on a very creditable three-finger version of "Ground Hog." Through the help of Pete Kuykendall (who was featured on one cut playing "Irish Washerwoman") and Tom Morgan, Mike managed to enlist into the project Junie Scruggs (an older brother of Earl) and, in Columbia, South Carolina, Dewitt "Snuffy" Jenkins, whose performances from the late 1930s are now widely acknowledged as the first recorded examples of the style that Scruggs later popularized.[36]

Jenkins played versions of ten songs, including "Lonesome Road Blues" and "John Henry."[37]

The definitive origins of the three-finger style will probably never be known, but Jenkins had become aware of it as early as 1927, when he played in a trio with Rex Brooks and Smith Hammett, two early proponents of the technique. Jenkins popularized his own version of the three-finger roll on radio broadcasts in the Carolinas in the 1930s and 1940s and had performed and recorded with a variety of string bands, including the well-known band led by J. E. Mainer. Great banjo players like Don Reno and Ralph Stanley had always been quick to acknowledge that Jenkins was the first "Scruggs style" banjoist that they had ever heard. Jenkins was still an active musician in 1956, playing mostly in the area around Columbia with fiddler Homer "Pappy" Sherrill in a band called the Hired Hands. Mike recorded Jenkins at WIS in Columbia in a studio where he had played since 1937.

Mike's tireless efforts bore fruit in 1957, when *American Banjo Scruggs Style* (Folkways FA 2314) was issued with liner notes written by Ralph Rinzler. The inclusion of liner notes, while pretty common for Folkways' products, was unique for rural or country music.[38] While *American Banjo Scruggs Style* might be considered the first album devoted to bluegrass music, Mike's next project, *Mountain Music Bluegrass Style*, proved to be even more significant in the dissemination of bluegrass in the North. This seminal album was Mike's idea and virtually a natural extension of his experiences in Baltimore. It was also an opportunity to spread the gospel of a conviction that had been steadily taking shape in his mind: he believed that bluegrass music was the logical and inevitable outgrowth of the music made by the old-time string bands in the 1920s and 1930s. Dick Spottswood had introduced Mike to some of the older varieties of bluegrass while he was living as a teenager in Washington. But in Baltimore he became immersed in the genre and, through the Dickens family, became intimately aware of the values, aspirations, and day-to-day concerns of the people who made the music. In large part, the album was an anthology of Baltimore-based musicians, including Mike himself and his old friend Bob Baker, Don Stover and Bea Lilly (who were on temporary leave from the Lilly Brothers while Everett Lilly was touring with Flatt and Scruggs), Tex Logan, and the exciting Earl Taylor with his Stoney Mountain Boys. Partly because of the ascendancy of rock and roll, bluegrass was experiencing a temporary lull in activity, and the underemployed musicians in the Baltimore/Washington area were eager to have their talents advertised. An association with Mike Seeger and Folkways promised to give them some access to a new audience. The music made for the album, while not always polished and smooth, was nevertheless exciting. Some of the songs performed by Earl Taylor, for example — such as "White House Blues" and "All the Good Times Are Past and Gone" — were among the most scorching and dynamic performances in the emerging bluegrass field. This was the first LP that explicitly linked bluegrass to Appalachian music and culture. In his liner notes, Mike presented a schematic history of bluegrass — probably the first written account of the style ever attempted — and he in fact lent currency to the use of "bluegrass" as the identifying term for the genre.

Bearing the prestigious Folkways imprimatur, *Mountain Music Bluegrass Style* reached an audience that otherwise might have paid little attention to this emerging body of music. The album contributed to two perceptions central to the music's acceptance by northern urban fans: the idea that bluegrass was "folk" music and that its roots were in the Appalachian South. Above all, the LP inspired scores of musicians who became emboldened to experiment with elements of the bluegrass style. David Grisman, now recognized as a major innovator in mandolin playing and a leading architect of acoustic jazz style, spoke for many musicians when he commented on the influence that the album exerted on his life and music. As an impressionable teenager in Passaic, New Jersey, Grisman had become attracted to the mandolin and to roots music through the mentorship of his older neighbor Ralph Rinzler. Grisman later declared that the Folkways collection "was the first bluegrass I ever heard. It had extensive liner notes, a booklet with pictures, and the whole story of bluegrass at the time. I used to read those notes over and over."[39] One should not discount the importance of liner notes to youthful and well-educated urban fans who were in or about to go to college and were looking for scholarly legitimization of the music they heard. Their parents, after all, had long been familiar with the presence of well-researched and explanatory notes in the jazz albums that they purchased.

Recalling the Baltimore days and his role in making bluegrass music widely known, Mike later said, "I had this feeling of mission." He seized every opportunity to demonstrate the value of this exciting musical form and introduced the best of what he had heard to the famous folklorist Alan Lomax. Lomax had recently returned from self-imposed exile in Europe, where he had gone in 1950 to flee the repressive anticommunist movement that had emerged in the United States. Lomax had been listed as a subversive character in the notorious publication *Red Channels*. After returning to America in 1958, Lomax was anxious to get reacquainted with American folk music and to explore its present contours.[40] Mike introduced him to both ends of the bluegrass continuum in the traditional music of Earl Taylor and the Stoney Mountain Boys, who Mike heard at Club 79 in Baltimore, and the "progressive" sound of the Country Gentlemen, who played in a club in downtown Washington. Lomax was swept away by what he heard. He invited Taylor's band, which had been featured on *Mountain Music Bluegrass Style*, to appear at Carnegie Hall in New York in April 1959 as part of a concert called Folksong '59. Although no country-and-western act was asked to perform, the concert presented a fairly judicious sampling of current "folk music" activity, including Jimmy Driftwood (of "Battle of New Orleans" fame), Muddy Waters, Memphis Slim, Pete and Mike Seeger, and, most daringly, a rock-and-roll group called the Cadillacs. Lomax ruffled the feelings of some people in the audience when he described rock and roll as a blending of black and white folk styles and asked his listeners to abandon their prejudices against the music. The country boys in Earl Taylor's band approached the concert in the august auditorium with considerable trepidation. Surveying the packed house from backstage, fiddler Curtis Cody remarked to banjoist Walter Hensley, "Walt, I don't think they'll like us a bit."[41] The audience, however, received each number from the Stoney Mountain Boys with thunderous applause and shouts of delight. Soon thereafter, Lomax helped to get Taylor and the group a recording contract with United Artists, which resulted in the widely circulated album *Folk Songs from the Blue Grass* (UAL 3049). Lomax's encounters with Taylor and other bluegrass bands culminated with his famous article for *Esquire* magazine in 1959 in which he referred to the style as "folk music with overdrive" and described it as "the freshest sound" in American folk music. Dubiously but enthusiastically, he also called bluegrass "the first clear-cut orchestral form in five hundred years of Anglo-American music."[42] With encomiums such as these coming from America's best-known folklorist, Mike Seeger could not help but believe that his "mission" was being achieved. He had contributed to the music's official recognition in American popular culture. Its vital presence in the urban folk music revival also seemed secure.

Bluegrass documentation and popularization, however, did not exhaust Mike's drive, passion, and sense of mission. Nor had he abandoned his love for old-time music. Mike continued to seek out and record old-time musi-cians and to present a few of them to the world through Folkways LPs. In the winter of 1957–58, in the midst of his varied and busy activities in Balti-more, he still managed to make several trips to Libba Cotten's row house in downtown Washington to record her eclectic repertoire. At the end of her busy workday, and often after she had put her grandchildren to bed, Eliza-beth sat on the edge of her bed and sang and played into Mike's hand-held microphone. Playing on three different guitars, including Mike's Martin D-28, she recorded the songs that in 1958 appeared on her first Folkways album.

When Mike returned home from his first trip south on his quest for Scruggs-style banjo pickers, he fulfilled another personal ambition. On October 4, 1956, he stopped at Wade Ward's house near Independence, Virginia. Mike had loved Ward's music ever since he heard it on the old records of the Bogtrotters' band. During this session, he collected twenty-three tunes from Ward, who played both fiddle and banjo. In many ways, this experience was much more rewarding for Mike than his bluegrass recordings had been. Not only did Ward's music bring back memories of the records Mike had heard as a child, but, describing Ward as "a very calm, graceful, country guy," Mike also said that the event was his "first experi-ence seeing a Virginia musician at home." Ward had succeeded in build-ing a comfortable country life, free of nine-to-five restraints, wage labor, and factory-imposed discipline. The meeting was still vivid in Mike's mind thirty years later when he decided to make Virginia his home.[43]

In late 1956 and early 1957, Mike recorded other old-time musicians, such as the fiddler J. C. Sutphin in Wittman, Maryland; the fine husband-and-wife team E. C. and Orna Ball in Rugby, Virginia, who had made com-mercial recordings and field recordings for Alan Lomax; and Ernest and Hattie Stoneman in Carmody Hills, Maryland. The Folkways LP that was issued in 1957—*Old-Time Tunes of the South*—included ten songs by Ernest and Hattie (and two of their children) and eleven songs by Louise Fouracre, J. C. and Vernon Sutphin, J. J. Neese, and H. N. Dickens (Hazel's father, who was heard playing the banjo and singing portions of three songs).

By August 14, 1957, Mike was back at Wade Ward's home, but this time to record the music of Kilby Snow, an unorthodox Autoharp musician who had been recommended to Mike by Ernest Stoneman. At the time Mike met him, Snow was working on a construction site not far from Indepen-dence. Mike had already developed a new respect for the Autoharp, the lowly instrument that had once been virtually dismissed as a child's toy or as a simple instrument that even the most tone-deaf amateur could strum. For one thing, after hearing Ernest Stoneman and Maybelle Carter play the instrument, he had learned that distinct melodies could be played on it. Then, during a trip to Nashville as part of his expedition to record the McGee Brothers and Arthur Smith, he saw Maybelle on the Grand Ole Opry and learned that she held the instrument against her chest when she played, as opposed to Sara Carter's fashion of laying the instrument flat on a stand. Snow's playing brought further revelations, for not only was he playing melodies note for note on the instrument, but he was also bending and slurring the notes. Snow strummed the Autoharp left-handed, below the chord bars; he produced what he called "drag notes" and demonstrated that blues and ragtime tunes could be played on the instrument. Mike became increasingly aware that a vital but undocumented tradition of Autoharp playing existed in the rural South. He also regularly incorporated the instrument into his own performing repertoire, but without the innovations made by Snow. Mike's forte, heard most compellingly on old ballads such as "When First unto This Country," was the straight-ahead melodic rendition of the song that he chose.[44]

While Mike's lengthy and growing list of documentary recordings was only one of his many accomplishments, he still was having trouble making ends meet and had no clear-cut idea about what his future would be. Inspired by a precedent set by his good friend Pete Kuykendall, Mike considered the prospects of a career in radio. Like his earlier inspiration, Don Owens, he thought he might find some economic stability as a radio disk jockey and yet still have the time to make music on the side. From 1956 to 1958, armed with financial support provided by Charles Seeger, Mike went to the Commercial Radio Institute, a radio school in Baltimore, hoping to become a radio announcer. The institute, as Mike remembered it, consisted of two teachers—an elderly man who taught math and a younger fellow who taught electronics. Once sufficient knowledge of the radio business was obtained, a student could then enroll in further courses dealing with the television business. Mike obtained a radio telephone license with the intention of fulfilling his old dream of moving to Galax, Virginia, to become a country radio disk jockey. The Galax job never materialized, but Mike did take a test for a position at a station in Havre de Grace, Maryland, where Ola Belle and Bud Reed worked. However, he read poorly for the position and could not pass the audition.[45] In the fall and winter of 1958, he worked at WCBM in Baltimore reading meters at the transmitter. If trouble occurred, he called the engineer. He took some preliminary training briefly in 1957 to be a Wearever salesman (selling aluminum pots and pans), but he seems never to have actually worked in that capacity. He also worked two stints briefly as a file clerk at the Social Security Administration (SSA) and for a few months received unemployment insurance. On July 10, 1958, during his second stay at the SSA, he found himself an innocent victim of "Seeger politics." He was quizzed by the FBI and asked about the alleged communist involvement of Charles, Pete, and Peggy. Mike would offer no information on his family, but he personally denied being a communist. He avowed that he had not been aware of his father's reported communist activities and said that, as a conscientious objector, he "could not believe in the overthrow of the government by force."[46]

When it came time to reenroll at the Commercial Radio Institute, Mike began looking for additional means to pay the tuition. At Alyse Taubman's suggestion, he contacted the Central Scholarship Bureau, a Baltimore organization that since 1924 had provided economic support for students who desired to further their professional or business growth.[47] The bureau recommended that he enroll in college instead. He rejected the advice, but he did agree to consult a psychologist. Mike quit his job at WCBM, and with the endorsement of John Dildine, who had worked at the company, he got a job at Capitol Transcriptions, a recording studio in Washington. He relocated to that city in January 1959 — a move that signaled new dimensions in Mike's life far larger than a change in residence and employment.

4

The New Lost City Ramblers

Creating the Old-Time Music Scene

In January 1959 Mike moved into what he called a "dreary little apartment" on Douglas Street in Northeast Washington. His job as a recording engineer at Capitol Transcriptions was sometimes interesting, but it was not totally satisfying. He was not yet married and was still unsure about what to do with the rest of his life. With members of his family under siege because of their political beliefs, Mike was busy trying to make music as often as possible and yet steer clear of the taint of "Seeger radicalism." Apparently, Mike had tried and failed to get a job in the Archive of American Folk Song, prompting Charles to say to him later in the year, "I doubt any Seeger could get a job with the U.S. government at this time."[1]

Mike's destiny, however, had been set the previous spring when he joined with two of his friends to form the New Lost City Ramblers, the trio that changed the sound of American folk music.[2] By the time Mike moved into his Washington apartment, the Ramblers had given a few concerts and had recorded their first Folkways album, which was released in January 1959. However, the group had not yet received any assurance that it would become popular in the folk music community. At the time, Capitol Transcriptions seemed to be Mike's only viable option for making a living. His work there brought him into contact with a wide range of people—anyone who wished to record their music or voice for private, business, political, or entertainment purposes, including a fledgling rock-and-roll band called Rockin' Robin, Korean and American translators, and the famous evangelist Billy Graham. Capitol's "bread and butter," though, came from remote recordings of major political and social events that were produced mostly for the Westinghouse Corporation to be broadcast later on its radio stations. Mike devoted a considerable amount of time to taping the press conferences of politicos like Senate Majority Leader Lyndon Johnson or Speaker of the House John W. McCormack or recording visits from foreign dignitaries at sites such as Andrews Air Force Base or the National Press Club. The visit made to the United States in September 1959 by Nikita Khrushchev, premier of the Soviet Union, was clearly the most important event documented by Capitol Transcriptions during Mike's employment there.

Although his work at Capitol was generally uninspiring, Mike nevertheless was able to take advantage of the position to make significant contributions to the exposure and popularization of bluegrass music. For example, he supervised a session by Bill Clifton and the Dixie Mountain Boys, playing the Autoharp, Dobro, and mandolin on some of the recordings (including one of the first album-length recorded tributes ever made to the Carter Family).[3] Now that Mike had produced a handful of albums that emphasized the down-home or rootsy side of bluegrass, he felt the need to show that some bluegrass bands were venturing into modern material and styles. He had become acquainted with the music of one of the most experimental bands, the Country Gentlemen, who played regularly in the greater Washington area; through Pete Kuykendall, Mike had met John Duffey, the leader of the band. The Country Gentlemen had recorded earlier for Nashville's Starday label, but they eagerly accepted Mike's invitation to record in the Capitol studios, realizing that the Folkways LP that would follow would introduce them to the folk revival audience. Though firmly grounded in the bluegrass tradition and resolutely wedded to the use of acoustic instruments and high-tenor harmony singing, the Country Gentlemen nevertheless played a brand of eclectic and stylistically wide-ranging music that borrowed from rock, jazz, popular, country and western, and traditional balladry. The Gentlemen, in short, played a style of music that would soon be described as "progressive bluegrass." Kuykendall helped select some of the material for the session and John Cohen took the photograph for the cover, but Mike assumed full responsibility for the actual recording that came to be considered as the "classic" Country Gentlemen—Duffey on mandolin, Charlie Waller on guitar, Eddie Adcock on five-string banjo, and Tom Gray on the stand-up bass.[4]

Mike never lost interest in bluegrass, and over the years he performed and recorded extensively with such musicians as Bill Clifton, Don Reno, Red Rector, Don Stover, Ralph Stanley, the Country Gentlemen, Hazel and

Alice, and other entertainers in that genre. He was beginning to feel, however, that bluegrass had become predictable and unchallenging, and that Scruggs-style banjo playing, for all its technical brilliance, lacked the diversity and soulfulness of the old-time styles. Therefore, despite his immersion in the bluegrass scene, Mike's heart remained wedded to the old-time sounds and styles that he first heard when he was a child.

The opportunity to play a profound role in the rediscovery and renewed appreciation of old-time music had actually occurred while Mike was still living in Baltimore. John Dildine, who hosted a folk music radio show on WASH-FM in Washington, had invited Mike to play on one of his broadcasts, and he had issued a similar invitation to New York musicians John Cohen and Tom Paley. Mike was already familiar with them: he had played with Cohen at Pete Seeger's cabin in Beacon, New York, and at Washington Square, and he had become acquainted with Paley at either a session at Myron Edelman's in Baltimore or at a hootenanny hosted by Paley and Cohen at Yale. The three of them met again at Dildine's show on May 25, 1958.[5] None of them realized that the influential career of the New Lost City Ramblers was about to begin.

Cohen and Paley had played music with each other since at least 1952, when they organized the first "hoots" (or hootenannies, folk music jam sessions) at Yale. Their introduction to folk music had come through their parents' interest in square dancing and left-wing politics, and at the "progressive" summer camps where such famous musicians as Pete Seeger and Leadbelly sometimes serenaded the campers. Both young men, separately, had already discovered the beauty and charm that lay in the old hillbilly records and had become avid collectors as teenagers. As early as 1948, Cohen had become fascinated by the old-time sounds he heard on the reissued material of old 78-rpm recordings produced by Alan Lomax — *Listen to Our Story* and *Mountain Frolics* — and by the music made by Woody Guthrie on *Dust Bowl Ballads*. In 1950 he also found an enormous cache of old hillbilly records in a store in San Francisco. The appearance of Harry Smith's *Anthology of American Folk Music* in 1952, then, reaffirmed Cohen's already strong interest in the old recorded music. Cohen and Paley had also learned much about southern hillbilly music by listening to and learning from Harry and Jeanie West, genuine hillbillies who had moved from North Carolina to New York in the 1940s.[6]

Paley had already established himself in New York as a professional folk musician — he had met Leadbelly, had played with Woody Guthrie, and had recorded an LP for Elektra in 1953 titled *Folk Songs from the Southern Appalachian Mountains*—by the time he arrived with Cohen at the Dildine show. Cohen was a photographer and a filmmaker whose loft in Greenwich Village was located right in the vortex of scenes frequented by abstract expressionist artists, Beat poets, and musicians. He later spoke of the Village's "convergence of creative imaginations" as an anticipation of the counterculture and a harbinger of cultural revolution in the United States. Cohen's photographs of people like Guthrie, Jack Kerouac, Allen Ginsberg, and a very young Bob Dylan earned him a reputation as a first-rate artist and documenter in both of those cultural worlds.[7]

Seeger, Cohen, and Paley practiced only minimally before their appearance on Dildine's show, but they felt very good about their thirty-minute session, playing old-time songs like "Soldier's Joy," "Make Me a Pallet on Your Floor," and "Colored Aristocracy."[8] They had played these songs together earlier at various jam sessions, although never as a threesome. Cohen volunteered to contact Moe Asch about obtaining a possible Folkways recording contract for the trio. Without even asking for an audition tape and acting largely because the three young men had such strong reputations, Asch agreed to supervise a session in September.

On September 28, two days prior to the session, they gave a concert at the Carnegie Chapter Hall in New York that had been arranged by Israel Goodman "Izzy" Young. Young had first been attracted to folk music through his participation as a teenager in Margot Mayo's New York square-dance group and now was the owner of the Folklore Center, a small shop on MacDougal Street in Greenwich Village that had become the chief focal point for folk music enthusiasts in New York. He had stacked the Folklore Center's small space with books, magazines, used instruments, and records and was a fount of information about all of the folk music that was being made in New York. He also edited a gossip column on folk music called "Frets and Frails" in *Sing Out!* magazine and had coined a popular term, "folkniks" (inspired by the recent orbiting of the earth by the Russian satellite, Sputnik), to describe the young folk music fans that were proliferating in the city. Young had been arranging small concerts at the Folklore Center and at other venues like the Carnegie Chapter Hall, so it was no wonder that Bob Dylan made the center one of his favorite hangouts when he came to New York in 1961 and even wrote a long, humorous poem (apparently never recorded) about Young and his store.[9]

After their successful concert in the small recital hall—and even after their Folkways recording session two days later — the trio still had no official band name. At the Carnegie performance, publicity material had merely billed them as "Seeger, Cohen, and Paley." There are conflicting memories regarding the way that the name New Lost City Ramblers came into existence. Moe Asch apparently provided the initial inspiration when he said that they should include "city" in their name because none of them had ever lived in the country. Paley has always insisted that the Ramblers were named through a joint effort. Both Seeger and Cohen, however, remembered Cohen as the principal creator: he evidently came up with the name sometime after dinner following the recording session while he was working on the cover of the LP. New Lost City Ramblers, Cohen said, was a playful, affectionate tribute to old-time country bands like the Skillet Lickers and the Fruit Jar Drinkers who had often used self-parodying names to describe themselves. If any one group, though, served as their model, it would have been Charlie Poole and the North Carolina Ramblers, a three-piece fiddle band from the North Carolina piedmont that had always impressed fans of old-time music with its drive, precision, and infectious rhythms. Mike later chuckled about what he described as the Ramblers' naïve belief that they could recreate the sound of that historic band.[10]

The first New Lost City Ramblers LP, called simply *The New Lost City Ramblers* (Folkways FA 2396),[11] and Mike's important Folkways project *Mountain Music Bluegrass Style* both came out in January 1959. Neither record sold in great quantities, but both were distributed widely in New York folk music circles and exerted tremendous influence. The two albums showcased Mike's expertise as a documentarian and musician. With Mike and Tom working full-time as a recording engineer and university mathematics professor, respectively, the group had little opportunity for extended tours outside of the Northeast. Consequently, the Ramblers gave few performances during the first year and a half after their initial recording and concert. They did, however, spend a good deal of time practicing, either in New York or Washington; they recorded their second LP in June 1959; and they managed to put on shows at the American Youth Hostel in New York City (February 28, 1959), Pierce Hall in Washington (April 17), Mills College in New York City (June 13), and Manny Greenhill's Ballad Room in Boston (sometime in November). The Ballad Room show was especially memorable because the Ramblers opened for two distinguished blues performers, Memphis Slim and Willie Dixon. Dixon even played bass with them when they performed "Dallas Rag."[12]

The New Lost City Ramblers in 1960. From left: John Cohen, Tom Paley, and Mike Seeger. (Photo courtesy of Alexia Smith)

The single most important incident in the emerging career of the New Lost City Ramblers came, to their astonishment, in July 1959, when they were asked to appear at the first Newport Folk Festival in Rhode Island. Since the previous year, when the Kingston Trio's recording of the old North Carolina murder ballad "Tom Dooley" was released to an immensely popular reception, the country had been in the throes of a major folk music revival dominated largely by urban interpreters of traditional or tradition-based music. Unlike the revival of the 1930s, which was heavily colored by left-wing assumptions and dreams, the folk music boom of the late 1950s and 1960s (later described by folksinger Bruce "Utah" Phillips as the "Great Folk Scare")[13] cut across generational and class categories and received support from conservatives, liberals, and radicals.[14] The Newport Folk Festival was top-heavy with commercially oriented musicians (generally singers of folk songs rather than true folksingers), but its organizers, George Wein and Albert Grossman, attempted to provide some diversity.[15] They chose a few country acts, including Earl Scruggs, the Stanley Brothers, and Jimmie Driftwood (James Morris), the Arkansas schoolteacher whose "Battle of New Orleans" had given him national exposure. The New Lost City Ramblers had won a host of eager admirers in the New York folk community with their first two Folkways LPs and a smattering of concerts, but their newly won fame would hardly have been enough to garner them a position on the festival stage without the allure of the Seeger name, as well as the prominence of Tom Paley as a local performer. But once they launched into their sets, festival fans were impressed with their musicianship and intrigued by the fact that the Ramblers' distinctive sound set them apart from other acts. No one else in the entire revival scene had attempted to recreate the string-band styles of the pre–World War II South, and no other urban band had used the fiddle as a defining instrument. The musician and reviewer Billy Faier summed up the feelings of many listeners when he said "these three young folksingers have accomplished something that is considered impossible by most. They have successfully reproduced the folk style of another culture. They have recaptured the sound of an entire instrumental and singing heritage." Others were charmed by the novelty of the Ramblers' act or by the archaic aura projected by their sound and stage presence. But many fans had become aware of old-time music through the Harry Smith collection and other reissues of old 78-rpm recordings. Now, for the first time, they saw examples of this music actually being performed on stage. The Ramblers came away from Newport convinced that their brand of old-time music would gain a respectful and enthusiastic audience among folk revival devotees.[16]

Despite the growing appeal of the New Lost City Ramblers, Mike did not yet feel free to make music his full-time profession, even though it occupied most of his waking hours. This was an intensely stressful time for him, as he struggled to balance his musical obsession with his full-time work at Capitol Transcriptions. In addition to frequent practices with the other Ramblers, Mike memorized songs learned from tape recordings on the bus while going to work.

Mike's personal life, however, began to take a positive upswing when he met Marjorie (Marge) Ostrow in the summer of 1959 at New River Ranch. An ardent country music fan and fledgling musician from New York City, the seventeen-year-old Marge had come to the country music park with two of her classmates from Antioch College, Jeremy Foster and his wife, Alice Gerrard. Jeremy had been one of Mike's Woodstock high school chums, and he and Alice had already been busy bringing bluegrass music to the attention of students at Antioch. An Osborne Brothers concert that Jeremy and Alice organized at Antioch on March 5, 1960, is generally considered to be the first bluegrass show ever held on a college campus. Marge was an attractive, dark-haired young woman whose skills on the guitar, banjo, and Autoharp could only have made her doubly appealing to Mike. It is fair to say that Marge fell head over heels in love with Mike and with the music that consumed him. The two became constant companions, and in July they drove together to the Newport Folk Festival. In her letters to him, she said that she had "rarely been so happy" and wore his jacket to work even though it was the middle of summer; she also spoke of her infatuation with the banjo and noted that she had been "playing ceaselessly."[17] The couple married on December 20, 1959, at the New York Society for Ethical Culture on the Upper West Side adjacent to Central Park. Marge was probably not aware that she was marrying more than a handsome and talented young musician; she was also committing herself to his compulsive and all-consuming musical career.[18]

In the summer of 1960, Mike made the decision to devote his life fully to music. He quit Capitol Transcriptions and took a broken-down tape recorder as his final payment. The Ramblers' career took off that same summer. Albert Grossman, a major folk music promoter and the codirector of the Newport Folk Festival, invited the Ramblers to do a three-week stint at the Gate of Horn, his upscale jazz and folk music club in Chicago. The club hosted most of the big-name acts in jazz and folk music, including Bob Gibson and Joan Baez, but it gained its most enduring notoriety as the place where comedian Lenny Bruce was arrested in December 1962 for an allegedly obscene monologue. The time spent in Chicago was exhausting but exhilarating for the band. All three Ramblers and two wives (Marge and Claudia Paley; Cohen was not yet married) stayed in the same small apartment, and the trio played each night at the Gate of Horn from about nine o'clock until three or four in the morning. They practiced constantly in their apartment, listening to old songs on the tape recorder not only to learn the lyrics but also to absorb the feeling and style of the original performances. It was a tough and demanding life, but the long hours of performance permitted them to hone their styles, sharpen their repertory, and develop compelling stage shows.

When the Gate of Horn gig ended, the Ramblers flew to New York and then took a small chartered plane to Newport for the second folk festival. At the end of the festival, Mike, John, and Tom set out on a grueling and harrowing series of flights on an unscheduled prop plane to California, stopping in various cities along the way before reaching their final desti-

Mike, Kim, and Marjorie Seeger recording a live performance.
(Photo courtesy of Alexia Smith)

nation of Burbank. Playing the Berkeley Folk Festival was their ultimate goal. Meanwhile, Claudia and Marge set out on the long trip to California in Mike's Volkswagen. Marge was six months pregnant and acting against the advice of her father-in-law and Pete's wife, Toshi.[19]

Like all of the other folk music festivals, the affair in Berkeley, organized by Barry Olivier, was an event that was designed to combine traditional and pop performers.[20] Again, the New Lost City Ramblers offered a unique fare and were popular with many fans because of their attempts at authenticity. Unlike the other musical acts that proliferated in the revival, the Ramblers never described their music as "folk," since the term had become largely meaningless through its widespread and careless usage. Nor did they often use the name "hillbilly" as a description for the songs and instrumental tunes that they performed on recordings and in concerts. Instead, they embraced the label "old-time" or "old-timey," a practice that Ruth Crawford Seeger had followed in 1953 when she compiled her book *American*

Folk Songs for Christmas. She noted that "old-time music is a folk name for folk music"—that is, a term used by plain working people to describe the familiar music that they loved.[21]

By the time they reached California, the Ramblers had assembled a repertoire of songs typified by, but not confined to, the music heard on their first two Folkways LPs.[22] The music that defined their stage shows included instrumental pieces, children's songs, frolic or dance tunes, ballads and love songs, and occasional religious pieces, all learned mostly from the old commercial 78s or, in a few cases, from Library of Congress recordings. This was rural *southern* music, even though Mike and John (who did most of the written annotations for the trio) typically tried to link the music with more geographic specificity to "the southern mountains" in their album notes and popular published song collection, *The New Lost City Ramblers Song Book* (an attractive paperback book filled with vintage photographs—many from the collection of Farm Security Administration photographers—and with lyrics and song transcriptions by Harriet Elizabeth "Hally" Wood, a classically trained musician who also transcribed songs for the Lomaxes).[23]

Although the Ramblers had made crucial departures from the ways in which folk music had been defined and studied in the United States—particularly in their recognition that commercial performance had been an important source and means of dissemination of "folk" material—they nevertheless clung to one presumption that had colored the thought of previous folk enthusiasts: they exhibited the romantic fascination with the Appalachians that had been present in American folk music circles since at least the time of Cecil Sharp in the early decades of the twentieth century. The Ramblers could not resist the temptation to equate "Appalachian music" with "old-time music." John Cohen alleged in their songbook that "the music we play is from the Southern mountain repertoire, a tradition which has come to be called 'old-time music.'" And Mike Seeger declared further that "most of the songs that we sing and play now were originally recorded by commercial companies and the Library of Congress in the Southeastern mountains between 1925 and 1935."[24] Many of the songs embraced by the New Lost City Ramblers did indeed come from the repertories of mountain musicians and from recording sites that lay in the southern hills. But a closer look at their repertoire reveals that they also borrowed songs from people like the Gant Family from Austin, Texas; Uncle Dave Macon, who lived near Nashville, Tennessee; Cliff Carlisle from central Kentucky;

Cover of *The New Lost City Ramblers Song Book*. (Courtesy of the Southern Folklife Collection, University of North Carolina at Chapel Hill)

Charlie Poole from the North Carolina piedmont; and Eck Robertson, who lived in Amarillo, Texas. A few of their songs had even been collected in California at Farm Security Administration camps, and Okies were clearly *not* Appalachian.[25]

More positively, the Ramblers demonstrated a habit of song attribution or documentation that was unprecedented among urban folk musicians at the time. While the mountain mystique may have sometimes clouded their judgment concerning the widespread provenance of old-time music, the Ramblers nevertheless did make original and vital contributions to the understanding of American roots music by scrupulously striving to give the sources of the music that they played. The mere acknowledgement that *commercial* sources—phonograph records, radio broadcasts, songbooks, and other ephemeral material—were indeed legitimate areas of scholarly interest marked a major advance beyond the earlier assumptions that had long dominated folk music scholarship. On album liner notes and in their songbook, Mike, John, and Tom provided the names of performers from whom they had chosen songs, as well as the names of record labels, record release numbers, and original dates of recordings. People who bought their LPS or attended their concerts not only heard an expert rendition of, say, "The Battleship of Maine," "Colored Aristocracy," or "The Story of the Mighty Mississippi," but they also learned that Red Patterson and the Piedmont Log Rollers, Eck Robertson, and Ernest Stoneman had originally recorded the songs. Such arcane information could be quickly forgotten, or it could become the basis for a fan's or scholar's deeper immersion in old-time music culture. The Ramblers hoped that, ultimately, such interest might even persuade the commercial record corporations to dig into their vaults to reissue new recordings of the old material.

The Ramblers were profoundly respectful of the music that they heard on the old records, and they strived mightily to present "authentic," faithful recreations of the material they had chosen. Critics differ as to how well they succeeded. Alfred Frankenstein of the *San Francisco Chronicle* saw them at the Berkeley Folk Festival on June 30, 1960, and concluded that they played and sang with "great precision and a very high polish of virtuosity," but he then went on to describe them as "eggheads with a genius for mimicry."[26] Many years later, Mike's good friend Ralph Rinzler, in an interview with Richard Straw, expressed the opinion that the Ramblers' performances were little more than contrived imitations of the original hillbillies' playing and singing. While he was impressed with their scholarship and showmanship, Rinzler said that "they sounded to me like poor, very poor imitations" of vintage hillbilly material performed by the likes of Uncle Dave or Charlie Poole.[27] The Ramblers, of course, were in an awkward, almost no-win, position. If they strayed too far from the music of their old-time heroes, they would lose the support of traditionalists. But if they labored too hard to sound exactly like them, they ran the risk of being accused of "slavish imitation" or of slumming in poor white culture. The Ramblers actually succeeded admirably in recreating vintage string-band styles. Vocally, they always sounded like John, Tom, and Mike — three city boys who had fallen in love with old-time southern rural music. And, to their credit, one really finds little evidence of them trying to affect a southern or rural twang or mannerism.[28] Most important, they communicated effectively with a host of listeners. They infectiously conveyed their excitement about old-time music to their audiences and inspired untold numbers to try their hand at the music. And while they could never sound like Charlie Poole or the Skillet Lickers, they encouraged modern fans to seek out these and other seminal musicians. Critic Jon Pankake has correctly argued that the Ramblers were among the very few in the folk revival who faithfully interpreted traditional material without losing their own performing integrities.[29]

Although the Ramblers performed the old material with great fidelity, it should be noted that their choices of songs and styles did not encompass the whole of the southern rural music tradition. If, as "crusaders for old-time music" (as they liked to describe themselves),[30] they hoped to convey the diversity and totality of southern homegrown music, they did not succeed. For example, they did not experiment with songs or instrumental styles such as cowboy, honky-tonk, or western swing, which came out of the Southwest. Musicians like Charlie Poole and Gid Tanner were their inspirations, not Tex Ritter, Ernest Tubb, Milton Brown, or Bob Wills. They did perform some nice versions of the country blues (such as "Johnson City Blues" or "Worried Blues"), but they did not include a single song from the catalogue of Jimmie Rodgers, the Mississippi Blue Yodeler who is now acknowledged as the "Father of Country Music." Pete Seeger had acknowledged the influence exerted by Rodgers when he recalled a statement made by a man in a Montana saloon—"Everything he sings is true"—and then said that it was "the highest praise a folksinger could ever have."[31] Even when the Ramblers borrowed songs from their southeastern mentors, they ignored some of the most crucial elements of that repertory. Frank Walker, who in the 1920s had overseen the recording of Columbia's historic hillbilly 78s (the 15,000-D Series), had once told Mike Seeger that the four basic themes of early country music had been heart songs (that is, sentimental songs), gospel numbers, event ballads, and jigs and reels.[32] The Ramblers' repertory was strikingly devoid of songs in Walker's first two categories. They did occasionally perform Carter Family songs, but one cannot imagine them doing a song like "If I Could Hear My Mother Pray Again" or "The Little Rosewood Casket," even though such songs were staples of the hillbilly trade. Similarly, the Ramblers' audiences almost never heard them do gospel songs, which also appeared frequently in the song bags of entertainers throughout the rural South. Cohen and Paley, in fact, could laugh over the spectacle of two Jewish boys performing songs that came from the evangelical Protestant tradition. Once, when Moe Asch referred to "jubilee" songs, Paley had laughed and said, "Oh, sure, we could call them "Jew Billy songs." And he remarked to Mike, "You'll have to change your name to Siegel." The song selections that the Ramblers made were certainly legitimate choices, and they lent themselves effectively to the young men's skills and styles of performance. But they were not enough to educate the folk revival audience about the full spectrum of southern rural musical tastes.[33]

Authenticity in style and repertory nevertheless seemed inevitably to link the New Lost City Ramblers to the era that had spawned some of the most vital sounds in old-time music: the Great Depression. Identification with the 1930s and the Great Depression symbolically suited Mike because of his father's involvement during those years with the New Deal agencies, the Resettlement Administration, and the Works Progress Administration. After all, the Library of Congress field recordings of American folk music, brought into the Seeger house and studied by Charles and Ruth, had initially introduced Mike to American roots music. The New Lost City Ramblers' preoccupation with the rural music of the Depression years also seems to have meshed with an enduring and often recurring public fascination with the hard times of the 1930s and with the audacity of the New Deal's response. People seem to find irresistible the idea that clear divisions of good and evil existed during those years, as well as the belief that under the pressure of hard times, Americans had become united in their efforts to build a better society. In many ways, this nostalgia reaffirmed the romantic Jeffersonian belief that our strongest virtues lay in the nation's rural areas, which were under siege by the forces of industrialism. Bored with the materialism and complacency of modern urban life, many people in post–World War II America longed for feelings of engagement and honest human emotions that they believed were evident in the strivings and endurance of Depression-era Americans. John Cohen, for example, has spoken of his own alienation from society and says that the three Ramblers were in rebellion against the 1950s.[34]

The Ramblers exploited Depression imagery as early as June 1959, when they were preparing for their show at Mills College in New York. The promoters of the show, Lee Hoffman (publisher of two small but influential folk music magazines called *Caravan* and *Gardyloo*) and Dick and Kiki Greenhaus, had reckoned that since most of the Ramblers' songs came out of the 1930s, their concert should be promoted with a Depression/New Deal theme. Dick Greenhaus, too, was aware that the Ramblers were preparing a Depression-themed LP. Someone remembered that the New Deal's National Recovery Administration (NRA) had promoted economic recovery by asking American businesses to follow certain government-mandated codes. Cooperating businesses had advertised their compliance by placing in their windows NRA posters depicting a Blue Eagle and featuring the slogan "We Do Our Part." Banjo player Winnie Winston prepared numerous three-by-four-and-a-half-inch tags on card stock with strings attached that could be worn around the neck or dangled from instruments. The tags depicted a Blue Eagle gripping a banjo and guitar, with accompanying slogans that said "NLCRA Member" and "We Do Our Part." The back of the card declared: "I am lost. Please return me to 1932." The cards were then handed out at Washington Square and at Izzy Young's Folklore Center.[35]

The photographs and other visual imagery used by the Ramblers on their record jackets and songbook also conjured up memories of the 1930s. John Cohen's knowledge of and facility for documentary photography made him aware of the most appropriate illustrations, particularly the vivid photos taken under the auspices of the Farm Security Administration during the Depression. Photographs taken by Ben Shahn, Dorothea Lange, Russell Lee, Walker Evans, and other government-employed photographers appeared on the jackets of early New Lost City Ramblers' LPs and throughout their popular book, *The New Lost City Ramblers Song Book*. A few of Cohen's own photographs, taken during his trip to eastern Kentucky and clearly inspired by the FSA precedent, also appeared in the songbook.

In a trip funded in part by the money he had made from selling photos of Beat poets to *Life* magazine, Cohen had gone to eastern Kentucky in early 1959 to get a feel for the gritty reality of rural poverty. He expected to utilize his insights in the forthcoming LP of Depression music that the Ramblers were planning.[36] Cohen could have found plentiful examples of poverty in his own home state of New York, but a mythicized view of rural southern life drew him southward. The spectacle of heavily wooded mountains and glens populated by a musical people who were struggling to survive was enough to fire the imagination of any young folk music fan who felt alienated from modern urban society.

The New Lost City Ramblers' LP of Depression songs—*Songs from the Depression* (Folkways FH 5264, 1959)—was one of two topical albums that they recorded (the other was the 1962 LP *American Moonshine and Prohibition*, Folkways FH 5263). The Depression LP has remained, arguably, their most influential album. Songs such as "How Can a Poor Man Stand Such Times and Live," "Breadline Blues," "NRA Blues," "Franklin D. Roosevelt's Back Again," "All I Got's Done Gone," "Old Age Pension Check," "Wreck of the Tennessee Gravy Train," "Serves Them Fine," and "No Depression in Heaven" circulated widely during the folk revival and are still known and sung today. The New Lost City Ramblers' LP inspired the reissuance of such material, and modern fans have come to know the beauty and charm of the original performances made by artists like Blind Alfred Reed, Ernest Stoneman, Slim Smith, Billy Cox, and the Carter Family. Whenever film-makers or other social documentarians concentrate on the 1930s, they inevitably draw on these songs as backdrops for the stories of economic distress, hope, and human resilience.

One of these songs, "No Depression in Heaven," has had a highly unexpected impact on American popular music. Originally titled "There's No Depression in Heaven," the song was written by the Tennessee gospel composer James D. Vaughan, published in his songbook *Sweet Heaven*, and recorded by the Carter Family in 1932. As a fatalistic response to hard times that held out no assurance of relief in this world, the song seemed a highly unlikely choice for inclusion in a rock music album. But in 1990, country-rock band Uncle Tupelo recorded the song in a version derivative of the New Lost City Ramblers' performance. The recording surprisingly became an inspiration for the "alternative country music" movement. A website was devoted to the short-lived phenomenon of "alt-country" musicians (those who presumably mixed rock and country sounds), and a published journal, *No Depression*, became the official organ of the movement.[37]

Although the emphasis on authenticity and the employment of Depression-era imagery figured strongly in New Lost City Ramblers performances, many fans just enjoyed the music and performances without any concern for context. Seeger, Cohen, and Paley were three good-looking young men who played beautifully and knew how to put on an engaging show. After their initial appearance at Newport in 1959, when they dressed casually if not slovenly, they began trying to look like the commercial hillbilly musicians of the 1920s and 1930s. When the Ramblers performed unkempt or in casual clothes, they had to ask themselves, "Would Charlie Poole have dressed this way?" The answer, of course, was no. Photographs of Poole and other early musicians invariably showed them looking straight ahead at the cameras and wearing suits, hats, ties, and decorous dresses, the kind of Sunday-go-to-meeting attire that rural musicians chose when they played before the public. The Ramblers consequently began wearing white dress shirts, dark trousers, vests, and ties—a clean-cut and traditional look that further separated them from their contemporaries in the folk revival.[38]

The Ramblers also offered a mix of corny, self-deprecating, but sophisticated humor that many fans found appealing.[39] All three young men were gifted at wordplay and puns, a skill they found particularly useful to kill time while the musical perfectionist Paley was tuning his instruments. Seemingly interminable periods of tuning by Paley became expected features of New Lost City Ramblers' concerts, and he would sometimes tell his audience that he was performing an ancient Chinese piece known as "Tu Ning." The Ramblers also sometimes jokingly admonished each other with inside quips that would have been understandable only to knowledgeable folk music fans: "Your guitar's Flatt, Lester." "Oh yeah, well your fiddle's Sharp, Cecil." "Oh, don't be such a Child, Francis." On at least one occasion, Cohen destroyed an old guitar onstage, slamming it against the floor and stomping on it as a pretended act of rage provoked by Paley's incessant tuning. Seemingly unperturbed, Paley looked at the wreckage, deadpanned "Your guitar's flat, John," and then launched into an instrumental piece. The Ramblers also occasionally performed risqué tunes, such as "Sal's Got a Meatskin" and "Women Wear No Clothes at All"; they even produced a short seven-inch album of such tunes called *Earth Is Earth* under the name the New Lost City Bang Boys (inspired by their knowledge that in 1936, Roy Acuff's band had sometimes performed similar material under the disguised name of the Bang Boys), with the musicians adopting the pseudonyms Wilbur Cohen, Delmore Paley, and McKinley Seeger. This was, apparently, one of their most popular albums.[40]

Above all, the Ramblers regaled their audiences with a bewitching mix of folkloristic erudition and versatile musicianship. During their shows, they moved from one instrument to another, typically including performances on the fiddle, banjo, guitar, Autoharp, mandolin, Hawaiian steel guitar, harmonica, Jew's harp, and panpipes. No feature of a New Lost City Ramblers' concert was more appealing to young fans than the spectacle of the three musicians moving from one instrument to another and playing them in a variety of tunings and styles. Chris Darrow, one of the founding members of the experimental rock band Kaleidoscope, spoke later of the formative period of his own band: "It was no big deal for us to pick up a fiddle, then a Dobro, then a banjo. We were all learning the instruments simultaneously, because we wanted to be like our idols, Seeger, Paley, and Cohen."[41]

The Ramblers' respect for the old commercial recordings, and their strong reliance on them as sources for their music, led them to a vital interrelationship with collectors. Most of the record collectors were informed amateurs, but a few were academic folklorists. Mike, of course, had already borrowed extensively from Bob Travis, Dick Spottswood, Pete Kuykendall, Eugene Earle, Joe Bussard, and other collectors back east; on the West Coast, he became acquainted with a new fraternity of collectors that included Bob Pinson, Fred Hoeptner, and Ed Kahn. These men had formerly comprised a rather tight-knit community who shared their knowledge of records and other commercial music ephemera only with each other, largely through mimeographed auction lists and such magazines as *Disc Collector*, *Record Research*, and *Country and Western Spotlight*. They prized the rare recordings issued mostly between 1922 and 1942, the period that Australian collector John Edwards described as "the Golden Age of Hillbilly Music." These collectors were also inspired to search for information about the men and women who had made the music. When they heard the New Lost City Ramblers, the collectors were intrigued that a contemporary trio of musicians were breathing new life into the old songs and styles and, best of all, were scrupulous in crediting their sources.[42]

Some of these collectors were academicians, such as John Greenway, Ed Kahn, Norm Cohen, and D. K. Wilgus, while others had a folkloristic bent, like Archie Green (who later became an academician). These academics were part of a small fraternity of scholars who became known as the "hillbilly folklorists," men who recognized the value of early country music and saw it as a commercial extension of earlier traditional styles and a repository of material that the "folk" had absorbed or created. The 78-rpm record, they believed, was a valuable document that should be preserved as a repository of, and a clue to, older and largely forgotten styles and songs. The commercial record was also a vehicle for the dissemination of music that might evolve into traditional material. D. K. Wilgus, a distinguished folklorist who first taught at Western Kentucky University and later at UCLA, even referred to the 78-rpm hillbilly record as a "modern broadside"—an allusion to the medieval, black-letter broadsheets that circulated in Great Britain, Ireland, and early America and introduced songs to plain men and women.[43]

Archie Green was an intellectual who had been a ship's carpenter, a self-styled left-wing libertarian, and an avid member of the United Brotherhood of Carpenters and Joiners of America.[44] His passion for labor lore had led him to the study and collecting of old phonograph records and ephemeral music journals (in which many labor-related items were advertised) and

Mike Seeger's mentor: labor folklorist Archie Green in 1993. (Photo by Hazen Robert Walker)

to associations with other collectors. Before the New Lost City Ramblers were organized, Green had corresponded with Mike Seeger in search of information about the Chattanooga duo the Allen Brothers (Austin and Lee), who in 1928 had recorded a coal-mining song called "Tiple [sic] Blues."[45] When the Ramblers traveled to the Berkeley Festival, Green sought Mike out and encouraged him to explore the labor or working-class dimensions of the music he was performing. And he urged Mike to search for David McCarn, the North Carolina textile worker who in the 1920s had recorded a series of biting textile songs, including "Cotton Mill Colic" and "Serves Them Fine."[46] Green persuaded Mike that, through his work as both a performer and a collector, he was making a political statement that was every bit as legitimate as the protest songs done by his brother Pete. (Green, admittedly, was repulsed by Pete's "Stalinism.") Green believed that Mike's musical decision to perform the songs originally made by southern working people in the decades before World War II lent dignity and a sense of affirmation to those people and their culture.[47]

While Mike was becoming aware of the full dimensions of his and the New Lost City Ramblers' work, he also began to see the stylistic fruits of their music. Already, young musicians were beginning to borrow songs from the Ramblers' catalogue and perform them in styles inspired by the Ramblers' music. It is impossible to document the earliest examples of imitation because many young musicians borrowed the songs and approximated the styles of the New Lost City Ramblers but never made recordings. The experience remembered by Rick March, the longtime state folklorist of Wisconsin, was probably not unlike that of scores of young musicians who encountered the New Lost City Ramblers in the early sixties. March and a high school buddy, Theodore Gustafson, heard the Ramblers at the Ash Grove Club in their hometown of Los Angeles. They bought matching vests the next day, named themselves the Old Time Real Guys, and, with Autoharp accompaniment, began a brief period of singing songs from the NLCR repertoire. March did not embark on a professional music career, but he did preserve his interest in traditional music, earning a PhD in Indiana University's folklore department before eventually becoming an authority on American polka music, European tamburitza stylings, and other forms of ethnic music.[48]

It was probably a rare college campus in the early sixties that did not have a campus folksong club and at least one string band that emulated the New Lost City Ramblers. John Cohen had said as early as August 1960 that he knew of at least three such bands at Harvard and others at Yale, Amherst, Dartmouth, Oberlin, Antioch, the University of Michigan, and the University of California, Berkeley.[49] The names of these bands have not endured, but at least a couple of campus-based groups remained active throughout the sixties and played important roles in the preservation and documentation of traditional rural music. The Philo Glee and Mandolin Society emerged in 1961 from the Campus Folk Song Club at the University of Illinois at Urbana-Champaign. Spurred by the example of the New Lost City Ramblers and by the encouragement of faculty sponsor Archie Green, who had become a librarian at the university's Institute of Labor and Industrial Relations, the society performed and recorded old-time country songs and sought out musicians in the community who sang and played such music.[50]

Uncle Willie and the Brandy Snifters were an old-time string band that was loosely associated with the University of Minnesota's folk song club. Like many old-time music enthusiasts in the United States, the group played music learned from Library of Congress field recordings and from the Harry Smith collection. Named for Willard Johnson ("Uncle Willie"), who had a huge collection of commercial 78-rpm recordings, the group began holding jam sessions in 1961 at the student union at the University of Minnesota and hosting concerts by the New Lost City Ramblers (probably beginning in 1964) and other folk music acts.[51] The Brandy Snifters maintained a close relationship with the NLCR during the following decades, and two of its members, Jon Pankake and Lyle Lofgren, built reputations as learned authorities and critics of old-time music. For about six years after 1962, Pankake was the coeditor, with Paul Nelson, of the *Little Sandy Review*, a small Minneapolis-based journal that was widely read and respected by old-time music fans and musicians.[52]

While the NLCR exerted influence wherever they played, the West Coast proved to be their most fertile ground of operation and a scene of immediate and lasting influence. For at least three years after their initial appearance there, the Ramblers typically remained on the West Coast for several weeks at a time. They used the Ash Grove Club in Los Angeles as their home base, sometimes playing and teaching at Idyllwild Summer Camp and making periodic forays into other cities and colleges in California. During their stints at the Ash Grove, the Ramblers learned that their music's appeal extended far beyond their original New York locus. They found that fans and musicians who were looking for an honest, down-to-earth alternative to the pop groups that dominated the folk field were beginning to gravitate toward them.

The Ash Grove was a nondescript coffeehouse located at 8162 Melrose Avenue in a working-class neighborhood in East Los Angeles.[53] It was the brainchild of Ed Pearl, a left-wing visionary, guitar player, and passionate folk music fan who had first become involved in music promotion at the age of seventeen when he helped to promote an off-campus concert by Pete Seeger in Los Angeles. When he opened the Ash Grove in 1958, Pearl hoped to combine music, art, and political advocacy under one roof. Lectures, music workshops and instructional classes, art exhibitions, and musi-

THE NEW LOST CITY RAMBLERS

Publicity photo for the New Lost City Ramblers. From left: Mike Seeger,
John Cohen, and Tracy Schwarz. (Courtesy of the Southern Folklife Collection,
University of North Carolina at Chapel Hill)

cal concerts were all part of the Ash Grove mix, and when musical acts appeared, photo exhibits and other displays provided context for the cultures represented by the musical presentations or performers.

Pearl initially seemed most receptive to flamenco guitarists and the urban interpreters of traditional music. But when he and his wife, Kate Hughes, a dancer and batik artist, traveled to the Newport Folk Festival in 1959, they heard the music of the New Lost City Ramblers and were swept away by the trio's breadth and command of the material they played. Pearl felt that he was being introduced to the roots of all the forms that were then being paraded as "folk." Pearl invited the Ramblers to the Ash Grove and began leaning heavily on Mike for advice about other acts that should be invited to the venue. Over the years, the Ash Grove played host to the biggest names in folk, bluegrass, country, blues, Tex-Mex, and other roots styles. At Mike's urging, folks like Clarence Ashley, Maybelle Carter, Dock Boggs, Ernest Stoneman, Doc Watson, Bill Monroe, the Stanley Brothers, and other pioneer acts came to the Ash Grove. Years later, Pearl told a reporter that "the change in the Ash Grove was from singing songs about other people to songs *by* other people."[54]

The young musicians who soaked up the music played by the NLCR and the visiting old-timers did not always remain exclusively wedded to the styles of their mentors; instead, as noted in the case of the rock band Kaleidoscope, many took the music to new dimensions. Ry Cooder is another example. He frequented the Ash Grove as a teenager in the early sixties and took guitar lessons from Tom Paley and Mike Seeger. "That band clarified everything," Cooder later said. "They got me going on open tunings and all sorts of stuff." Soon after he heard the Ramblers, he began listening to reissued LPs of Charlie Poole and other old-time musicians. Cooder remained a student of roots music in all of its manifestations and a consummate acoustic musician, even though he moved far beyond the styles learned from the Ramblers.[55]

Clarence White similarly used his early Ash Grove musical indoctrination as a stepping-stone to a brilliant career as a musical innovator. Memories differ as to how Clarence and his brother Roland came to be involved with the club. Mike recalled that he had taken Pearl to a show in Burbank expressly to hear a little bluegrass band called the Country Boys. Roland White, on the other hand, thinks that he met Mike and the NLCR at the Ash Grove. At any rate, the band included brothers Clarence and Roland White (originally LeBlanc), who had moved with their family in 1954 to California from their native Maine. Already a superb musician and much influenced by the hot electric guitar playing of the West Coast performer Joe Maphis, Clarence began to see the full potential of the acoustic guitar when he heard Doc Watson playing fiddle tunes on the instrument at the Ash Grove. Watson played the Ash Grove for about three weeks in March and April 1962, along with Clarence Ashley, Fred Price, and Clint Howard. Clarence sat wide-eyed in the audience every night, soaking in every detail of the Doc Watson style. Roland had gone into the army in 1961, and when he returned in September 1963, he said that his brother was "playing the hell out of the guitar." Clarence's sensational flat-picking style dazzled guitarists everywhere in the burgeoning acoustic music business of the 1960s. Until he and his brother moved east to follow their career on the bluegrass circuit (with the support of Marge Seeger, who arranged bookings for them at the Club 47, Gerde's Folk City in New York, and Ontario Place in Washington, D.C.), Clarence had been virtually the house musician at the Ash

Grove, playing music often but also taking tickets, running the sound system, working at carpentry repairs, and performing any other task that Pearl required.[56]

The New Lost City Ramblers typically played for five or six weeks at the Ash Grove and used the club as their headquarters for additional forays to Stanford and other sites in California. Their trip to Stanford introduced their music to student Jerry Garcia, who at the time was playing with Mother McCree's Uptown Jug Champions.[57] He became a lifelong disciple of the Ramblers and of old-time music. Mike found life on the road exhilarating but stressful, causing him to lose his voice at one point. During the first trip to Los Angeles, Mike and Marge stayed briefly with Charles Seeger, who was teaching ethnomusicology at UCLA and conducting experiments on his invention, the Melograph. More often, though, the Seegers lived in small and dreary apartments near the Ash Grove. All of Marge and Mike's sons were born in the same hospital in Los Angeles under the care of the same doctor. When Jeremy was born on April 3, 1963, Toshi Seeger clipped out a small ad for Planned Parenthood from a telephone book and sent it to Mike and Marge.

Neither Jeremy nor Arley had yet arrived, though, when Mike, Marge, and baby Kim headed back east after the first extended gig at the Ash Grove. They were essentially homeless, and for several months they only survived through the good graces of friends and family members who took them in. At varying times, for example, they lived with Toshi and Pete Seeger in Beacon, New York; at the University Settlement House in Beacon, where Toshi's father served as the manager; with Alice and Jeremy Foster in Leesburg, Virginia; and with Bill and Sarah Lee Clifton in Warrenton, Virginia.[58]

Their wanderings finally came to an end in September 1961, when Ralph Rinzler helped them find a house in Roosevelt, New Jersey, about an hour south of New York City—close enough to satisfy Marge, who still had a strong attachment to the city, and far enough to satisfy Mike, who longed for some greenery and space. Roosevelt had been a planned New Deal community known as Jersey Homesteads that was designed as a self-sufficient community for Jewish garment workers who might relocate from New York. By the time the Seegers moved into a house rented from the writer and artist Ben Appel, Roosevelt had lost much of its working-class identity and was becoming an artists' colony. Built on concrete slabs with cement-poured, cinder-block walls, the houses were "pretty stark looking" but nevertheless affordable for young families like the Seegers. Some of

Mike's musician friends, such as Paul Prestopino, lived in Roosevelt, as did the famous photographer and artist Ben Shahn. Shahn's large fresco mural commemorating Jersey Homesteads as a refuge for Jews who had been persecuted in Europe is still on display at Roosevelt High School. Mike and Marge moved out of the rented house in August 1962 and bought a home in Roosevelt, where they resided until the summer of 1966.[59]

The New Lost City Ramblers found 1961 to be a banner year. They began recording, for example, with producer Peter Bartók (the son of classical composer Bela), who supervised their Folkways sessions in a state-of-the-art studio housed in a library in Pequot, Connecticut. Paneled with nineteenth-century wood and plaster, the little studio provided them with the best acoustics they had ever had; the sound equipment used by Bartók, they believed, typified the kind usually used to record fine chamber music.[60] The Ramblers continued the touring pattern that had been set the previous year, playing mostly in the northern United States at universities, folk festivals, and folk music clubs. While they did schedule a few engagements at schools in "border" states (such as the University of Virginia in Charlottesville, the University of North Carolina at Chapel Hill, and the University of Texas at Austin), their circuit of universities and colleges tended to include such institutions as the University of Michigan, the University of Illinois at Urbana-Champaign, the University of Minnesota, the University of Chicago, the University of Wisconsin, Stanford University, and the University of California, Berkeley. They also returned to the Ash Grove again in 1961 for another five-week engagement. True to form, the Seegers' second child, Arley, was born on September 26, 1961, during that tour.

While the Ash Grove gigs were played mostly to the Ramblers' reliable blend of students, beatniks, and folkniks, another performance in New York City in the summer of 1961 introduced them to a very different audience. This contact and its reception also led to a welcome, if brief, period of national exposure. They appeared at the Blue Angel, an upscale nightclub, before a "sophisticated" audience that was generally receptive to their brand of music but not quite sure whether to take the Ramblers as hayseed comics or as serious entertainers. The Ramblers had chosen this venue because they thought it might win them critical reviews, as well as engagements at other "respectable" clubs. The influential *New York Times* critic Robert Shelton — who is best known for writing the first laudatory review of a Bob Dylan concert — did review their show favorably, applauding their gifts as musicians and treating their songs with respect.[61] Shelton's review garnered widespread attention for the New Lost City Ramblers and was largely responsible for their first television appearance, a short stint on NBC's *Today Show*. Their appearance occurred at the time of the Cuban Missile Crisis, and the Ramblers chose to sing "The Battleship of Maine," a humorous song about a reluctant soldier that had been inspired by the Spanish-American War of 1898.While the Ramblers' performance seems to have been well received, a promised second appearance never materialized. A probable reason for this was the fact that Tom Paley had refused to apologize for having belonged to an alleged Communist Front square-dance group[62] during his earlier days in New York. Mike Seeger must have been bemused by the fact that, this time at least, Seeger politics had not been responsible for controversy in his career.

While the Ramblers could not help but be pleased by the favorable reception given their music in folk revival arenas, they were frustrated by the seeming indifference shown in the region that had originally spawned their music: the rural South. Young southerners who were interested in roots-based music had generally embraced organic adaptations of old-time music, such as bluegrass, country and western, blues, and Cajun. Old-time string-band music too often seemed like a relic of their grandparents' worlds and something that only exotica-seeking urbanites could like. Political tensions also probably contributed to the lukewarm response made by southerners to traditional music performed by "outsiders." Although the crucial years of student protest and antiwar demonstrations came a few years later than the New Lost City Ramblers' debut, civil rights unrest in the early sixties made it problematic for three "Yankee" boys, two of whom were Jewish, to feel very comfortable in any southern setting.

Interest in the New Lost City Ramblers' performances may have been most enthusiastic in the North and on the West Coast, but a southern re-awakening was actually well under way by 1961. The seeds for a rebirth had been planted, in large part, through the actions of people like Mike Seeger, John Cohen, and Ralph Rinzler, as well as by Alan Lomax, who in 1959 had embarked on an extensive two-month expedition through the South in search of traditional song material. Lomax had found there a wealth of tradition-oriented music being played by both white and African American musicians. He later boasted that after these discoveries, there was "no more talk about the dominance of Washington Square."[63]

For his part, Mike Seeger was not content merely to recreate the old songs and styles; he also wanted to present southern traditional musicians to the revival and general public. His joint billing with Libba Cotten at Swarthmore in January 1960 had been, arguably, the first major solo performances for each of them. The 1960s would see him appearing constantly with her and other southern rural musicians. Not only did he introduce previously unknown entertainers like Kilby Snow to the general public, but he also brought such venerable performers as Dock Boggs, Cousin Emmy, and Lesley Riddle out of retirement. Several of Mike's friends in the folk revival shared his sentiments. For example, Mike Fleischer, the president of the Chicago Folklore Society, had become a close friend of Mike during the Ramblers' Gate of Horn shows in the summer of 1960. Like many traditionalists, Fleischer was upset with the Newport Folk Festival's practice of booking mostly commercial folk acts. He wanted to give old-time performers — and modern acts that tried to be faithful to traditional styles — a setting where they could perform. Consequently, on February 3–5, 1961, the University of Chicago Folk Festival[64] hosted a roster of mostly traditional musicians, the first venue that had ever done so. A few urban musicians, such as the New Lost City Ramblers, Frank Warner, Sandy Paton, Marshall Brickman, and Fleming Brown, also appeared, but they were all committed to traditional performance either as musicians or as promoters of old-time acts. The real sensations of the festival, though, were Horton Barker, a traditional ballad singer from Virginia; Libba Cotten; Roscoe Holcomb (recently found by John Cohen in Kentucky); Frank Proffitt, whose version of "Tom Dooley" had inspired the popular version by the Kingston Trio; Arvella Gray, a blind blues street singer from Chicago; the Stanley Brothers; and Bob Atcher, a long-time fixture on Chicago's National Barn Dance.

In New York City in December 1960, John Cohen, Ralph Rinzler, Israel Young, Margot Mayo, and Jean Ritchie had created an organization called the Friends of Old Time Music (FOTM). Designed to make the New York City folk music community aware of the best traditional southern rural musicians, the FOTM presented fourteen concerts between 1961 and 1965 (not all of them in New York). Each concert included one or more genuine rural acts and a "presenter" (someone like Mike Seeger or Ralph Rinzler) who would explain something about the music and help in the selecting and sequencing of the songs performed. The FOTM held its first concert on

February 11, 1961—only one week after the Chicago Folk Festival—at P.S. 41, a progressive school in Greenwich Village that was known for its high percentage of parents who were artists, musicians, and intellectuals.[65]

The roster of performers at this first concert seems to have been carefully calculated to introduce traditional musicians to a New York audience in a context of urban-oriented performers whose music was rural-based but also palatable to middle-class city tastes. Jean Ritchie, for example, was a Kentucky-born ballad singer and dulcimer player, but she was well known to New Yorkers because she had lived in the city since 1946 (when she had gone to work at the Henry Street Settlement House), had recorded for Alan Lomax and the Library of Congress, and had recorded several commercial LPs of her music. The other urban acts—the New Lost City Ramblers and the Greenbriar Boys, a New York bluegrass band that included Rinzler— were familiar to most northern folkniks. The Greenbriar Boys were one of the earliest bluegrass bands to emerge in the North. The real feature of the concert, however, and its actual reason for being, was Roscoe Holcomb. Holcomb was a clawhammer banjo player and finger-style guitarist from Daisy, Kentucky, deep in the heart of Appalachia, who sang with a powerfully emotional and high-pitched voice. John Cohen had become aware of Holcomb during a 1959 research trip to Kentucky, where he traveled looking for insights and material for an album of Depression-era music that the New Lost City Ramblers were preparing. Meeting Holcomb, and hearing him perform his music, were happy by-products of his Kentucky trip. In introducing this living embodiment of rural musical tradition to the revival, Cohen also introduced a term—"the High Lonesome Sound"—that was first used in a film of the same name and then on an album of Holcomb's music. It has persisted as a description of much of Appalachia's music and even of bluegrass.[66]

Holcomb was one of several southern traditional musicians who emerged in the early 1960s to become part of the urban folk revival circuit. It was an exhilarating experience for many fans to learn not only that some of the performers on the Harry Smith collection were still alive, but also that other heretofore undiscovered musicians were still making music similar to that heard on the collection. Fans of the Grand Ole Opry, of course, had long known about Maybelle Carter, the guitar player and alto singer of the original Carter Family, because she performed with her gifted daughters (Helen, June, and Anita) each Saturday night on that venerable Tennessee radio barn dance. Little by little, other country and blues singers who had been featured on the 78-rpm records resurrected by Harry Smith or on other commercial reissues emerged out of long years of retirement to find worshipful young fans who were more than ready to celebrate their new careers. Mississippi John Hurt, Furry Lewis, Sleepy John Estes, Buell Kazee, Ernest Stoneman, Dock Boggs, and Clarence "Tom" Ashley were among those enjoying their unexpected new acclaim in urban America. For the most part, these old-time musicians were both elated and humbled by the adoration given to them by young fans and pleased to know that their careers could be renewed. Tom Ashley, for example, said that "my life is like a flower, and is now blooming a second time."[67] On the other hand, Clayton McMichen may not have been alone in questioning the motivations and sincerity of these newfound fans. This venerable Georgia fiddler and longtime mainstay of such country acts as the Skillet Lickers and the Georgia Wildcats lectured his listeners at the Newport Folk Festival in 1964 by complaining that people like him were admired only because they were old or considered to be museum pieces. "I could play the worst fiddle in the world," he said, "and you'd still applaud."[68]

The first revelation that life for surviving Harry Smith musicians extended beyond the grooves of the Folkways LPS came in 1960, when Ralph Rinzler and collector Eugene Earle found Ashley at the Union Grove, North Carolina, fiddle contest. Rinzler, who was scheduled to play at the contest with the Greenbriar Boys, was bowled over when he found that the spry and humorous old man that he met in a backstage dressing room was the same Clarence Ashley whose banjo playing and singing of "The Coo Coo Bird" on the Harry Smith anthology had intrigued revival fans.[69] Mike Seeger hurriedly brought his tape recorder into the room to document this exciting and unexpected moment. The next revelation came a short time later at a show in East Tennessee, when Rinzler heard Arthel "Doc" Watson playing in the string band that backed Ashley. He was immediately impressed with Watson's guitar proficiency but was dismayed by the fact that the musician played an electric guitar. A native of Deep Gap, North Carolina, Watson was a blind musician who had been making his living playing in a rock-and-roll and country swing band near his home. Rinzler persuaded Watson to learn (or relearn) some of the old songs that his family had known and to take up the acoustic guitar when he played future dates with Ashley—not fully realizing just how multitalented the singer was, nor how influential his guitar style would become. In the spring of 1961, Watson, Fred Price, and Clint Howard accompanied Ashley when the old-time musician headlined the second concert sponsored by the FOTM in New York. This concert was doubly enlightening for New York fans, showing them that some of the heroes from the Harry Smith collection were still capable of making vital music and that younger southern musicians like Watson could be inspired to return to the roots. Watson's brilliant career as a solo musician was launched in December 1962, when he played his first independent gig at Gerde's Folk City in New York.[70]

Despite the New Lost City Ramblers' exhaustive schedules and major contributions to American music, they made little money from their ventures. Their first album sold only about 400 copies, even though it seems to have enjoyed wide circulation and was heard often (in public libraries, for example). By the end of the summer of 1960, each Rambler had netted about $2,000; and at the end of that year, their four Folkways albums had sold a grand total of 1,090 copies.[71] With royalties of thirty cents a copy, no one got rich from the group's recording enterprises. Conditions did not improve dramatically for the young men in 1961 and 1962. Their efforts to find a booking agency that would actively promote them had not been successful, and they had to scuffle to find engagements. Frankly, they were ceasing to be an original or unique act. They also were not united in their desire to pursue music together as a full-time career. Tom Paley, who had taken a leave of absence from the mathematics department of Rutgers University, wanted the group to continue only on a part-time basis. He felt that he could not make a living playing with the Ramblers. A competitive friction, too, had marred the relationship between Paley and Cohen ever since their student days at Yale. Although there is little evidence for the claim, Paley said he was dismayed by what he considered to be his partners' indifference concerning racial segregation in the South.[72] Mike and John, it is true, did play without Tom at the University of the South in Sewanee, Tennessee. But Tom and John had had a strong argument a week earlier in California, and Tom had missed two other engagements (Marge had filled in for him at shows in Colorado and Kansas). Tom left the group in 1962 and soon thereafter organized the short-lived Old Reliable String Band with Artie Rose and Roy Berkeley. He moved to Sweden in 1963 but by 1965 had taken up permanent residence in England, where he became a mainstay of that country's traditional music scene.[73]

Cohen and Seeger resolved to carry on without Paley, and in the interim months before a full-time replacement was found, Marge Seeger filled in on guitar for a few Ramblers gigs. Mike and John tried to hire Doc Watson as a replacement for Paley (and the imagination is staggered by the thought of how awesome that band would have been!). Family responsibilities, however, prevented Watson from committing to the kind of intensive schedule that the Ramblers followed. The Ramblers would certainly have been a different group with Watson, but it is now impossible to believe that his superb talents could ever have been subsumed by membership in any band. Although Watson was a consummate performer of old-time music, his preferences in fact lay with the performance of country blues music (both black and white).

The Ramblers found a musician of great compatibility and versatility when Tracy Schwarz joined them in late 1962.[74] Schwarz, who was then living in Washington, D.C., had played informally with Mike Seeger off and on for at least a couple of years. Although born the son of an investment banker in Montclair, New Jersey, Schwarz developed an early love affair with country life and had lived for several years in rural New England, where he easily linked his preference for all things pastoral with a fondness for rural styles of music. He always bridled angrily at any suggestion that he was a "folk revivalist," arguing that his long rural residence had made him a genuine practitioner of country music. Schwarz brought not only considerable musical skills to the group but also an eclectic interest in both vocal and instrumental performance styles. He shared the Ramblers' love of old-time string-band music, but he was also fond of bluegrass, Cajun, and mainline country music. His facility for a cappella balladry, Cajun fiddling, and bluegrass tenor-harmony singing set him apart from most old-time music performers. He could sing both the oldest varieties of traditional music and the most modern forms of country music. In a sense, he took the New Lost City Ramblers further back in time with his a cappella balladry and forward with his affinity for bluegrass.

The new version of the New Lost City Ramblers made its debut in August 1962 with a concert at Galax, and the group followed up that performance with shows later in the year at Vassar, Yale, and the Gate of Horn in Chicago. (Mike Seeger's solo engagements were becoming more numerous at this time, and his efforts to balance home and family with his career were becoming more challenging. New Lost City Ramblers concerts, while extremely important, were only part of the mix that consumed his life.) In the months and years that followed, the group continued the familiar pattern of performances and recordings that they had pursued since 1959, but they also added visits to Europe and other foreign countries to their schedule. In

1965 Manny Greenhill arranged a tour of Australia for the Ramblers, which took them to Adelaide, Brisbane, Melbourne, and Sydney. In September of that same year, through the intercession of promoter Roy Guest and musician Bill Clifton, they played eighteen engagements in England, starting at the Cecil Sharp House in London and moving on to both small folk clubs and larger arenas across the country. England continued to provide the Ramblers with good performance opportunities for the rest of their career.[75]

Since 1958 Clifton had been a pivotal influence, and a loyal friend, in Mike's life. Mike had been aware of his music because Clifton and his band, the Dixie Mountain Boys, managed to get several songs—such as "Goodbye, Mary Dear," "The Little Whitewashed Chimney," and "The Girl I Loved in Sunny Tennessee"—on country radio shows and in jukeboxes in the midfifties. Clifton was an ardent fan and student of old-time country music and had become a close friend of A. P. Carter, who was still living at the old home place in Virginia. Of all the people in Mike's circle of friends, Clifton was the only one who had actually met all three of the original Carter Family trio (A. P., Sara, and Maybelle). He had also compiled a popular paperback songbook, 150 Old-Time, Folk, and Gospel Songs, that circulated widely among country and bluegrass fans. Mike learned about Bill's whereabouts from Bill's sister, Ann Hoffman, who had done the illustrations for the book and was listed in its frontispiece as a resident of Baltimore. Mike called up Bill, who was living in Charlottesville, and the two of them soon began a warm friendship and musical collaboration, playing for small events in Virginia and, with Paul Clayton, for a cruise on the Chesapeake Bay.[76]

Born William August Marburg on April 5, 1931, in Riderwood, Maryland, Clifton had fallen in love with old-time country music as a child when he heard the music played on the radio in the home of tenant farmers who worked for his family on their estate near Baltimore. To Bill, the decent, down-home values held by these people was mirrored in the music that they loved. Although Clifton lived a varied and busy life—he earned a master's degree in business administration at the University of Virginia, served as a U.S. marine, and did a stint in the Peace Corps—he maintained his involvement in country music and became one of its most fervent spokesmen. He performed actively as a bluegrass musician and served as a member of the board of directors for the Newport Folk Festival. In 1963 he moved to Sevenoaks, England, and did much to spur interest in bluegrass and American old-time country music in that nation through a series on the BBC called *A Cellar Full of Folk* and through concerts in folk music clubs like the Cecil Sharp House and in auditoriums like London's Royal Albert Hall. The first direct consequence of the work that Clifton did in England was the emergence of a popular bluegrass band called the Echo Mountain Band (who also profited from the American bluegrass recordings that Marge Seeger sent to them).[77]

Chris Strachwitz, an influential patron of American roots music, provided further contacts on the European continent. Strachwitz, whom the Ramblers had met during their first trip to Berkeley, was the founder of the Arhoolie record label and owner of Down Home Music in El Cerrito, California. Although he had immigrated to the United States in 1947 from his native Lower Silesia, Strachwitz had become one of the most knowledgeable students of American roots music in the world and had strived tirelessly to document the music of Cajun, Tejano, blues, and country performers.[78] The contacts he maintained with music people in Europe enabled him to link the Ramblers to some influential promoters in Germany. Through Strachwitz, the Ramblers booked a lengthy tour extending from late February through March that carried them to sites in Germany, Switzerland, and Denmark. The tour was a memorable one for the Ramblers because they were accompanied by an array of old-time, bluegrass, and Cajun musicians, including Cousin Emmy, Roscoe Holcomb, the Stanley Brothers, and Adam and Cyprien Landrineau.

Mike had been a fan of the Stanley Brothers since he first saw them perform at New River Ranch, but this tour marked the first time that he had ever been with them for an extended period of time. The Ramblers and the Stanley Brothers shared bus rides, living quarters, and concert stages during the tour. The group had originally traveled from New York to Boston (where they held a concert) and then flew to Germany. On the Continent, they traveled from show to show mostly by chartered bus. Observing their heroes close up on a day-to-day basis, the Ramblers received glimpses of their complete humanity, with both its nobility and faults. Some practical jokes could be harrowing as well as humorous, like the time Carter Stanley filched and hid George Shuffler's passport just before it was demanded by a security guard. The musicians' jokes and earthy repartee, while sometimes disconcerting, could be funny—unless they were racist in nature, which they sometimes were. Those moments, though, were accompanied by touching scenes of musical intimacy, as when Ralph Stanley and Roscoe

Holcomb sat in the tour bus and sang songs like "Village Church Yard" from the *Baptist Hymnal*. Although the tour drew only moderate audiences, it provided memorable moments and also built a small but hardcore contingent of old-time music fans in Europe.[79]

Most fans seem to have embraced the new version of the trio with enthusiasm. Critic and editor Jon Pankake spoke for many of them in 1968 when he reviewed the ten-year history of the New Lost City Ramblers. Pankake presented a favorable assessment of the group in both its older and newer manifestations, noting that the band had persisted through major changes in American life and music. He argued further that the Ramblers' career was "a noble monument to the fact that the Revival was more than simply another pop music fad, that it was a discovery of a forgotten corner of the American soul." Pankake nevertheless indicated that he and many others missed the spontaneity, humor, and instrumental virtuosity that Tom Paley had provided. The Ramblers, Pankake argued, "have never been so purely entertaining since the departure of Tom Paley in 1962. Jolly Tom was the master showman of the group, the entertainer who made their concerts jump and who could best reach out to and amuse members of the audience who may not have cared less for old-timey music itself." With the addition of Tracy Schwarz, who Pankake praised for his versatile musicianship, the Ramblers had nevertheless moved away from entertainment and toward the presentation of "chamber music art."[80]

Fans of traditional string-band music, though, had no reason to despair when they heard the performances of Seeger, Cohen, and Schwarz. On their first album, *Gone to the Country*, released on January 1, 1963, fans could find the familiar variety of fiddle tunes, banjo pieces, Carter Family songs, old love songs, and ballads—all performed with great verve and competence and in the spirit of the original hillbilly versions. Schwarz's eclecticism in some ways surpassed the considerable skills of his partners. He was heard on this album playing a bluesy style of fiddle, singing an unaccompanied version of the old cowboy song "Tom Sherman's Bar Room," and adding a bluegrass-style tenor harmony to the murder/suicide ballad "Little Glass of Wine." With the performance of songs like "Little Glass of Wine," the Ramblers indicated a willingness to venture into modern expressions of tradition-based music that had not been apparent in their Tom Paley phase.

Later albums recorded by the group exhibited their familiar fondness for traditional songs, but "modern" songs (those originally recorded in the

1950s or after) sometimes appeared alongside the vintage numbers. Some, such as the Cajun pieces "Parlez-nous A Boire" and "La Valsse Des Bambocheurs," probably reflected Schwarz's personal preference and his growing absorption with Cajun fiddling. The appropriately named album *Modern Times*, recorded in 1968, included a number of socially relevant songs, such as "From 40 to 65" (concerning the problems faced by older workers), "Dear Okie" (about the false hopes held by migrants who moved to California), "The Death of Ellenton" (about a South Carolina town that vanished in the wake of the building of the Savannah River nuclear plant), and "Truck Driving Man" (an example of a genre that has become central to the modern country music repertoire). The album even included a Vietnam era item, "Private John Q," a humorous but biting song about a reluctant American soldier written by the country music superstar Roger Miller.

The New Lost City Ramblers never officially disbanded. Their last LP appeared in 1975 (*On the Great Divide*, Folkways FTS 31041) and had been recorded live at the Boarding House in San Francisco. By the time they did their twentieth-anniversary concert at Carnegie Hall on September 30, 1978, the Ramblers had become thoroughly immersed in their own separate and private enterprises. And while they were always able to make good music together, private frictions between Mike and John often made their associations painful.[81] The trio continued to give occasional concerts as late as 2008. (Tracy and John, in fact, performed under the name New Lost City Ramblers at the Appalachian String Band Festival at Clifftop, West Virginia, in August 2009, only a few days before Mike's death.)[82] But by 1968, when *Modern Times* was recorded, their heyday had passed. The folk revival had already begun to ebb by 1964, the year that the Beatles came to America and dramatically changed the complexion of American music. America's youth moved on to a new musical fascination, one that was closer to their urban sensibilities than the rustic folk revival had been. The revival's influence, though, could still be felt, particularly in California. Young musical acts like the Grateful Dead, David Lindley, the Byrds, Jefferson Airplane, and Janis Joplin, who had cut their teeth on bluegrass, blues, and other roots styles, moved easily into rock music but fused the older sounds with the new. One consequence was the emergence of folk-rock music.[83] John Cohen later argued that the Ramblers had "served as a gateway for city kids to pass through" on their way to rock and roll and other forms of modern pop music.[84] The trio of young men who had once been hailed for their freshness and originality now confronted the fate that awaited all groups that stayed around for several years. The Ramblers were now considered to be old-timers, "founding fathers" of the string-band movement. However unwelcome, this transition was as much a tribute to the importance of their work as it was an indication that American popular culture had moved on to new enthusiasms.

While the folk revival ebbed significantly in the American consciousness, it did not die. Folk entertainers no longer appeared on the cover of *Time* and other popular magazines, nor did they dominate the pop music charts like the Kingston Trio had at the beginning of the sixties. Self-styled folk musicians moved to less-crowded and less-publicized arenas, such as coffeehouses and local clubs, and many soon found refuge in a renewed string-band movement. The ascension of Black Power and the escalation of the Vietnam conflict affected the content and style of many songs, and the idealism and innocence that had once surrounded folk music dissipated, imploding the NLCR's fan base. But Mike Seeger was not deterred. He clung to his mission and pushed it in different directions.

5

Music from the True Vine

Mike Seeger and the Search for Authenticity

During his involvement with the New Lost City Ramblers, Mike Seeger never ceased making music on his own or being active in a multitude of ways in the emerging old-time music scene. When he made the decision in 1960 to devote his life fully to music, Mike invested his total energy and passion. That decision exacted a costly toll on his health, marriage, and family life. He worked indefatigably over the ensuing decades, often as a member of the Ramblers but increasingly on his own as a missionary for old-time music. Mike was the supreme multitasker: he gave innumerable solo concerts; recorded LPs; worked as a session musician with Bill Clifton and others; performed frequently with the Ramblers, the Strange Creek Singers, and his second wife, Alice Gerrard; and produced important documentary recordings of Dock Boggs and other seminal musicians. Increasingly, he also participated in workshops and seminars; held a variety of college residencies; and served on the boards of directors of the Newport Folk Festival, the Southern Folk Cultural Revival Project, the American Folk Festival, the Smithsonian Folk-Life Festival, the Mariposa Folk Festival in Canada, and the National Endowment for the Arts Folk Arts Program.

Mike's most distinguished contribution to America's traditional music, however, came through his own musicianship. The other members of the New Lost City Ramblers had been valued for their talents and eclecticism, but in many ways, Mike always stood out from the pack. Jon Pankake isolated a crucial component of Mike's unique gift in a retrospective of the group that he wrote in 1968 for *Sing Out!* Seeger's performances were "the most beautiful and personal of the Ramblers," Pankake claimed, because they arose from his intimate identification with the persons from whom he learned the songs: "We are so moved by his performance of 'Freight Train' because Seeger has been so moved by Elizabeth Cotten."[1] Many young musicians, on the other hand, were more impressed by Mike's versatility and his seemingly effortless ability to move fluently from one instrument to another. Chris Darrow, for example, a founding member of the experimental rock band Kaleidoscope, spoke for many young musicians when he said: "If you asked Ry Cooder, if you asked Taj Mahal, if you asked David Lindley, if you asked me, you would all get, 'I wanted to be Mike Seeger.'"[2]

Still others were drawn to Seeger because of his commitment to and seeming mastery of stylistic authenticity. Bob Dylan referred to this when he noted in a lengthy, rambling, Whitmanesque poem written in 1963 for a short-lived folkie magazine called *Hootenanny* that "Mike Seeger is really real."[3] In the first volume of his autobiography, *Chronicles*, Dylan was more explicit in his acknowledgment of Seeger's influence on his own budding career. He remembered that he had first seen Mike perform solo at a couple of music parties in New York City, including one at Alan Lomax's loft on 3rd Street. Dylan claimed to have discerned very early that Mike already possessed the qualities that he himself was struggling to attain. Mike was "extraordinary," he wrote, "the supreme archetype. He could push a stake through Dracula's black heart. . . . What I had to work at, Mike already had in his genes, in his genetic makeup. Before he was even born, this music had to be in his blood. Nobody could just learn this stuff." Since Mike had already cornered the market on "real" performance in folk music, Dylan would have to do something else: "[M]aybe I'd have to write my own folk songs, ones that Mike didn't know."[4]

Mike's earliest solo performances are hard to document because he appeared occasionally at very small venues and his shows were not always remembered or reviewed. He, in fact, had given programs at elementary schools and children's nurseries in the year or so after his high school graduation. His two most important early concerts, however, were in April 1959 and January 1960 at Carnegie Hall and Swarthmore College, respectively. On April 3, 1959, Mike performed at Carnegie Hall as part of Alan Lomax's Folksong '59 concert. He played briefly in two segments with his brother Pete and Jimmy Driftwood, and he also did a short set by himself. The reviews of Mike's performance were generally favorable, but he must have been particularly pleased with the assessment made by his close but critical friend, Ralph Rinzler, who said that Mike had been "very cool, very musical, and very old-timey. I thought it was spectacular."[5] The Swarthmore concert in early January the following year also marked one of Libba Cotten's first formal music concerts. Mike was pleased to share his talents and love for old-time music with the world, but he was also humbled and moved by the opportunity to be on the same stage with Libba, this grandmotherly presence who only a few short years before had baked him cookies and cleaned his family's house.[6]

Since those initial performances, Mike appeared in a staggering array of venues in the United States, Canada, the European continent, the British Isles, Australia, New Zealand, various African countries, and Japan. As early as 1960, when the New Lost City Ramblers were at their peak, Mike was already earning at least half of his income from solo gigs. These appearances—at private parties, festivals, clubs, coffeehouses, colleges (including classroom presentations), and, less frequently, on television and radio shows—were often booked in conjunction with NLCR tours. Mike consistently gave programs of traditional songs borrowed from Library of Congress field recordings and old 78-rpm commercial phonograph recordings, and he presented them with his trademark instrumental versatility and faithfulness to the original stylistic performances. Mike's singing was never his strong suit, but he presented convincing interpretations of songs with a simple, unadorned vocal style that emphasized the song rather than the performance. He surmised correctly that an attempt to recreate southern backcountry vocal phrasing would be difficult and probably scorned.

Instrumentation, though, was another matter: Mike's playing undoubtedly did justice to the people from whom he had learned. With a minimum of stage patter and a self-effacing style of humor, he played guitar, banjo, fiddle, Autoharp, harmonica, Jew's harp, and panpipes (usually called quills) during a typical engagement. Other performers sometimes joined him onstage, as Dylan did when Mike played at Gerde's Folk City in New York, or when the famous bluesman John Lee Hooker was persuaded to do a short impromptu set in 1961 at the Chessmate Club in Detroit. One night during a show at Club 47 in Cambridge, Massachusetts, Mike played to an audience that included Dylan, Buffy St. Marie, Eric Anderson, Bill Keith, and Joan Baez (who came over after a gig in Boston). Before the evening was over, Baez stepped on the stage and sang a version of "Engine 143" joined by Mike on Autoharp, Bill Keith on banjo, and Bob Siggins on guitar.[7] Mike enjoyed the companionship and musicianship of his contemporaries in the folk revival, but he much preferred playing with the old-timers. They gave him the same sense of comfort that he had received from the aluminum disks that he played during his childhood. Peggy even surmised that he probably received a "sense of belonging" that he had never gotten from his family.[8] He could now pay homage to the old-timers for the memories of hearing their music and take delight in getting to know the people behind the voices. Throughout the 1960s and beyond, Mike increasingly invited such performers as Maybelle Carter, Cousin Emmy (Joy May Carver), Ralph Stanley, Dock Boggs, and Tommy Jarrell to share the concert stage with him.

At one time or another, Mike played at every club on the American folk revival circuit, as well as in Ottawa, Manitoba, Winnipeg, and other Canadian sites. In 1964 he made his first trip to England in a grueling series of concerts arranged principally by Bill Clifton. Mike welcomed the opportunity to travel and to be reunited with Peggy, who had lived in England since the midfifties. Clifton had relocated in England the year before and had already become a fixture in English folk music circles, dispensing his repertoire of Carter Family material, vintage hillbilly tunes, and early bluegrass. American hillbilly music's growth of popularity in England can be traced directly to Clifton and to the tours made by Mike and the New Lost City Ramblers in the years that followed.

Mike began his English tour with a joint gig with Clifton at the Sevenoaks School, not far from where Clifton lived. He then set out on a grueling schedule of one-night stands. Traveling mainly by train or in Clifton's automobile and laden with a cumbersome assortment of luggage and instruments (guitar, banjo, Autoharp, and fiddle), Mike visited towns throughout England and Scotland, staying in bed-and-breakfasts and playing mostly for "folk song clubs," which typically met in rooms above or near pubs and attracted audiences that ranged from fifty to a hundred people. The trip was not without its awkward moments, at least for Clifton. One night, some people in the audience who were aware that Marge was also a musician (probably members of the English bluegrass band the Echo Mountain Band) shouted for her to join Mike onstage. Marge borrowed a guitar from Clifton and went up there; after she finished playing and was walking down the stage steps, she stumbled and broke the neck on the guitar. Not quite as painful, but nevertheless frustrating, to Clifton were some of the compulsive habits that Mike displayed on the trip. Mike, for instance, insisted on removing his baggage and all of his instruments from the car each time they made a pub stop to eat or relax. When Clifton noted wryly that Pete Seeger was not nearly as careful, Mike replied, "Pete loses a lot of instruments."

Bill Clifton playing with Mike Seeger on Mike's first trip to England.
(Photo courtesy of Bill Clifton)

Most of Mike's British shows were solo engagements, but he did play with others on a BBC radio show in early January, at the Cecil Sharp House in London with Peggy in the same month, and at least once with Clifton.[9]

Mike's first independent recordings of his own music had occurred in 1957 as part of a joint project with his three sisters: *American Folk Songs Sung by the Seegers* (Folkways FA 2005). Recorded at Swarthmore and produced by Ralph Rinzler, who played guitar or mandolin on several cuts, the LP was more "folkie" than hillbilly. The album nevertheless revealed the instrumental prowess that Mike had attained on the mandolin, banjo (both frailing and Scruggs style), guitar, and fiddle. The first recorded example of his fiddle playing, in fact, appeared in his version of "Old Molly Hare." Mike's singing sounded tentative, but he and Peggy achieved some fine duet harmony on "Goodbye, Little Bonnie" and "The Brown Girl."[10]

Mike's first two solo albums, *Old Time Country Music* (Folkways FA 2325) and *Mike Seeger* (Vanguard VRS-9150)—recorded in 1962 and 1964, respectively—closely followed the pattern of his live concerts. Like the LPs recorded with the Ramblers, each album consisted solely of material drawn from hillbilly records or Library of Congress field recordings and was presented with Mike's singular contribution to folk music performance: a fidelity to the original stylistic sources. This faithfulness to original style set him apart from other musicians and certainly from other musical members of the Seeger family. Peggy, for example, was skeptical of Mike's stylistic singularity of purpose and once asked him if he was still "drowned in hillbilly."[11]

Old Time Country Music, arguably Mike's best album, was a milestone recording in the launching of the old-time music movement and was still influencing musicians ten years and more after it was first issued. One of these musicians was Henry "Hank" Sapoznik, who has had distinguished careers in both old-time and klezmer music. He said that the LP inspired him and many of his friends in New York City to take up the performance of old-time music. Sapoznik did not hear the record until 1972 but was staggered by the sweep and lush diversity of the performances heard on it—everything from full string-band sound to a cappella. Mike, he said, had not only mastered the content and styles of old-time music but had also recognized the potential of multitrack recording in demonstrating his own diverse skills and in recreating a full band sound.[12] The songs heard on the album reflected the affection for traditional music that Mike had developed as a child in suburban Maryland; a few of them, in fact, had been first collected by old Seeger family friends (like Herbert Halpert and Sidney Robertson Cowell) and other people who had worked as Charles Seeger's field assistants at the Resettlement Administration.

Although Mike was committed to authenticity in both song selection and stylistic performance, his work was never marred by simple imitation. In his thinking, "authenticity" had never meant the literal recreation of an old-time performer's style or sound. Instead, it suggested a faithfulness to the musical culture that produced the songs, and it permitted individual creativity within those traditional bounds. Indeed, it was inevitable that a performer would produce, consciously or unconsciously, his own modifications. One always heard a distinctive "Mike Seeger" sound. In the liner notes to *Mike Seeger*, UCLA folklorist D. K. Wilgus expressed his admiration for Mike's subtle reinterpretations of traditional material, commenting that Mike had "mastered a range of variations within the tradition, without slavishly imitating individual performers."[13] Reviewers Jon Pankake and Paul Nelson declared that Mike had "attained a stunning maturity of expressiveness" and that his Vanguard album was, in their opinion, "the best single LP yet produced by a single city singer."[14] Like virtually all performers who have utilized traditional material, Mike frequently mixed

FOLKWAYS
· FA 2325

Old Time Country Music, Mike Seeger's first solo LP for Folkways. (Courtesy of the Southern Folklife Collection, University of North Carolina at Chapel Hill; photo by John Cohen)

verses and styles from assorted sources in order to come up with the ideal arrangement. His version of "John Hardy," for example, was a composite taken from the Carter Family and a field recording made in 1936 by Sidney Robertson Cowell. "I'm a Man of Constant Sorrow" came from recordings by Emery Arthur and Ralph Stanley, as well as from a version by Juanita Moore that Mike taped in 1956 at New River Ranch. The text used for "Wild Bill Jones" mixed verses taken from the singing of George Reneau and the Stanley Brothers. The banjo style on the song, however, came from Dock Boggs.

Mike's third album, *Tipple, Loom, and Rail: Songs of the Industrialization of the South* (Folkways FH 5273), recorded in 1966, was Mike's most explicitly historical album. It explored an idea that had unconsciously undergirded Mike's earlier music: the fact that southern rural music documented the industrialization of the South and its people. Mike had avoided immersion in the political radicalism of his family, but he nevertheless managed clearly to link the music he loved to southern working-class identity. He did not attempt an exhaustive survey of the various forces that had marked the rural South's transformation from agriculture to industry but instead concentrated on songs that reflected life in three of the most powerful industrial entities: coal mining, textile mills, and railroads. Mike recorded the album at the suggestion of the labor folklorist Archie Green, who was then

Mike Seeger (Vanguard), Mike's second solo LP. (Courtesy of the Southern Folklife Collection, University of North Carolina at Chapel Hill)

working as a librarian at the Institute of Labor and Industrial Relations at the University of Illinois and serving as the faculty sponsor of the campus folk music club. Green's comprehensive and authoritative album notes presented an eloquent testimonial to the value of hillbilly records, calling them "the best single source for southern industrial folksong" along with the material collected after 1933 by the Library of Congress.[15]

The songs that Seeger and Green chose for the album spanned several decades of southern industrial change but also included a very rare version of "A Factory Girl," a song learned from Dorsey Dixon's sister that had originally commented on women's labor in the New England textile industry in the 1840s. In *Making People's Music: Moe Asch and Folkways Records*, Peter Goldsmith compared *Tipple, Loom, and Rail* to an album made about ten years earlier by Pete Seeger titled *American Industrial Ballads* (Folkways FH 5264): "Mike went to considerable length to recreate the originals [earlier hillbilly performances] musically. The significance of the songs was to be found—in part at least—in the style in which they were performed. The younger half brother recreated them as a means of transporting his audience to a previous era, when there was little in the way of romance but a great deal of hard-headed dignity."[16]

While collections like *Tipple, Loom, and Rail* paid tribute to the older styles and sounds of working-class culture, Mike's most satisfying contributions came through his "discovery," reinvigoration, and popularization of

Tipple, Loom & Rail (1966), Mike's musical survey of southern labor history. (Courtesy of the Southern Folklife Collection, University of North Carolina at Chapel Hill; photo by John Cohen)

the people who had made the music in the first place. Mike felt that it was not enough simply to borrow their songs or recreate and teach their styles in workshops or on instructional recordings (as he did increasingly beginning in the 1980s). Like his colleagues in New York's Friends of Old Time Music, he also felt the need to introduce, or reintroduce, the old-time musicians to the public. Mike, of course, had been recording old-time musicians since the midfifties, but his earliest ventures had been motivated primarily by his desire to learn the songs and styles that he had heard. The chance encounter with the music of Libba Cotten in the Seeger's Chevy Chase home, and the eventual recording of several of her songs, did ultimately result in the documentation of her important work. But Mike's real emergence as a conscious documenter came after he moved to Baltimore and produced his seminal Folkways albums of Scruggs-style banjo and bluegrass musicians.

As mentioned in chapter 3, Mike had begun documenting some of the pioneer country musicians as early as 1955. He collected the music of people like Marshall Louis "Grandpa" Jones, Sam and Kirk McGee, and Bill and Charlie Monroe on his portable tape recorder at country music parks such as New River Ranch and Sunset Park.[17] He recorded others closer to home. Displaying a knack for being at the right place at the right time, Mike found one of the most venerable musicians, Ernest Stoneman, still living nearby in Carmody Hills, Maryland. The relationship led not only to

Stoneman's rerecording on the Folkways label but also to Mike's acquaintanceship with Kilby Snow and the realization that a vital tradition of Autoharp playing existed in the South.[18]

America's most famous Autoharp player, of course, was Maybelle Carter. Mike was aware of her unique style of holding the instrument against her chest as she played, but he did not have a protracted relationship with her until she appeared in 1963 at the Ash Grove in Los Angeles. He described the encounter as a "very special experience" — Johnny Cash had even come in one night as her substitute — and when Mike saw people bringing in stacks of old 78-rpm records for Maybelle to autograph, he came to understand the strong affection that fans had for the Carter Family. He also learned that she was a resilient and road-hardened trouper. Maybelle rode with Mike and the other Ramblers to a show in Tucson, Arizona, and willingly took the wheel for her turn at driving. The Ramblers marveled at the fact that she changed her guitar strings about a half hour before the show and still managed to get them in tune.[19]

During the Ash Grove sojourn, Mike, Maybelle, and the young UCLA folklorist Ed Kahn (who was working on a doctoral dissertation on the Carter Family) drove to Angel's Camp, California, to visit Sara Carter Bayes and her husband, Coy, who lived there in a mobile home. They spent the night interviewing the Carter women, playing music, feeding the chickens, and watching Coy's peacocks roaming in the yard. The visit inspired a brief musical reunion of Maybelle and Sara and an album by them on the Columbia label.[20]

Like the association with Maybelle and Sara Carter, some of Mike's most important documentary efforts were by-products of his tours with the New Lost City Ramblers. Driving back home from the California trip, Mike encountered another pioneer of country music's first commercial generation: Alexander Campbell "Eck" Robertson. Mike had learned about Robertson's whereabouts from the University of Texas folklorist Roger Abrahams after one of Abrahams's students found the fiddler in Amarillo, Texas. Mike, Marge, and the kids (who at the time were age two and a half, one and a half, and two months) stopped off in Amarillo to visit the veteran fiddler. This encounter put Mike in intimate touch with the very beginnings of commercial country music. As a commercial entity, the hillbilly field had neither emerged nor been given a name in 1922 when Eck and an old fiddler friend, Henry Gilliland, traveled to New York and made their first test recordings for the Victor Talking Machine Company (later RCA Victor).[21] One of Eck's initial recordings, "Sallie Gooden," is considered to be one of the virtuoso performances of old-time music. Amazingly, in 1963 he was still playing his fiddle in contests in Texas and Oklahoma. John Cohen and Tracy Schwarz had visited and recorded Eck the previous year, but Mike — during this visit and another in 1964 — recorded an entirely different set of tunes, several of which were later released on the County label. Like most of the other pioneer hillbilly and blues musicians who were being rediscovered during these years, Eck was both delighted and humbled to learn that a brand-new audience was becoming available to him. Mike made sure that Eck was soon booked at the UCLA Folk Festival, at Newport, and at other venues.[22]

Mike's association with Maybelle Carter also led to the uncovering of another old-timer who had been linked to the Carter Family. To Mike's surprise, he learned from Maybelle in 1963 that Lesley Riddle was still alive. Riddle, an African American musician who was born in Burnsville, North Carolina, and reared in Yancey County, Tennessee, had taught Maybelle how to play the bottleneck blues style of guitar and had traveled with A. P. Carter on some of his song-hunting expeditions, supplying him with such songs as "Cannon Ball Blues" and "Lonesome for You." Riddle also sometimes came down to the Carters' home place in Maces Spring, Virginia, to spend a few weeks and share his songs with A. P. After a long search that first took Mike and Marge on a fruitless visit to Riddle's hometown of Kingsport, Mike finally learned from the bluesman Brownie McGhee, who also came from the Kingsport area, that Riddle lived in Rochester, New York. In October 1963 Mike finally found Riddle in Rochester working as a shoe-shine man in a barbershop. The reclusive Riddle was reluctant to record or perform, but after a series of meetings in the following years, Mike persuaded him to record several numbers and to appear publicly at the Newport, Mariposa, and Smithsonian festivals.[23]

Mike's documentary net extended far and wide, encompassing both the old-timers — whose musical careers extended back to the beginnings of country music history — and younger musicians who built upon roots foundations, such as the Lilly Brothers, Merle Travis, Jimmy Martin, and the Country Gentlemen. For example, when Mike found out that Travis was scheduled to appear in a joint concert with the Lilly Brothers at Jordan Hall in Boston on November 21, 1959, he borrowed an Ampex 600 recorder from Capitol Transcriptions and set out by car from Washington to document the event. Mike was aware that Travis's name and style of guitar picking had been well known in the folk music community, principally because of a ten-inch, 78-rpm album of four records titled *Folk Songs from the Hills*, which Travis had recorded back in 1947. Songs like "Dark as a Dungeon" and "Sixteen Tons," though written by Travis for the album, had attained such widespread circulation that they were presumed to be traditional ballads of unknown vintage. The CD that eventually emerged from the Boston concert reintroduced Travis's musical genius to a new generation of roots-music fans.[24]

Except for his role in the discovery of Libba Cotten, Mike may have found his most satisfying achievements in his recordings of Dock Boggs and the relationship that developed between him and that singular musician. Boggs had been instrumental in Mike's parents' introduction to commercial old-time music. Back in 1932, when Thomas Hart Benton played Boggs's recorded versions of "Pretty Polly" and "Danville Girl" (originally recorded for Brunswick in 1928) for Charles and Ruth, the event had opened up for them an exciting new world of folk music expression. It was, in many ways, one of the turning points in American folk music scholarship. Boggs was also a vital part of Mike's youth and of his personal discovery of the music when, as a child, he listened repeatedly to these and other old-time records. Boggs's music had also been one of the distinctive features of the Harry Smith anthology and had greatly excited young fans. Mike said Boggs's "sound was so wild and otherworldly to me. His music seemed to be both a 'mixture of Africa and the wilder side of England.'"

While Mike may have succumbed to a bit of romantic hyperbole in his description of Boggs's music, he nevertheless echoed the feelings that many young fans had when they heard the great Virginia country musician. Like his contemporaries in the 1920s, Boggs's new fans marveled at his penchant for playing the melody rather than the chords on his five-string banjo as he sang. Above all, they were fascinated by his eclectic repertoire of ballads, blues tunes, and gospel songs and by the rough and lonesome sound of his voice. Judged exclusively by his stark style of singing and his choice of songs like "Country Blues," "Pretty Polly," "Oh Death," "The Rowan County Crew," and "Wild Bill Jones," Boggs's music seemed to be the expression of a tragic and violence-ridden life. And in some ways, this image was correct. Boggs had spent much of his life working in the coal mines of southwestern Virginia and eastern Kentucky; he carried a gun (although he never used it); he had several violent encounters; and he drank heavily. But he was also drawn to the life and music of the Holiness Church, particularly through the influence of his wife, who looked askance at his music making and the wild temptations that seemed to go along with it. When Mike met him, Boggs had been long retired from both coal mining and music, but he had also recently begun thinking about making music again on his beloved banjo.[25]

In June 1963, as Mike and Marge were driving home from California, they decided to take a detour through the southern hills. Having been informed by the collector Gus Meade that Boggs was still alive and living somewhere in the region of eastern Kentucky or western Virginia, they decided to seek out some of the places where Boggs had lived on the outside chance that he or someone who knew him might still be around. Their diligent search through the small towns of Appalachia proved anticlimactic and unnecessary, however; Mike and Marge eventually learned that Boggs was living in Norton, Virginia, by looking in a local phone book. Boggs told them that sometime earlier, he had retrieved his five-string banjo from the friend who he had pawned it with and was more than ready to play it again. Mike conducted the first of several interviews with Boggs and soon managed to book him at the American Folk Festival in Asheville, where he performed for a crowd of 10,000 people. Mike eventually produced four LPs of Boggs's music and interviews for Folkways.[26] Boggs found a new audience at folk festivals and colleges around the country, and though he never felt completely at ease in these new surroundings, he once said in an interview that "when Mike Seeger found me, he asked if I would like to play again. I told him it had been my heart's desire to put my old songs on records so the younger generation could learn them if they wanted to."[27] Several years later, Molly Tenenbaum, in a review of the CD compilation reissue of Boggs's 1960s LPs, noted the ubiquity of Mike's presence in Dock's life: "Everywhere you go in the Land of Boggs, you find Mike Seeger's name. It was he who took the trouble to locate Boggs, and who introduced him to new audiences. Seeger recorded his music, recorded his conversation, took photographs and has provided much of this material for every Dock Boggs project I run into. I'd say that, besides Dock Boggs himself, we have Mike Seeger to thank for this music."[28]

Mike's multiple undertakings—and his all-consuming commitment to see them accomplished—inevitably placed strains on both his health and his marriage. Grueling road trips, concerts, recording ventures, and practice took up many of his days, and all too many of his nights were filled with song transcribing, record editing, and business and personal correspondence. Mike once commented that when he went to bed, ideas about various musical projects filled his head and often kept him from sleeping. "I really liked to work so much," he said, "I'd just keep working. I'd jump out of bed, go to work writing or learning songs or recording someone, or write letters until I'd go to sleep." Judging from Mike's experiences, it is easy to see that despite its emphasis on simplicity, nonmaterialistic values, and rural placidity, the world of old-time music was no more immune from the stress-producing anxieties associated with modern urban life than were the cultures of more commercial forms of music. Musicians who followed schedules as rigorous as Mike's experienced difficulties in reconciling the emotional highs of public performance with the letdowns that inevitably set in when they left the stage and went back home. As early as 1960, when he was still working at Capitol Transcriptions, putting out records with the New Lost City Ramblers, and supporting a newly pregnant wife, Mike began experiencing physical ailments and psychic stresses that remained with him, off and on, for the next twenty years and more. Complaining of chest pains, anxiety, and the inability to sleep, Mike sought the support of doctors and therapists who advised him to alter his lifestyle, which was difficult for him to do. Medical consultation and prescriptions also introduced him to a variety of amphetamines and tranquilizers, including Miltowns (meprobamate), which was then a relatively new drug on the American market. In 1965 he also began using marijuana—what he called "the illegal weed"—in order to induce relaxation and sleep.[29]

Mike's physical complaints were troublesome, but they paled in comparison to the blow he received in 1966 when Marge asked for a separation. While he insisted that her request took him by surprise, it seems that it should not have. Mike alleged that the breakup was "a result really from wanting to have different kinds of lives," and that Marge, a native New Yorker, was "really a city person." But life with Mike Seeger could not have been easy, even though Marge loved and supported the music that consumed his existence. Their good friend Bill Clifton, who knew and loved them both, said that life with Mike must have been "very difficult."[30] Marge occasionally gave guitar lessons after they moved to Roosevelt, New Jersey, and she worked as a phone receptionist in a computer firm for a lengthy period to help support the family. Marge played guitar during a few of Mike's concerts and with the New Lost City Ramblers when Tom Paley was easing his way out of the group, and she played the same instrument on at least a couple of Mike's LPs, his first solo effort for Folkways, and a budget banjo recording that he did with fiddler Tex Logan. She also tried her hand at booking musical acts, first with the White Brothers (Clarence and Roland) and the Echo Mountain Band and then with the old-time performers Dock Boggs and Mississippi John Hurt. She also made extensive tapes of the music of the Stanley Brothers and other pioneer bluegrass acts and sent them to the Echo Mountain Band in England so they could become more acquainted with the songs and culture of American musicians. While Mike was struggling to put bread on the table, Marge raised their three children, spent an enormous amount of time on the road, and lived in a wide assortment of homes and apartments before settling down in their own home in Roosevelt.[31]

The first two years of separation were, in Mike's words, "a sad time," and not solely because of the breakup of his marriage. He continued to make music with the New Lost City Ramblers, but his association with John Cohen had never been an easy one. In 1975 the friction that often marred his personal and musical relationship with John led Mike to contemplate disbanding the New Lost City Ramblers or even creating two such organizations.[32] The folk music revival had ebbed, and many of Mike's friends had retreated to rock and roll or other kinds of electric-based music. Mike left Roosevelt and moved back to the familiar confines of Greater Washington, settling down in a small D.C. apartment ostensibly because it was close to the Upper South and the music that he loved.

Familiar surroundings brought some comfort to Mike during these difficult years, but music, as always, provided his greatest salvation. His musical energies never flagged. Hunkering down in his tiny apartment with his Magnechord recording unit, he began splicing tapes and completed production of two more Folkways LPs that he had long been working on: Libba Cotten's second album, *Sugaree*, and *McGee Brothers and Arthur Smith: Old Timers of the Grand Ole Opry*, a collaboration made by the old-time Grand Ole Opry stars. Mike continued to play numerous solo gigs and concerts with the New Lost City Ramblers, including the Chicago Folk Festival, the tradition-oriented venue that had always been close to his heart. The Ramblers also played at their first rock festival, the Sky River Rock Festival and Lighter than Air Fair, in rural Washington State near Sultan, north of Seattle, on August 30, 1968. They shared the stage with acts like Santana, Country Joe and the Fish, and the Grateful Dead. The tie-dyed shirts, long hair, bizarre clothing styles, and open use of hard drugs provided a culture shock to these seasoned performers of the more benign folk scene. Reminiscing about the event many years later, a nostalgic fan, Walt Crowley, recaptured the spirit of those euphoric counterculture days. He noted that the day after a heavy rain had turned the grounds into a sea of mud, "the denizens of Sky River Rock stirred from their huts and greeted the day. Blouses and bras, pants and briefs were discarded. A dance began and soon linked hundreds in a spontaneous ritual of purification around and within a deep pool of ooze." The Ramblers never disclosed whether they partici-pated in this "ritual," but they were pleased by their young audience's en-thusiastic response to their performance and discovered that their music might possibly have an appeal outside of the old-time music crowd.[33] Mike and the Ramblers also toured England in February 1967, and later that year, they journeyed to Australia and New Zealand.

Back home, Mike spent a considerable amount of time playing and recording with John Duffey, Ralph Stanley, and other musician friends. He even got a strong taste of hillbilly barnstorming when the veteran blue-grass musician Don Reno, looking for a replacement for his recently hospi-talized partner, Bill Harrell, asked Mike to play guitar on one of his tours. Mike met Reno in the latter's Hyattsville, Maryland, home, practiced a few songs, and soon set out on a grueling tour in Reno's "well-worn" Chrysler Imperial. With the bass tied to the top of the car in classic hillbilly fash-ion and the other instruments packed in the trunk along with the group's traveling clothes, Mike, Reno, George Shuffler, and Reno's son Ronnie trav-eled to Meriden, Connecticut; to Buffalo, New York; on through New Jer-sey; down to Louisville, Kentucky; to Bean Blossom, Indiana; back to New York; and then to Baltimore. Mike soon found out that he was not quite suited to play the style of bluegrass guitar that Reno wanted, so he shifted to the bass for most of the one-night stands that they played. The music was exhilarating and the schedule exhausting; but the entire experience was an "adventure" that Mike would never forget, as he listened to Reno and Shuf-fler spinning tall tales and reminiscing about life on the road — or cringed as Reno carried on his lengthy monologues while driving and looking back through the rearview mirror.[34]

During these years of separation from Marge, Mike's longtime relation-ship with Alice Gerrard gradually evolved into romance. Mike had first met Alice in 1956, when she and her future husband, Jeremy Foster (Mike's former high school classmate), were both attending Antioch College in Yellow Springs, Ohio. The three friends traveled frequently to New River Ranch and other country music parks but also found immediate compat-ibility in singing old-time country music; Mike described their first musical encounter, singing either a Carter Family song or an early bluegrass song, as "absolutely wonderful."[35] Alice, born in Seattle but California reared, had matriculated at Antioch, where she became a good friend of Marjorie Ostrow. Alice was playing the piano and still influenced by her family's classical background when she began listening to the music collected by Jeremy and heard dorm mates singing folk songs. An introduction to Texas Gladden's "One Morning in May" and the Harry Smith collection con- verted her to folk music, but living in Washington, D.C., introduced her to the area's burgeoning bluegrass scene. Although she had gone to Washing- ton as part of a required social outreach plan for Antioch students, Alice did not permit academic responsibilities to dim her passion for music. She frequented the bluegrass scene at the Famous Restaurant and showed up often at bluegrass parties in Washington and Baltimore.

One night at a party in Baltimore (probably at the house where Mike and Alyse were living),[36] Alice became acquainted with Hazel Dickens, and they soon began singing with each other. As unlikely as this partnership be- tween an upper-middle-class girl from the West Coast and a working-class girl from Appalachia might seem, Alice and Hazel found immediate vocal compatibility, impressing their listeners with their soulful harmonies and passionate phrasing. Their rural tenor and urban contralto meshed beauti- fully. They sang informally for several months but ventured into the realm of public performance when they sang onstage at the old-time fiddlers' con- vention in Galax, Virginia. In 1965 their first album, *Who's That Knocking?*, was released on the Folkways label. It featured the instrumental backing of David Grisman on mandolin, Lamar Grier on banjo, and Chubby Wise and Billy Baker on fiddle. Although this first Folkways LP received critical ac- claim in the bluegrass community, it was not well promoted, and a second album (actually recorded only a few months after the first one) did not ap- pear until 1973. By this time, Ken Irwin and the Rounder label had signed them to a new contract, and Hazel and Alice had become popular fixtures on the bluegrass festival circuit.

The sounds heard on the Folkways and Rounder records were significant departures for bluegrass music and milestones in the Women's Movement. Hazel and Alice sang in the duet style usually associated with men like the Louvin Brothers (Ira and Charlie)—a low lead topped by a high tenor. Their song lyrics, along with the fact that they had written many of them, proved singularly appealing to women. Hazel and Alice's performances have since been described as the beginning of the "feminization of bluegrass," and

Alice Gerrard (left), Hazel Dickens, and Mike Seeger performing together.
Hazel and Alice was the first influential women's group in bluegrass music. (Courtesy of
the Southern Folklife Collection, University of North Carolina at Chapel Hill)

many women in that genre now look upon them as pioneers and mentors. To their great surprise, feminists began to see them as role models, and some of their songs, such as Hazel's "Don't Put Her Down, You Helped Put Her There" and Alice's "Custom Made Woman Blues," became anthems to many women. Hazel and Alice appeared often in festival workshops that were devoted to women's issues.[37]

Jeremy Foster was killed in an automobile accident in 1964, leaving Alice a young widow with four children. By 1966 she and Mike had become constant companions, and when Mike's children came down from New York to visit him, they usually stayed with Alice and her kids in her apartment in Maryland. During the years of their courtship and marriage, Mike and Alice often sang together in various combinations but recorded only one album on their own: *Mike Seeger and Alice Gerrard* (Greenhays, 1980).[38] As fans and historians of old-time music, they occasionally wrote articles and reviews for *Bluegrass Unlimited* and other music journals, sometimes as collaborators and sometimes alone. Alice and Mike's musical preferences were quite similar and even encompassed people from the country-and-western circuit, such as George Jones and Tommy Collins. Alice, for example, wrote a well-received article on the popular and populist superstar Merle Haggard.[39]

One of Mike and Alice's most important musical collaborations came as part of a group called the Strange Creek Singers, formed with Hazel Dickens, Tracy Schwarz, and Lamar Grier. Stories differ (at least subtly) as to why the name was chosen. Returning from a fiddlers' contest in West Virginia, Mike and Alice had been bemused by a little community they passed through in Braxton County called Strange Creek. But Tracy claims that the couple had gotten lost in the area and decided to choose the name because they had invested so much time in the region.[40] The Strange Creek Singers fulfilled Mike and Alice's desire to have a band that could perform both bluegrass and traditional material. Listeners would hear a little touch of the New Lost City Ramblers, Hazel and Alice, the bluegrass sound of Tracy's tenor and Lamar's five-string banjo style and, of course, the individual styles of all the musicians. The Strange Creek Singers made only one LP and traveled infrequently, but the group did make an extensive tour of the West Coast and, in October 1975, one European tour. Ranging from Tracy's haunting "Poor Old Dirt Farmer" and the Louvin Brothers' "Get Acquainted Waltz" to the old religious piece "When I Can Read My Titles Clear," the song selections on the LP indicate the breadth and diversity of the group's repertoire and arrangements. Hazel's first recording of "Black Lung," a song inspired by the death of her brother Thurman from the grim disease pneumoconiosis, appeared on the LP and became a classic dirge of protest.[41]

In 1966 Mike and Alice also became involved with the Southern Folk Cultural Revival Project, the brainchild of two women, Anne Romaine and Bernice Reagon. Romaine and Reagon hoped to employ music to promote the cause of racial brotherhood and justice in the United States. Like Hazel and Alice, the two seemed total opposites in background and looks. Anne had grown up in North Carolina in comfortable middle-class surroundings, but she was imbued with a strong missionary social consciousness, first expressed as a medical worker and youth counselor for the Presbyterian Church. She and her husband, Howard (who was on the staff of the Southern Student Organizing Committee), became deeply involved in the civil rights movement while attending graduate school at the University of

Virginia. Anne was an avid fan and singer of country music, fronting for a short time a band called Anne Romaine and the Honky Tonk Angels, and she recorded at least one LP, *Gettin' on Country* (Rounder 3009), which was composed of feminist songs, economic protest songs, and mainline country and western. Bernice was an African American from the Deep South who had been a member of the Student Nonviolent Coordinating Committee and a powerful singer of freedom songs in Mississippi and other racial battlegrounds. Of course, she has since become famous as a historian of black religious music and as a founder and member of the popular singing group Sweet Honey in the Rock.[42]

The Southern Folk Cultural Revival Project was an interracial troupe of musicians (constantly shifting in personnel) who took their music — usually under the name of the Southern Folk Festival — to racially mixed audiences in the South. Colleges generally hosted the festival tours, but the project also traveled to various communities, typically presenting high school assemblies in the afternoon and community concerts in the evening. A strong array of roots musicians traveled at one time or another with the project, including Dock Boggs, Johnny Shines, Reverend Pearly Brown, Roscoe Holcomb, Libba Cotten, Bessie Jones, the Balfa Brothers, and such younger musicians as Hedy West, Phyllis Boyens, Billy Edd Wheeler, John D. Loudermilk, Sparky Rucker, and Hazel and Alice. Each year, the project typically conducted one tour in the Deep South and one in the upper South. The troupe's unique goal was to promote the music of the region and to reveal the interrelationship of racial and ethnic musical styles, while at the same time focusing on racial brotherhood and justice. Reagon later said that "we grounded our work in the historic reality that Black and White southern music cultures crossed racial boundaries that the actual peoples who created those cultures could not cross."[43]

Everyone who became involved in the Southern Folklore Project seems to have been permanently affected by its idealism and dream of racial brotherhood. Above all, the project suggested that interracial working-class harmony was possible in the South — a vision far different from the racial bigotry that had so long dominated the region. For Hazel Dickens, involvement in the tours constituted a decisive turning point in her life and music. She particularly enjoyed the give-and-take of the workshops held by the project, where she talked about her music and its roots in her personal life and culture: "Sitting in a semi-circle onstage, interacting with and supporting each other — it really encouraged me with my own performing and songwriting." She abandoned her embarrassment about her West Virginia working-class roots, developed pride about her origins, and began to write explicit songs of protest. Hazel began making appearances with, and on behalf of, worker groups and became a zealous battler on behalf of black lung legislation and other workers' needs.[44]

Mike became involved in the Southern Folklore Project in 1966 when the New Lost City Ramblers gave a concert and workshop in Charlottesville at the University of Virginia and Anne Romaine invited them to join her tours. After an initial moment of embarrassment for Mike when he saw the project's posters advertising the group as "Mike Seeger and the New Lost City Ramblers," he became a staunch supporter of Anne's project. He was intrigued by the fact that while Anne was politically liberal, she was also committed to all kinds of country music. Anne, on the other hand, was impressed with Mike's musicianship but unsure about his commitment to "real" country music, and she asked him what he thought about one of her heroes, Loretta Lynn. He apparently gave her a satisfying answer, because the two of them became close friends and passionate champions of working-class music.[45]

Mike was emotionally affected by the Southern Folk Festival tours. They constituted another milestone in his equating old-time music with working-class values, as well as a reaffirmation of his conviction that southern rural music was a fusion of black and white styles. Only three days after Martin Luther King Jr. was assassinated, the Ramblers joined the festival for appearances on five college campuses in North Carolina, Tennessee, and Virginia. Ray Allen argued that "by appearing with a troupe of traditional black and white musicians and acknowledging the biracial origins of the southern music they championed, the Ramblers positioned themselves as ardent supporters of integration and equality without having to demonize white southerners."[46]

While Mike had rejected "Seeger politics," he nevertheless promoted his own brand of democratic egalitarianism. He had become increasingly convinced that old-time music *itself* was inherently a political statement because it embodied and demonstrated the innate worth of average people. The Southern Folklore Project also meshed neatly with Mike's desire to revitalize old-time music in the South and renewed his determination to convince northern listeners that old-time southern musicians were not universally the reactionary bigots that many presumed them to be. Mike participated only in the Upper South tours, but he found much there to reinforce the relevance of the old-time music that he had always loved. His most vivid memory of the project was of a show in North Carolina given to piedmont cotton-mill workers who were trying to win union recognition. The workers particularly liked the old tune "Cotton Mill Colic," learned from the great textile music poet David McCarn, who had intrigued both Mike and Archie Green.[47]

Mike and Alice were married in August 1970 in an apple orchard in York County in southern Pennsylvania, with Hazel's dad, Hillary Dickens, officiating at their wedding.[48] The orchard was located on an old farm near New Freedom that Mike had bought back in June 1969. Tracy Schwarz already lived in the area and had told Mike and Alice about the site. The couple lived in the stone house there from 1970 to 1976 with Alice's four children—Cory, Jenny, Joel, and Jesse—who were frequently joined by Mike's three kids. The newlyweds appreciated the space that surrounded the house and the good schools in the area. Mike's idealization of the life of Wade Ward, who had managed to live simply and independently in rural Virginia, also probably influenced his desire to live in the country. The house was ideally located for a couple of people who valued and, indeed, mythicized the rural past. It was situated on a seventy-five-acre site at the mouth of a hollow about two and a half miles off the interstate. Surrounded by abundant farmlands, the house had once been a thriving agricultural enterprise, replete with about fifteen or twenty outbuildings that included a springhouse, corncrib, toolshed, and barns. While the rural surroundings were attractive, the house's central location also permitted Mike to occasionally run down to Washington, D.C., only an hour and a half away, to fulfill his growing board and advisory obligations and to perform in the concerts that filled so much of his time. Although the new home seemed ideal in many ways, the place required an immense outlay of repairs and renovation—work that entailed more time and money than was usually available to a couple of old-time musicians who had other time-consuming priorities. Given the circumstances, these upkeep responsibilities undoubtedly contributed to the tensions that soon surfaced in the marriage.[49]

Musically, however, Mike and Alice were well matched. Both were totally immersed in the culture of old-time music, and both had an insatiable desire to learn as much as they could about it. But they generally pursued separate careers. Alice still performed regularly with Hazel Dickens and, after 1980, as part of a trio called the Harmony Sisters (with Irene Herrmann and Jeanie McLerie);[50] and Mike, Alice, and Hazel did occasional gigs with the Strange Creek Singers, including a European tour from October to December 1975. The Strange Creek Singers traveled to Europe by Icelandic Air, the cheapest but slowest way to fly, and then rented a Volkswagen bus in Germany. They depended on the language skills of Tracy Schwarz to navigate them through the Continent (he had played a similar role in 1966 when the New Lost City Ramblers toured Europe with a group of bluegrass and old-time musicians). Israel "Izzy" Young, who had moved to Sweden, arranged some bookings for them in Stockholm and other parts of that country. Then they went to Hamburg, Bremen, Wales, Manchester, Belfast, Bern, Lausanne, Paris, and Brittany.[51]

Mike still performed occasionally with the New Lost City Ramblers but became increasingly consumed with his own concerts and multifaceted enterprises. He had been heavily involved in advisory work since 1963, when he replaced Bill Clifton as an adviser to the Newport Folk Foundation. Alan Lomax also joined that board for the first time, and he and Mike became persuasive spokesmen for the inclusion of traditional acts on the Newport Festival. Through their influence, too, Ralph Rinzler became a full-time field-worker for the board and another advocate of traditional performers. Board work was time-consuming, but Mike willingly took it on because he saw these board activities as indispensable opportunities to promote the interests of traditional artists and to use the foundation's grant money to further the interests of traditional arts throughout the country. Mike also served as the director of the touring Smithsonian Folk-Life Company from 1968 to 1976, and he sometimes did fieldwork for the organization to help choose artists for the annual folklife festival on the National Mall in Washington.

In 1973 Mike began a stint on the advisory panel of a small folk music program within the Jazz, Folk, and Ethnic Music Division of the National Endowment for the Arts (NEA). Created largely through the determined advocacy of Archie Green and Ralph Rinzler, the NEA folk-arts program lent a certain degree of equity to the appreciation of the music, arts, and crafts of untutored people in the United States. Mike served as an adviser on applications for grants, but he soon became upset with the "public sector" folklorists. Since they were dependent on government funding and public taxation, they tended to promote traditional musicians or "artists who were actually community-based tradition bearers" instead of "outsiders" or people like him. Increasingly, he found it difficult to get musical gigs at the Smithsonian Festival and similar affairs unless he was willing to be an an-

Mike Seeger with Alan Lomax (in white short-sleeved shirt), Julius Lester (next to Mike),
and Hazel Dickens (background above Lester) at the Newport Folk Festival.
(Photo by Aaron Rennert of Photo-Sound Associates; courtesy of Ronald D. Cohen)

nouncer, facilitator, or panel participant. Even his longtime friend Rinzler favored the folklorists' position. Ironically, after many years of determined advocacy of traditional acts, Mike now found his own career adversely affected by the uncompromising stance taken by the public folklorists. Ray Allen noted that Mike and the other Ramblers felt like "victims of their own success who were suddenly on the outside looking in."[52]

Mike nevertheless remained very busy on a variety of projects, including various documentary LPs (such as a third one by Dock Boggs) and his first LP for a major label, *Music from the True Vine* (Mercury SRM1–627), produced by Paul Nelson and recorded in 1971 at the Mercury Sound Studios in New York. Nelson, a former editor of the *Little Sandy Review* and a longtime fan of Mike and the New Lost City Ramblers, carefully fashioned a well-produced LP that was free of the studio embellishments found in most of the products produced by major labels. This was apparently the first time that Mike used the term "True Vine" to describe the music that he collected and performed. The True Vine, he argued, was "the home music made by American Southerners before the media age." It was music that had grown out of "hundreds of years of British traditions that blended in our country with equally ancient African traditions to produce songs and sounds that are unique to the United States."[53] Instrumentally, the LP was a tour de force: Mike played guitar, Autoharp, banjo, harmonica, fiddle, and dulcimer and showcased a variety of styles. For the first time on one of his recordings, he also played the Jew's harp, adding its distinctive sound to an old nonsense song called "Old Blind Drunk John." He selected a wide assortment of old songs, ranging from an unaccompanied version of "Black Is the Color" to tunes like "Roving Cowboy," played with fiddle accompaniment; "Don't Let Your Deal Go Down," featuring both fiddle and harmonica backing; and "Rattlesnake Daddy," complete with a yodel-like refrain and single-string picking on the resonator guitar (a guitar that was amplified with a metal diaphragm or disc).

Mike also increased his level of academic participation in the mid-1970s. He had enjoyed a close relationship with academic students of folk music ever since the beginning of his musical career. D. K. Wilgus, Archie Green, Ed Kahn, Arthur Palmer Hudson, and others had been intrigued by the unique scholarship exhibited by Mike and the Ramblers. Consequently, Mike sometimes took his music into classrooms, as he did in December 1971 when he spent three or four days in Green's class at the University of Illinois at Urbana-Champaign. During the spring semester of 1974, he even undertook a full-time residency in the English department at Fresno State University in California. When Professor Gene Bluestein went on leave, Mike rented his house and assumed full responsibilities for the teaching of a course on American old-time music.[54] He and Alice and three of her children (Jesse, Joel, and Jenny) drove to California in her Chevrolet van and made their home in that state for about five months.

Mike taught a lecture class at Fresno containing 130 students and a small seminar with fifteen students. He provided his classes with tape recordings and films of varying musical genres, gave musical demonstrations, and held extended one-on-one discussions with his students. Mike invited a variety of old-time musicians to make guest appearances, and this proved to be a very popular feature of his classes. These included Cousin Emmy, Johnny Shines, local bar owner Otis Pierce (who played the Jew's harp), and Tommy Collins. Collins, a well-known country singer and songwriter, was part of the contingent of musicians (including Merle Haggard and Buck Owens) who had made Bakersfield, California, a thriving country music center. Collins drove down from Bakersfield in his pickup truck carrying a chainsaw and looking for nice pieces of wood. Mike and Alice continued to give concerts in California and elsewhere on the West Coast, as did the New Lost City Ramblers and Hazel Dickens, who visited with Mike and Alice for a couple of weeks. During the semester, Mike also managed to fly back to the Chicago Folk Festival and to the Indian Springs Bluegrass Festival in Maryland, where he played with Bill Clifton.[55]

When the residency was completed, Mike, Alice, and the kids took a circuitous route back home through Canada, playing at occasional gigs, such as Toronto's Mariposa Folk Festival, along the way. Mike's varied enterprises continued, but his friendship and collaboration with Thomas Jefferson "Tommy" Jarrell, a highly regarded local fiddler and five-string banjoist from Toast, North Carolina, brought a new and special experience to his and Alice's life. Tommy had worked for the North Carolina Highway Department for forty-one years as a road grader but had always found time to play music in the Round Peak area of North Carolina. After his retirement from the highway department in 1966, his music was introduced to the folk revival when his son, Benjamin Franklin "B. F." Jarrell, approached Alan Jabbour, a Duke University graduate student and fiddle enthusiast, and told him: "You ought to hear my daddy play the fiddle." Energized by Jabbour's support and by the patronage of County Records in New York, Jarrell became one of the guiding lights of a new phase of the old-time string band revival,[56] one that brought an additional retinue of southern-born musicians into the consciousness of old-time music fans.

Mike Seeger and the NLCR had contributed mightily to the awakening of interest in traditional string-band music, but they were not alone. Enlivened by the precedent of the Harry Smith collection and by his own childhood interest in southern hillbilly music, the New York–born collector Dave Freeman established in 1964 a record label called County devoted to the LP reissue of the old 78-rpm records and, a year later, a mail-order outlet for bluegrass and old-time country music called County Sales. In 1974 Freeman moved his operations to the tiny town of Floyd, Virginia. By that time, County Records had already become the dominant force in the reissue of old-time music and had helped to reawaken an interest in such music among southerners themselves. In the late 1960s, after having released an important body of reissued items, the County label changed its

focus to the recording of still-living old-time musicians and began issu-
ing their music on its 700 series. As part of his work for County, Charles
Faurot, a banjo enthusiast and alumnus of the famous Yale University folk
music "hoots," traveled in 1965 from New York to Galax and other communities in southwest Virginia and recorded an impressive array of clawhammer banjo players and fiddlers, including Fred Cockerham, Kyle Creed,
Ernest East, and other traditional musicians. By 1969 the 700 series LPS
had begun surpassing the County reissues in sales, and, according to Freeman, at least 60 percent of them were being bought by rural customers
throughout the nation.[57]

Released on three County LPS (701, 717, and 757), the songs collected
by Faurot influenced a new generation of folk revival fans and musicians.
Ray Alden, a New York collector and musician, was one of them. In 1967
he saw and heard Cockerham, Oscar Jenkins, and Tommy Jarrell at the
home of collector friend Loy Beaver in New Jersey. Alden fell in love with
the music played that night, and in 1968 he began making pilgrimages to
North Carolina, first to the Union Grove Old-Time Fiddler's Convention
and then to a section of Surry County where Cockerham and Jarrell lived.
He described the fiddle and banjo music he heard in Surry County as the
Round Peak style, named after a local mountain and distinguished by a
syncopated, double-noted clawhammer banjo style pioneered by Charlie
Lowe. Back home in New Jersey, Alden worked hard to learn this banjo
style and told friends about his exciting discoveries. Alden often took some
of his friends — including Bob Carlin, Paul Brown, and Hank Sapoznik —
with him on his southern jaunts, and they, in turn, took their fascination
with southern styles to new dimensions. Spurred by a good-natured question posed to him by Tommy Jarrell — "Don't none of you people have
none of your own music?" — Sapoznik, the son of an eastern European–
born New York cantor, became curious about his own ethnic and religious
backgrounds and undertook research that eventually made him the world's
leading specialist on klezmer and eastern European Jewish music.[58]

Florida-born Alan Jabbour, a classical violinist and medieval literature
graduate student at Duke University, came independently to country fiddling. He insisted that he had never heard the music of the New Lost City
Ramblers when he formed his own fiddle band, the Hollow Rock String
Band. Jabbour had become interested in folk music when he studied ballads in an undergraduate course at Miami University. Curious about folklorists' lack of interest in instrumental music, he began listening intently

to Library of Congress field recordings and then set out to collect the music of still-living country fiddlers. While he contributed directly to the national discovery of Tommy Jarrell, Jabbour's personal favorite among the old-time musicians was Henry Reed of Glen Lyn, Virginia. Reed's fiddle tunes became the bedrock repertoire of the music that Jabbour and his contemporaries played. Jabbour formed the Hollow Rock String Band (named for a little community between Durham and Chapel Hill) in the mid-1960s. In addition to Jabbour, the group included Tommy Thompson on banjo, Bobbie Thompson on guitar, and Bertram Levy on mandolin. Ignoring the music heard on the old 78-rpm records and instead specializing in the music of Reed, Jarrell, and other old-timers that Jabbour had collected, the Hollow Rock String Band, along with the Highwoods String Band of Ithaca, New York, contributed to a new revival of string-band music that has not yet run its course.[59]

Mike Seeger had become acquainted with Tommy Jarrell sometime in 1967 or 1968, probably at the University of Chicago Folk Festival, but the two of them did not become active musical partners until about 1974. Thinking that Tommy might enjoy playing with some younger musicians, Mike had obtained grant money to fund a tour of the West Coast for a trio including himself, Tommy, and banjoist Blanton Owen, as well as the African American string band Martin, Bogan, and Armstrong (Carl, Ted, and Howard) and the Cajun trio of Mark Savoy, Dennis McGee, and Sady Courville. Mike's repeated appearances at the Ash Grove Club and extended residencies in Los Angeles had provided him with contacts on the West Coast that always ensured bookings for his own music and that of the people whom he sponsored. And through his experience reading grant applications on the boards of the Newport Folk Festival, the NEA, and the Smithsonian Folk Festival, Mike also knew how to write successful proposals. Of course, having the name Mike Seeger on the proposal did not hurt either.

During the first three weeks of April 1975, Mike joined again with Jarrell as part of the American Old Time Music Festival. He picked up Tommy in Mount Airy, North Carolina, and flew with him from Winston-Salem to Dallas and then on to Salt Lake City, where they gave their first show. Giving workshops in the afternoon and concerts in the evening, the group followed an exhausting schedule that took them through much of California. They followed an even more rigorous schedule in 1976, starting in Calgary, Alberta, on March 30 and then traveling down the West Coast to San

Diego, where they concluded the tour in mid-April. Mike typically played the guitar as a backup for Tommy's fiddling, emceed the shows, and chose the artists. In addition to Tommy, performing acts included bluesman John Jackson, the Otha Turner Fife and Drum Band, Lily May Ledford, and the Cajun group the Balfa Brothers.

Amid all of this hyper musical activity, Mike and Alice made another major and disruptive move: they decided to return to the Washington, D.C., area. Only five years earlier, the move to rural Pennsylvania had been perceived, at least by Mike, in almost idyllic terms as a retreat from urban anxieties and pressures and as a place where Alice's kids would receive good schooling and the blessings of rural simplicity. However, Alice's oldest daughter, Cory, never liked the new home and went off to private school at the first opportunity. Her younger siblings enjoyed country life, loved having their own wing of the house where they could roam freely, and did not want to move back to a big city. Asked about the move several years later, Mike said that he did not remember why they decided to move and even averred that he really had not wanted to make such an abrupt change. Alice, on the other hand, was ready to move back to the D.C. area. She felt a bit isolated in Pennsylvania, found it difficult to keep up her partnership with Hazel, and had become increasingly frustrated in her attempts to find good babysitters. It seems evident that country life had proved to be harder and more unmanageable than they expected. "I didn't want to spend time working on a farm," Mike said, "but I found myself with a farm."[60]

In 1976 they moved to Garrett Park, Maryland, a progressive working-class community that was becoming middle class, and lived there until 1980. Residence in the greater Washington area brought Mike closer to the boards and panels on which he served and made it easier to find someone to help him with his office work. Alice's rehearsals with Hazel, who lived in Washington, were now easier to arrange. And while the promise of good schools had been one of the professed reasons for the move to Pennsylvania, Mike and Alice now believed that schools in Greater Washington would offer better and broader opportunities for their kids, particularly since Cory had already gone away to boarding school. They ultimately came to believe, however, that the move to Garrett Park was a mistake for the children because of the "bad crowd" with which they became involved. It must nevertheless be acknowledged that Alice and Mike's busy schedules also kept them away from their children at crucial times, and Pennsylvania country life had often had its moments of almost unmanageable chaos.

Mike's children and Alice's children with Libba Cotten in New Freedom, Pa., 1975.
Standing from left: Chris Arley Seeger, Kim Seeger, Libba Cotten, Jenny Foster,
Cory Foster, and Joel Foster; kneeling: Jesse Foster and Jeremy Seeger.
(Courtesy of Chris Arley Seeger; photo by Mike Seeger)

One gets some insight into this life through the note Alice appended to the song "Custom Made Woman Blues," which she sent in 1972 to *Sing Out!*: "To tell you the truth, I just can't get my thoughts together to write something coherent regarding my motivation for writing this song. There are seven children here at the house; the house is in dreadful need of cleaning, Hazel and I are trying to cut a record, and Mike and I are trying to practice for an almost-upon-us job."[61] Alice and Mike's busy careers undoubtedly got in the way of the kind of care and supervision that the kids needed. She later admitted that neither she nor Mike were much into parenting, and that they had too often followed a policy of laissez-faire in their dealings with the children. Mike expressed his guilt more than once in the days before he died about his and Alice's failure to deal adequately with the problems experienced by her two boys, especially Jesse. "I feel like I could have done better," he said.[62]

Mike and Alice's relationship with Tommy Jarrell became even more intimate after the move to Garrett Park. In 1977 Alice got an NEA Folk Arts

Apprenticeship Fellowship to study the fiddle with a "master" musician —
in this case, Jarrell. Through this program, the "apprentice" received some
expense money, while the master received a grant from the NEA.[63] Alice
and Mike spent a lot of time at Tommy's home in North Carolina, enjoying
his country food, partaking of his warm hospitality, reveling in his storehouse of tales and old songs, and, at his insistence, even occupying his
bedroom while he slept on a couch in the front room. Often, other young
people would drop in without warning to either listen to or make music
with them. Tommy had learned many of his tunes from his father, Ben,
who had recorded commercially with Da Costa Woltz and his Southern
Broadcasters in 1927 for the Gennett label, as well as from older local fiddlers, whose music dated in some cases from the era of the Civil War South.
Much of this music found its way to LPS made by Tommy and to a documentary film of his life and career made by Les Blank. Produced by Alice
Gerrard and Cecelia Conway and funded principally by an NEA grant, the
film was called *Sprout Wings and Fly* (a title inspired by a line from Tommy's
song "Drunken Hiccups"). Production of the film, of course, required extensive stays at Tommy's house and additional helpings of Tommy's home
cooking, droll humor, and warm hospitality — in addition to lots of good
music making.[64]

Mike and Alice were themselves the subjects of *Homemade American
Music*, a documentary film produced by Yasha and Carrie Aginsky and
filmed in 1978 and 1979. The Aginskys had set out to explore the ways in
which the young learn from the experiences of older people and had approached Pete Seeger as the possible subject of their documentary. Pete, in
turn, had recommended his brother Mike as a candidate for such coverage.
Filmed principally in Garrett Park but also in the homes of three old-time
musicians, at the Freight and Salvage Club in Berkeley, and at a couple of
festivals in California and Washington State, the documentary included segments featuring Lily May Ledford, Roscoe Holcomb, Libba Cotten, Tommy
Jarrell, and an assortment of younger musicians, such as Hank Bradley.
By including both older and younger musicians, the filmmakers hoped to
highlight the power of apprenticeship and to provide some insight about
the breadth of the string-band revival. Mike and Alice reminisced about
their musical backgrounds and the routes they took to old-time music and
were shown walking around in the woods near their home, but the bulk of
the documentary emphasized the musicians. Roscoe Holcomb was filmed

at his home in the Kentucky mountains, and Libba and Tommy were shown at their respective homes in New York and North Carolina. Lily May's clip showed her playing at the Freight and Salvage Club.[65]

The New Lost City Ramblers also celebrated their twentieth anniversary in 1978, marked by a concert at Carnegie Hall. The recording of the Carnegie Hall concert eventually received a Grammy nomination, the first of six that Mike received during his career.[66] The event proved anticlimactic, however, because the group made the first of their several "retirements" the following year. For Mike, 1979 was a year of both highs and lows. He remained musically active, touring in April on his familiar West Coast terrain with the Scottish singer Norman Kennedy, attending NEA meetings in Washington, giving workshops at events like the Augusta Heritage Festival in Elkins, West Virginia, writing a column of musical instruction for *Frets* magazine, and taking part in the "last" New Lost City Ramblers' concert at the Great Hudson River Revival Festival.

But 1979 was also a tough year for Mike. His father, Charles, died on February 7, 1979, in Bridgewater, Connecticut. Ruth's death had been a severe blow from which Charles never fully recovered, and he had sometimes expressed the impact of that loss in letters to Mike and his other children. He spoke, for example, of rereading Dio's letters and being "gripped by nostalgia." He may have even felt a twinge of guilt about the emotional distance that had once lain between him and Mike, saying that he had "copied out a letter" that Mike had dictated when he was eight. "How I wish we had more of the letters you dictated to your dear friends."[67]

Charles's intellectual curiosity, though, never flagged, and he continued to make impressive contributions to folklore and musicological scholarship for the rest of his life. Ann Pescatello notes that it was "fitting that when Seeger died his desk was covered with work to be done."[68] He had been a towering figure in American folk music and in the life of his children. Hillbilly music, of course, was something that he never fully embraced aesthetically, but he recognized its importance and supported its recognition and scholarly acceptance. And he was always quick to applaud any contribution that Mike made.[69]

In addition to dealing with his grief and working with Penny to settle the business and financial arrangements surrounding their father's death, Mike also had to contend with the physical and mental anxieties that had plagued him for years. He was still coping with his dependence on prescription drugs, doing Tai Chi exercises, and consulting counselors and social

Mike Seeger and Libba Cotten in 1979.
(Courtesy of Alexia Smith; photo by Paul Feinberg)

therapists. Mike also saw the number of his concerts decline in 1979 and 1980, partly because of the retirement of the New Lost City Ramblers but also because of the reluctance of the public-sector folklorists to recommend or fund his shows. Mike worked diligently to arrange bookings for himself and for Alice, and he even borrowed folksinger John McCutcheon's mailing list as a means of making vital contacts.[70] Nothing worked very well, though. High spots certainly existed, including an LP on the Greenhays label, which was recorded with Alice mostly at home in Garrett Park but also at the old Seeger home in Chevy Chase; a recording session with Bill Clifton for County; a Labor Day appearance with Hazel Dickens at the White House for President Jimmy Carter, which was arranged by Archie Green; continued reunions at Tommy Jarrell's home, where he met his future music companions Andy Cahan and Paul Brown; and, best of all, occasional tours with Libba Cotten.

Libba remained a godsend to Mike in a variety of ways. For one thing, she was good for his economic health. Mike's booking agent, John Ullman, arranged tours that included both Mike and Libba, including a four-month stint in 1980 that covered Ohio, Michigan, Idaho, Vancouver, and the West Coast and was topped off with a show at the University of California, Berkeley. Mike worked as Libba's road manager, emcee, record seller, and accompanying musician. When Libba was inactive, Mike's career was adversely affected. In a letter to Moe Asch, he noted that one of his tours had been canceled because of her illness (and this after three months of having no work). Working with Libba, though, was important to Mike beyond the economic opportunities that she created. "[Libba] fulfilled my feeling of mission," he said, "which is . . . to bring the traditional music, especially music of a brown-skinned woman, to city people."[71]

The two most important mother and father figures in Mike's life — Libba Cotten and Tommy Jarrell — could only have been shocked and saddened when they learned in late 1981 that Mike and Alice had separated and were contemplating divorce. According to Alice, "a lot of things" contributed to the breakup of their relationship, including their differences in temperament and style and Mike's inability to be a good, loving father. She noted that he could sit in judgment, for example, but not get involved in the kids' day-to-day lives. She even said that "it was a relationship that never should have been."[72] But marriages have often survived such personal incompatibilities. The problems in Mike and Alice's marriage were compounded by a more serious factor: Mike had become involved with another woman. He had come to know her during his advising days at the Smithsonian Institution in the late 1960s, but the relationship had ended when she married in 1972. Sometime in 1980, after an exchange of Christmas cards, they resumed their romance. Mike's aim, which he pursued relentlessly until sometime in 1982, was to persuade the woman to move into a house that he had bought in Virginia and then marry her.[73] Initially, however, Mike moved to an apartment in Washington. Alice remained in the Garrett Park house, but she eventually moved to Galax and became immersed in the music and culture of that region. The two of them fulfilled some musical dates that they were contractually obligated to play, but the team of Mike and Alice had come to an end, and Mike's life had entered a new and uncertain phase.

6

Lexington and Alexia

Home at Last

As Mike's marriage dissolved, his thoughts turned toward Virginia. In the months immediately following his separation from Alice, he lived in a Washington apartment, still beset with the anxieties, compulsive habits, and physical ailments that had long troubled him and dependent on prescription drugs and the support of counselors and therapists. With the help of David Winston, a chemist and five-string banjoist who lived in Natural Bridge, Virginia, Mike began checking out possible homesites in the Lexington area. Moving to Virginia was the fulfillment of a dream that probably began with his first trip to the fiddlers' convention in Galax with his father in 1941 and that took firmer root after 1956, the year he first visited Wade Ward's country home in Independence. Ward—and by extension, Virginia—seemed to embody the kind of rustic and meaningful life for which Mike yearned.[1] Mike hoped that his lady friend (who lived in Nashville) would join him at his Virginia rural retreat.

Lexington, in many ways, seemed ideal. It was both rural and cosmopolitan, a quality that befitted a back-to-the-lander like Mike who longed for the peacefulness of rustic life and the solitude that permitted the work that consumed him. Not actually in the mountains but not too far away from the Blue Ridge range, Lexington was a college town with many people of liberal or moderate views. Mike had also learned about the active musical scene there from the Highwoods String Band and other friends in the old-time music community. The region had been a thriving center of old-time music since about 1971, when Odell McGuire, a Washington and Lee University geology professor and a five-string banjo player, began hosting extensive jam sessions in his home.[2]

In February 1981 Mike found an old two-story house in Rockbridge County exactly one mile from the Lexington city line. He immediately began the arduous task of overseeing repairs of its leaky roof, faulty plumbing, busted tiles, and antiquated steam-heating system. He fixed up the servant's quarters in the back of the house and rented the renovated space to a young woman who was working as an intern at the local Stonewall Jackson House. He also added a concrete-block building to house his tapes and most valuable instruments. In many ways, it seemed like the Pennsylvania experience all over again. He moved into the only partially renovated house in June 1981 and lived there alone until 1993. Mike remembered being "very, very lonely" during the first couple of years of this period as he dealt with his physical and psychological problems, struggled to find gigs, tried to make the house livable, negotiated with lawyers to conclude his divorce from Alice, and attempted to secure his relationship with his Nashville friend. After protracted and constant communication by telephone and at least one lengthy stay in Nashville, the two of them decided in October 1982 to call it quits. Mike was now truly on his own.[3]

Although some of the local musicians initially perceived Mike as being overly serious and socially awkward—David Winston said that "his tension showed in his carriage, his facial expressions, and extremely measured speech"—they soon warmed to his graciousness and willingness to share his musical knowledge. Winston also remarked that "ours was a community filled with characters, and we welcomed one more."[4] Mike invited them into his home and played often in jam sessions with Winston, James Leva, Carol Elizabeth Jones, Brad Leftwich, and other old-time devotees. In 1986 he further strengthened his community involvement by working with the Parks and Recreation Commission of Buena Vista, Virginia, to establish the Rockbridge Mountain Music and Dance Festival. Mike hoped to make the venue available to older, traditional musicians while also incorporating the next generation of musicians, who were taking the string-band revival to new dimensions of style and performance. The first festival included the New Lost City Ramblers and an array of younger string-band performers, such as Mac Benford, Alan Jabbour, and the Horseflies. Mike relinquished direction of the festival after a couple of years, but it continued to be held annually at the Glen Maury Park in Buena Vista, located off the Blue Ridge Parkway about five miles east of Lexington. The festival website refers to "dancing and old-time music in a mellow setting with

magnificent views of the Blue Ridge Mountains." In 2011 Rockbridge celebrated its twenty-fifth anniversary.[5]

In the mid-1980s, Mike also began working with the Virginia Commission
for the Arts and presenting programs with museums and libraries all over
the state. For instance, on October 25, 2002, he gave a free concert at the
Virginia Library sponsored by a folklife grant from the commission, which
coincided with an exhibition called *Virginia Roots Music: Creating and Con-
serving Tradition*. In 1986, with the support of an NEA grant, he had organized
the Old Time Music Convention, held at Washington and Lee University in
Lexington. Mike wasted little time in becoming a fully committed citizen of
the community and state that he had adopted. He even helped to initiate the
successful effort to preserve the local Brushy Hills woodlands when Lexington put forward a proposal to sell portions of the tract for development.[6]

NLCR reunions came very rarely in the early 1980s. In fact, an appearance at the Chicago Folk Festival in 1985 was the only engagement of consequence that the group made during these years. Each of the musicians
had developed very busy independent careers. John Cohen now worked as
a full-time teacher of art and photography at Purchase College, State University of New York, located in upstate New York, but he continued to write
articles about and produce recordings of old-time music. Tracy Schwarz
had become a performer of Cajun music and was also a frequent entertainer with his wife, Ginny Hawker, an outstanding Virginia ballad singer.

Mike consequently depended primarily on solo gigs. Twenty years and
more of performance had left him with a host of valuable contacts, so he
could count on certain venues, such as Freight and Salvage in Berkeley,
the University of Chicago Folk Festival, and the Mariposa Folk Festival in
Toronto. The occasional tours with Libba Cotten served as both soul savers
and economic boons. In the summer of 1981, for example, he and Libba
shared a cabin in the woods for a week at a guitar camp called the Puget
Sound Guitar Workshop in Washington. Although these years had many
emotional and commercial low points, Mike did experience many rewarding moments. These included his gigs at the folklife festival held as part of
the Knoxville World's Fair, an event rich with traditional music acts that
was held from May 1 through October 31, 1982, and drew an estimated 11
million visitors; concerts in Alaska and Hawaii; his first appearance on the
radio show *A Prairie Home Companion* in November; and tours made in 1983
in Italy and various parts of Africa.

In Italy, Mike was introduced to the music of the Stefanini brothers (Rafe, Bruno, and Gianni), who had become enthusiastic exponents of American old-time music after first hearing the recordings of the New Lost City Ramblers. They had been performing in Italy as the Moonshine Brothers. Rafe, a brilliant mandolin player and fiddler, moved to the United States in late 1983 and soon became a pillar of the old-time music scene as a musician, workshop leader, and instrument maker.[7] The African tour — which also included fiddler Liz Carroll, Irish musician Mick Moloney, and two African American dancers — took Mike through Zaire, Cameroon, Senegal, and the Ivory Coast. Sponsored by the U.S. Department of State, the African tour suggested that the Seeger name no longer conveyed quite the sense of menace that it once held for sensitive government officials.

Mike also became involved with a new string-band venture when he joined with Paul Brown and Andy Cahan to form the Bent Mountain Band. Brown and Cahan had both been swept away by the magic of Tommy Jarrell and had spent many hours jamming with and learning from the old master at his home in Toast, North Carolina. Brown, in fact, like Alice, had served as an apprentice with Jarrell under an NEA grant. Informal sessions at Jarrell's home had encouraged Mike, Paul, and Andy to try their hands as a trio of old-time string-band musicians. Like many young revivalists, Paul and Andy had taken a variety of jobs, such as cabinet making, to support their music habits. Paul built furniture and musical instruments but soon went into radio work as an announcer and news director on WPAQ, a small radio station in Mount Airy, North Carolina, that prided itself on being the "Voice of the Blue Ridge" and a force in the preservation of the traditional music of the region. In obtaining a job as announcer on a small Virginia radio station, Brown fulfilled an ambition that Mike Seeger had sought but never achieved. Brown's mellifluous and authoritative voice can still be heard regularly on National Public Radio. The Bent Mountain Band played infrequently, but they did play at least one high-profile show: the Winnipeg Festival in July 1983. They also made a couple of musical "reunions" in the 1990s, and in 1996 Paul and Mike recorded a CD of old-time songs and tunes titled *Way Down in North Carolina*, which featured a wide variety of instruments and both duet and solo singing.[8]

In 1984 Mike's research moved in a significantly new direction when he launched the Talking Feet dance project. Mike was always an avid dancer and was certainly aware of the young cloggers and flatfoot dancers who generally showed up anywhere that the Highwoods String Band and other young bands appeared. He had long believed that dancing was an indispensable but overlooked ingredient of old-time music. Abundant evidence of the ubiquity and popularity of solo step dancing in rural America exists in old newspapers, travel accounts, county histories, and other printed data. The phenomenon, in fact, was noted in the first known published reference to fiddle contests in America: an account found in the *Virginia Gazette* in 1736. The newspaper gave notice of a fair in Hanover County at which prizes were to be given to winners in both dancing and fiddle competition. Regretting, too, that the known examples of solo step dancing in commercial country music — such as that done by Lew Childre, Chick Stripling, and Kentucky Slim — had been largely undocumented, Mike began looking for grants to support a film that would research the remnants of the tradition.[9]

With the invaluable assistance of Ralph Rinzler, Mike obtained a visiting scholar grant of $5,000 from the Smithsonian Folklife Festival and then an additional grant from the NEA. Joined by dance authority Ruth Pershing, a recent graduate of Wellesley and an active member of the Cane Creek Cloggers, Mike began his intensive research in October 1984 on a project that ultimately consumed three years and 300 hours of studio time, as well as significant cost overruns. He and Ruth did all the contact work with musicians and dancers, paid the participants, and, of course, handled all the paperwork. They traveled with a two-man camera crew ("on loan" from the Smithsonian) through southern West Virginia, southwestern Virginia, eastern Tennessee, and western North Carolina. Accompanying musicians were generally hired on location, but Mike occasionally played his fiddle or banjo as the dancers went through their improvised routines. He and Ruth documented a variety of solo dancers — black and white, old and young — who described their dances variously as "flatfooting," "clogging," "buckdancing," "hoedown," and "rural tap." The steps were not only exciting examples of social play in the South but they also presented prime demonstrations of the major theme that increasingly characterized Mike's work: evidence of the musical interchange that had always characterized African American and white musical cultures. The work eventually culminated in the production of a documentary film called *Talking Feet: Solo Southern Dance: Buck, Flatfoot, and Tap* (Smithsonian Institution, 1987). Mike also gave a presentation on solo dancing at a meeting of the American Folklore Society and produced a book on the project (with the same title) that was published in Berkeley by North Atlantic Books in 1992.[10]

By mid-1986 Mike's mental and physical health had begun to improve.

And he had begun to settle into the roles of Mentor or Elder Statesman/ Patriarch of old-time music. But he never stopped being an eager student. In his review of a concert that Mike gave at the College of William and Mary in August 2003, Tim Jones commented on this continued enthusiasm: "[E]ven in his capacity as teacher, Seeger's inner student shines through."[11] Mike was no longer consumed with the "discovery" or documentation of old-time musicians but seemed more concerned with learning and teaching their styles. In the last decades of his life, he became increasingly focused on making instructional videos and CDs.[12] Mike never stopped trying to learn new instruments and styles, and he always cringed a bit when someone suggested that he had "mastered" a particular instrument or style. He became increasingly fascinated with such ancient and esoteric instruments as the panpipes (flutelike reed instruments that are also known as quills) and the Jew's harp, and he began attending conventions of the International Jew's Harp Congress and other gatherings that concentrated on particular instruments.

Mike also received NEA apprentice grants to study the guitar style of Kennedy Jones and the song repertoire of Nimrod Workman. Along with Arnold Shultz, Mose Rager, and Ike Everly, Jones had been one of the creators and popularizers of the thumb-style guitar playing associated with Muhlenberg County, Kentucky, and most identified with Merle Travis. In this style, the guitarist plays a 4/4 rhythm with his thumb on the bass strings and a syncopated melody on the treble strings with one or two fingers. The effect is that of two or more guitarists playing together or perhaps one guitarist playing with at least three fingers. Jones was indifferent, if not hostile, to being interviewed by "folklorists," but he did agree to give a few lessons to Mike. One was conducted in a parking lot, and others took place in a motel not far from Jones's home in Cincinnati. Along with the lessons, Mike was able to record some of Jones's spoken commentary.[13]

Workman, on the other hand, was a very willing subject. He invited Mike into his home in Mascot, Tennessee, near Knoxville, on a few occasions and sang song after song from his enormous repertoire. This wizened veteran of the eastern Kentucky and West Virginia coalfields was a storehouse of old songs (both religious and secular), stories, and recollections of the industrial warfare that had long marked the struggles for workers' justice in Appalachia. He had worked in the mines for forty-two years and had been a militant member of the United Mine Workers of America and a political radical, but through the influence of his wife, Workman had also become a convert to the Pentecostal religious faith. His songs and stark, unadorned singing encompassed all of these crucial ingredients of his life. When Mike interviewed him in 1982, Workman was eighty-seven years old; he lived to be ninety-nine.[14]

As befitted the role of an elder statesman, Mike reached out to bring musicians of varying styles and ages together and to integrate the world of old-time music by showcasing traditional musicians and young string-band revivalists on the same stage. One of his more interesting projects involved a collaboration with David Grisman and John Hartford that humorously demonstrated how modern songs of rock, country, and bluegrass origin could be presented in old-time fashion. Titled *Retrograss* and released in 1999, the CD included Bob Dylan's "Maggie's Farm" (sung and played on the banjo by Mike in Dock Boggs style), Otis Redding's "Sittin' on the Dock of the Bay" (done in jugband fashion), Chuck Berry's "Maybelline" (featuring Mike on the Jew's harp), and other whimsical and imaginative performances.[15]

The mingling of generations and styles had actually begun in California in the 1960s, first at the Ash Grove in Los Angeles and later that decade when the Ramblers began giving concerts at the Freight and Salvage Coffeehouse in Berkeley. In Berkeley and San Francisco, the Ramblers found a countercultural community of fans and musicians like Sue Draheim, Eric Thompson, Mac Benford, and Hank Bradley, people who had cut their teeth on rock music but who were now eager to sample music that lay outside the mainstream. All of them had become active exponents of old-time string-band music. Draheim, Benford, and Jim Bamford, in fact, had formed one of the seminal bands of the young string-band movement: Dr. Humbead's New Tranquility String Band and Medicine Show. Benford later joined with Walt Koken and Bob Potts to form the Fat City Stringband, an exciting precursor of the Highwoods String Band. Often, after one of their concerts in the San Francisco area, Mike and the other Ramblers would go to fiddler Sue Draheim's house at 6018 Colby Street in San Francisco and join one of the all-night picking parties. They also sometimes took their music out into the Sierra Nevada foothills to Sweet's Mill east of Fresno, where they joined similar gatherings of hippies and old-time musicians for jam sessions at Virgil Byxbe's cabin. Mike also participated at least once in the local street scene at Sather Gate on the California campus in Berkeley, where he played with Hank Bradley and other musicians and even did an impromptu mock auction of the gate. This and other simi-

lar scenes probably marked Mike's and the other Ramblers' introduction to
the new routes that old-time music was taking.[16]

Mike was actually somewhat ambivalent about the young musicians. He
admired them and saw them as bearers of the tradition that he had promoted all his life. They were enthusiastic, highly skilled, and full of the
energy generally associated with rock-and-roll performance. He was also
thrilled with the sense of community that they shared with their fans, and
he was particularly fascinated by their fondness for dancing. Clogging and
other forms of step dancing seemed to be spontaneous and inevitable ingredients of most old-time string-band happenings. On the other hand,
Mike was troubled by the lack of singing among the young musicians and
by their seeming indifference to the history that accompanied the old
songs. He had told one interviewer: "They don't sing much; they don't take
the singing seriously. I never thought that would happen." The New Lost
City Ramblers, he felt, had been much more faithful to the totality of old-
time music than were the young bands.[17]

Mike nevertheless had paid tribute to this vibrant California scene in
1972 when he produced an LP anthology of these musicians called *Berkeley
Farms: Oldtime and Country Style Music of Berkeley* (Folkways FW 02436).[18]
He also began to bring young revival performers like the Highwoods String
Band and Ry Cooder into his own recording ventures as early as 1973, when
he produced *The Second Annual Farewell Reunion*. The hippie musicians of
Berkeley may have inspired the ironic sense of humor embodied in the
album's title. Back in February 1968, they had called one of their musi-
cal gatherings at Provo Park the 35th Annual Berkeley Old-Time Fiddlers'
Convention even though it was the first time that such a meeting had been
held. In 1985, with the aid of a Guggenheim Fellowship, Mike produced
Fresh Oldtime String Band Music (Rounder), an entire LP of new string-
band music featuring himself and the likes of Alan Jabbour, Norman and
Nancy Blake, Kirk Sutphin, James Bryan, and Paul Brown. In 1986 he also
produced and participated in a project called *Old Time Music Dance Party*
(Flying Fish 415) that included other string-band revivalists, such as Bruce
Molsky and Paul Brown. Since the songs were lengthy tunes designed
for dancing (both flatfoot and square dance), the music was playfully described as having been recorded by "A. Robic and the Exertions." In 1994, in
the whimsically titled *Third Annual Farewell Reunion* (Rounder 0313), Mike
paid tribute to both the older and younger performers who he had met and
played with during his lengthy career, revealing the multigenerational na-

Mike Seeger and
Alexia Smith having
fun—and making
music—at a party.
(Photo courtesy of
Alexia Smith)

ture of the old-time community. He recorded songs with such veterans as
Bob Dylan, Ola Belle Reed, Tommy Jarrell, Ralph Stanley, Jean Ritchie, and
siblings Pete and Peggy Seeger and with such younger performers as Bruce
Molsky, Dirk Powell, Rafe Stefanini, Tim O'Brien, Jody Stecher, Maria Mul-
daur, and Carol Elizabeth Jones.[19]

The arrival of Alexia Smith ushered in a new and refreshing phase in
Mike's life. She had been a friend of Mike's sister Penny, with whom she
shared a love for pottery, weaving, and other forms of art. Like Peggy,
Penny had been a favorite of her father. Mike and Alexia had seen each
other a few times during his visits to Seeger family gatherings in upstate
New York, but the pair did not begin to have a serious relationship until
after their brief conversation at Penny's memorial service after her death
from cancer in 1993. Not too many meetings and phone calls ensued before
Mike asked: "Are you moveable?" And Alexia responded by moving into his
house in Lexington.[20]

Alexia, the daughter of a geologist, grew up in California. She graduated from the University of California, Berkeley, in 1967 and then lived
for three years in Paris. As a child, she had played classical music on the
piano and sung to entertain herself and her siblings. Her favorite songs
were learned from the recordings of people like Jean Ritchie, Pete Seeger,

Mike Seeger
and Alexia
Smith in 1999.
(Photo courtesy
of David Holt)

Woody Guthrie, and Lee Hays, but while the world of old-time music
seemed familiar to her, she did not fully understand its breadth and diversity until she met Mike. After she moved to Lexington, she began learning
a few chords on a guitar that had belonged to Penny. Alexia proved to be a
good listener and a quick learner, and she quickly absorbed the harmony
style that she heard on the Carter Family records that Mike suggested to
her. "Going Down the Road Feeling Bad," in a sense, was a breakthrough
song for her because Mike felt that she had found a harmony that sounded
appropriately old-timey.[21]

Alexia and Mike married at their home on August 27, 1995, in a cere-
mony and celebration suffused with music. Mike joyously sang and danced
with such old friends and relatives as Hazel Dickens, Pete Seeger, Peggy
Seeger, John Cohen, Tracy Schwarz, Ginny Hawker, and Carol Elizabeth
Jones. Peggy Seeger and Irene Pyper-Scott sang "Autumn Wedding," a song
that Peggy composed for the occasion. Mike and Alexia then spent a short
honeymoon in the North Carolina mountains in Peter Gott's cabin home
in Madison County.[22] The solitude and peacefulness of this rural retreat,
and Alexia's gentle and soothing presence, seemed to reflect the life that
was now unfolding for Mike in Lexington. Playing and singing a few songs
in the evening and taking long walks in the woods with Alexia initiated a
routine of relaxation and deep comfort and compatibility that Mike had
never encountered or made time to include. David Winston noted later
that Mike had "assumed some of the lightness and grace of his favorite partner."[23] Alexia also accompanied him on many of his tours and even began

to sing publicly with him on some occasions. By this time, Mike had largely overcome the anxieties, drug dependence, and stress problems that had troubled him since at least 1960. Just as a new century unfolded, however, Mike received a sobering reminder of life's uncertainty: he was informed that he was suffering from a grave and potentially life-threatening disease.

In early 2001 Mike received the frightening news that he had lymphoma, a cancer of the circulatory system. He soon learned that of the many forms of lymphoma, the one that he had—chronic lymphositic leukemia, or CLL—was perhaps the most manageable. Though CLL could not be cured, it came with a long life expectancy; it was very slow growing and was treated as a chronic disease. Following some mild chemotherapy from which he experienced virtually no side effects, he had no need of treatment in the six years that followed. Mike already knew that his good friend and sometime music partner John Hartford suffered from CLL, and he was heartened by the way that Hartford dealt with the disease over a twenty-year span. Mike, however, also experienced increasing difficulty and pain from the progressive scoliosis that had been developing since adolescence, but he was largely able to maintain his normal workload. Despite these physical challenges, he never once thought of abandoning his musical mission, and he told one questioner that he had "a very full and happy life."[24]

Mike was certainly not guilty of overstatement when he said that he led a full life. He continued to involve himself in a remarkably diverse array of music-related activities, including the role of master artist for the Virginia Folklife Program with the Virginia Foundation for the Humanities (which meant that apprentices learned under his instruction). He even wrote occasional columns for *Frets*, a magazine that concentrated on the history and performance of string instruments.[25] By the time he entered this chapter of his life, Mike had become the complete musician. Within the old-time community, Mike, as a solo musician, had become virtually an anomaly in a movement largely dominated by string bands. But he reassured one interviewer that playing solo was very much in the old-time tradition: "A lot of old-time music, maybe most of it, was solo. I've considered my mentor in that respect, Hobart Smith, a musician and singer who played solo almost all of the time." Smith was a multi-instrumentalist and singer from Virginia who was the brother of ballad singer Texas Gladden. Both of them had played often at White Top Mountain and other folk festivals and had recorded for Alan Lomax and the Library of Congress. Mike reaffirmed his link to the tradition represented by Hobart Smith when he

Dom Flemons of the Carolina Chocolate Drops proudly holds a panpipe and a brochure advertising his mentor, Mike Seeger. (Courtesy of Dom Flemons; photo by Hubby Jenkins)

recorded, in 1991, his first solo recording in eighteen years: *Solo — Oldtime Country Music* (Rounder CD 0278). Several years later, the brilliant young African American musician Dom Flemons (a member of the popular Carolina Chocolate Drops) reasserted the importance of the solo tradition — and revealed himself to be a link in the chain — when he pointed to this particular CD by Mike as the indispensable catalyst for his own musical journey. He noted that he had first heard the CD while "pirating" music off the Listen Rhapsody website: "I was completely a Mike Seeger fanatic from that point on."[26]

Mike continued to dazzle audiences with his command of a multitude of instruments — the guitar, banjo, fiddle, mandolin, Autoharp, lap dulcimer, French harp, Jew's harp, quills — but this breadth was equaled by the depth that he brought to the playing of each instrument. In many cases, Mike understood and could demonstrate a variety of styles for each of the instruments that he played. Yet the banjo continued to remain his first love. His stylistic command of this instrument extended from the Scruggs style to the oldest known African American and British styles. He typically played his examples on period-piece instruments or ones that had been built to replicate vintage instruments, including those of gourd construction.[27]

Mike's knowledge of instrument design and his efforts to obtain only those instruments that were constructed with "original" materials and according to original purpose were as profound as his technical skills of performance. He was always on the lookout for luthiers who had expertise in vintage construction, such as Wayne Henderson, Pete Ross, Clarke Buehling, and Todd Cambio. Mike did not build instruments, but he knew how he wanted them to sound and had firm ideas about how the chosen luthier should proceed. Cambio, for example, who Mike met in 2003 at the Appalachian String Band Music Festival in Clifftop, West Virginia, built a replica of one of Mike's favorite guitars: Bradley Kincaid's "Hound Dog" guitar that had been sold in Sears, Roebuck catalogs in the 1930s. Following Mike's specifications that the guitar should contain only wood from North American trees, the Madison, Wisconsin–based Cambio built a lightly braced parlor guitar composed of white oak, red spruce, yellow poplar, persimmon, and maple (each material, of course, was used to construct a different part of the guitar). Instruments of vintage construction were particularly crucial to Mike's performances of banjo music, and he increasingly looked for instruments of gourd construction, which he believed were close to the original types brought to the South from West Africa or newly fashioned in the New World. Using gourd banjos enabled Mike to illustrate what he considered to be the formative component of Southern music: the fusion of African and Anglo elements. He gave specific voice to these ideas in 2005 when he produced, recorded, and performed on *Southern Banjo Sounds*, one of his most important anthologies.[28]

While Mike was preeminently concerned with persuading his listeners to enjoy the sounds of old-time music, historical expression had now become a central ingredient of his presentations, and education had become a major facet of virtually all of his concerts, workshops, recordings, and residencies. On his elaborate website, he announced that a Mike Seeger residency could include any number of options: a concert for either family or children, school assemblies, lecture demonstrations (with either or both live performance and recorded examples), and special topical presentations (such as Southern Banjo Sounds, from Africa to Appalachia; The Roots of Country Music, from "Barbara Allen" to "Wildwood Flower"; and

Tipple, Loom, and Rail: Songs of the Industrialization of the South). He also offered "master classes" in southern traditional vocal and instrumental music.[29]

Audiences were still entertained by Mike's versatility and wit, but above all, they were enlightened by the profundity of his knowledge about old-time styles and instruments. A few of Mike's programs that have been recorded and preserved, including his concert in May 2003 at the Oberlin Folk Festival (available on MP3) and a performance made in 2007 at the Sugar Maple Traditional Festival in Madison, Wisconsin (recorded by Tom Martin-Erickson of Wisconsin Public Radio). These examples provide a representative sampling of the nature and breadth of his presentations. In a very relaxed and extremely low-key fashion complete with subtle, understated wit and brief and cogent commentary, Mike took his audience through a broad panorama of old-time southern songs and styles. If he did not totally encompass the whole of traditional southern music, he came close to it. At the 2003 Oberlin concert, for example, he sang an a cappella version of a river boatman's song; he played instrumental tunes that featured, simultaneously, banjo and quills or fiddle and French harp (played in harmony!); and he did solo tunes on the fiddle, Autoharp, Jew's harp, guitar, and quills (while also moaning in syncopated fashion along with the latter instrument). At virtually all of his concerts, he also offered the expected tributes to some of his most important mentors, such as Maybelle Carter (on both guitar and Autoharp) and Libba Cotten (with his vocal and instrumental performance of "Freight Train"). He concluded his Oberlin show, supported with Autoharp accompaniment, with a religious song learned from the great Ozark ballad singer Almeda Riddle that spoke of the hopes for worldwide peace. The Madison show, on the other hand, closed with Mike and Alexia singing some Carter Family songs.[30]

Although Mike appeared in a wide variety of venues, college and university residencies had become the central locus for many of his presentations. These spanned the country, from William and Mary in Virginia to the University of Washington (Seattle) and UCLA, where he appeared as the guest of his cousin, Anthony Seeger, who served there as a professor of ethnomusicology. Typically, while Mike was presenting workshops or occasional informal lectures, his most effective teaching methods came through musical demonstrations and his informative responses to student questions. The student evaluations that have survived provide testament to his humility, technical proficiency, and friendly forbearance. Mike did not consider any

Mike Seeger with his favorite instrument: the five-string banjo. (Photo courtesy of Frank Baker)

question to be unworthy of a careful response, no matter how repetitive it may have been. Students marveled at his knowledge and his willingness to share it with others, but they also noted a strong contrast between the private and public Mike Seeger. For example, students in Professor Ron Pen's 2005 class at the University of Kentucky, a doctoral musicology seminar titled the History of Old Time Music, spoke of a "shy, fragile man" who became "playful, energetic, and hilarious" when he performed. "Talking with Mr. Seeger and sharing ideas with him was a wonderful experience, but watching him perform and share his passion with an audience was the most revealing time of his visit," wrote one student. "The opportunity to meet, sing, and socialize with such an icon in this field was once in a lifetime," wrote another. "Mike Seeger allowed the music to become alive and real to us. It was an amazing week!"[31]

In addition to his academic involvement, Mike also ventured from time to time into collaboration with classical musicians. While these ventures illustrate his receptivity to all kinds of music and the stature that his musicianship had achieved among artists of varying stripes, this classical phase nevertheless seems ironic given the indifference, if not resistance, that he had shown toward such music in his earlier life. Ruth Crawford Seeger could only have been pleased that her son, who had rejected piano lessons and classical theory of any kind, was now performing in the company of classically trained musicians. It should be noted, though, that Mike had not changed. While he shared the stage with these musicians, he continued to play "by ear" and not from a score, and he continued to perform the traditional numbers that he had loved all of his life.

Mike's partnership with classical musicians began as early as 1982 through a conversation with Scott Reiss and Tina Chancey in a parking lot at the Oak Grove Music Festival in Staunton, Virginia, where they were all performing. Reiss and Chancey were members of a musical group called Hesperus, organized in 1979, that specialized in Medieval music played on such period-piece instruments as the recorder, the viola da gamba, the cittern, and the theorbo. The three musicians recognized certain commonalities that early music and old-time music possessed: string instruments, gut strings, drones, modalities, and, of course, a preference for old songs and tunes. They also bemoaned the fact that gut strings were acutely sensitive to temperature changes and consequently were hard to keep in tune. Their conversations led to the convening in 1983 of an annual workshop called Song Catcher (a program designed to encourage students to learn old instruments by ear) and then to occasional collaborative concerts that featured the music of Appalachia.

Seeger, Reiss, and Chancey appeared at Oak Grove for ten days in 1984 through the sponsorship of a theater group run by Fletcher and Margaret Collins. Fletcher Collins was a longtime professor at Mary Baldwin College in Staunton and a student of prebaroque music who had collected folk songs for the Works Progress Administration in the 1930s and early 1940s.[32] After Oak Grove, the trio went on to give occasional concerts, mostly in Virginia. One of their larger shows was at an event in 2007 called Colonial Faire, a celebration held in honor of Jamestown's 400th anniversary. While no one, including Mike, could be certain about how early rural string musicians and songs actually sounded, he was rigorous in his efforts to present what was known to be factual and what was educated guesswork. Nevertheless, he had no problem recreating semblances of the fiddle and banjo styles that might have been popular among both white indentured servants and African slaves at the time of Virginia's founding.[33]

Mike was also involved off and on in a similar collaboration with the Ying Quartet, a chamber string ensemble composed of four Chinese American siblings who played violins, viola, and bass. The Yings experimented often with music far removed from the standard classical repertoire and created contexts far different from those usually seen at performances of string quartets. One of their most popular shows, *No Boundaries*, was first presented as a series at Symphony Space in New York City and featured collaborations with actors, dancers, nonclassical musicians, a magician, and even a Chinese noodle chef. Mike performed traditional songs during his stints with the Ying Quartet—including concerts at Symphony Space, Stanford University, and the Skaneateles Festival in New York—but he did them with a touch of theater. In an evening designed to show the connections between traditional and classically composed pieces, Mike stood in the glow of a spotlight at the side of the Symphony Space Theater and sang "Amazing Grace." His rendition was then followed by the Yings playing a setting of that melody composed by Jennifer Higdon. At a Presbyterian church in Skaneateles, Mike entered at the back of the church following intermission and sang an a cappella version of "Amazing Grace." When he finished the song, he walked down the aisle emitting a wild, backcountry holler.[34] Once onstage, he exhibited his normal display of virtuosity on the gourd banjo and other instruments; gave his tribute to Libba Cotten with his guitar version of "Freight Train"; and, finally, with the Yings performing as their backup band, Mike and Alexia concluded the set with a couple of duets.[35]

Despite the theatrical nature of these performances, Mike's program with the Ying Quartet resembled those that he gave elsewhere in other venues. Contrary to the publicity brochures that advertised the concerts, audiences did not hear a synthesis of classical and old-time country music, nor in Mike's performance did they receive insights about old-time music's alleged influence on contemporary classical composition. The Ying-Seeger collaboration was essentially a presentation of wonderful but largely un-related bodies of work by some very gifted musicians. On the other hand, Mike did participate occasionally in projects that illustrated attempts by classical musicians to appropriate folk tunes for high-art purposes, much like his mother and father had done back in the early 1940s. Ruth's arrange-ment of "Risselty Rosselty," for example, had become quite well known among concert musicians; and Charles's arrangement of "John Hardy," a ballad about a notorious southern bad man of the nineteenth century, had been performed in 1940 by the CBS Radio Orchestra. In April 2005 Mike had the opportunity to perform his father's song, and another one called "John Hardy's Dream," with the Knoxville Symphony Orchestra. "John Hardy's Dream" had been written by Jonathan Romeo, a classical guitarist, music teacher, and composer who soon became the executive director of the Crooked Road: Virginia's Heritage Music Trail.[36] On August 20, 2005, Mike and Peggy Seeger created still another program of classical music's occasional exploration of the hillbilly music repertoire when they gave a program called Aaron Copland and the Folk Revival. Presented at Bard College in New York as part of a major symposium called Copland and His World, the Seegers not only documented Copland's utilization of American rural music but also his specific indebtedness to Ruth Crawford Seeger and her transcriptions of songs for the Lomax collection *Our Singing Country*. Copland, for example, had borrowed directly from "Bonaparte's Retreat," a tune transcribed by Ruth from a version collected by Lomax in 1937 from Kentucky fiddler W. H. Stepp. In Copland's hands, the tune became "Hoe-Down" in his 1942 ballet *Rodeo*.[37]

Mike's occasional collaborations with classical musicians received con-siderable inspiration from his association with Judith Tick, the author of *Ruth Crawford Seeger: A Composer's Search for American Music* (1997), a biog-raphy of his mother. Mike met Tick in 1982 at the performance of a sonata written by his mother in the 1920s. He gave his wholehearted support to

Tick in her many years of research, including invaluable contact information on Lomax and Sidney Cowell, and she in turn dedicated her book to her husband and to Mike. It was through Tick's encouragement that Mike joined the Society for American Music and began a satisfying relationship with music educators and music scholars of all kinds. Many of his college residencies and school performances came about as a result of these connections.[38]

Most important, the collaboration with Tick reintroduced Mike to the multisided musical and social world of his mother. He acquired renewed appreciation of Ruth's many contributions to American music and a fuller understanding of the sacrifices she made in balancing her many roles as wife, mother, educator, scholar, and composer. Further confirmation of her pioneering work came through a conference sponsored by the Hitchcock Institute for Studies in American Music and held at the CUNY Graduate Center in Manhattan on October 26, 2001, that celebrated the centennial of her birth and documented her manifold achievements. Festival participants became reacquainted with Ruth's role in modernist music composition, the influence of leftist politics on American music, her work as a transcriber of folk songs, and, of course, the specific contributions she made with such compositions as "String Quartet, 1931." A panel called Remembering Dio: A Seeger Family Scrapbook, moderated by Judith Tick, permitted Mike, Peggy, and Pete to join with their old friend Bess Lomax Hawes in reminiscences of growing up with Ruth, watching her work, and listening to her make music. The three Seegers also concluded the festival with a musical tribute to Ruth, performing folk songs transcribed and arranged by her.[39]

Festivals like this one—and a very ambitious one sponsored by the Library of Congress on March 16, 2007, called How Can I Keep From Singing? A Tribute to the Seeger Family—reminded the public of the remarkable contributions made by this gifted family. The Seeger family tribute included some formal academic presentations, including an opening address by Librarian of Congress James Billington, but the most telling evidence of the Seegers' enduring marks on the American cultural landscape came through the music they presented. Sonya Cohen Cramer (the daughter of Penny Seeger and John Cohen) and Kate Seeger (daughter of Anthony Seeger) represented the young generation of singing Seegers. Sonya sang to Pete's guitar accompaniment, and Kate performed as part of a trio called the Short Sisters. On the night following the Library of Congress event,

Mike, Peggy, and Pete Seeger together onstage on March 17, 2007, in Washington, D.C.
(Photo courtesy of Ursy Potter)

Pete, Mike, and Peggy performed in an event sponsored by the Folk Music Society of Greater Washington. The three did a few songs together, but Mike, who opened the event, put the whole evening into perspective with a program that revealed the rural roots of everything that the Seegers did that evening. Beginning with a country holler, Mike ranged through a number of instruments—including the Jew's harp, quills, banjo, French harp, and fiddle—and returned his listeners to the front porch, where this music began. His intent, he told the audience, was to evoke a time before the world was "guitarized."[40]

The symposia devoted to his mother and the entire Seeger family brought honor to Mike as part of a historic tradition. These tributes, however, were only a small part of the plethora of honors and awards that he received in the last few decades of his life. His being awarded a John Simon Guggenheim Fellowship in 1984 initiated the recognition of his contributions, and his most prestigious award, the Bess Lomax Hawes National Endowment for the Arts National Heritage Fellowship, capped the list in 2009. In between those achievements, Mike had also been awarded four grants from the NEA; an Honorary Membership Award from the Society for American Music; a Heritage Award from the Uncle Dave Macon Days Festival in Murfreesboro, Tennessee; a Master Music Award conferred by the "Swannanoa Gathering" and Warren Wilson College; the Ralph J. Gleason Award from the Rex Foundation; and six Grammy nominations. The last two accomplishments probably most emphatically revealed the impact that

Mike's music had made on the broad world of American popular music. Funded by the Grateful Dead, the Ralph J. Gleason Award took notice of the wide circulation of songs Mike had recorded and of their appearance in the repertories of popular musicians.[41]

Unfortunately, the terrible news of a new and fatal illness countered whatever satisfaction such recognition brought. Mike had managed to live with lymphoma, although he suffered from the pain caused by scoliosis. Despite these infirmities, Alexia later recalled that "he functioned beautifully," mainly by spacing his engagements more carefully and tempering his work with restful naps and walks. Mike, in fact, was heavily booked through 2009 and into 2010. He even managed to work in a flight to the West Coast, where he met with Hazel Dickens and Elaine Purkey on April 23, 2009, at the Labor Archives and Research Center at San Francisco State University for a tribute to his old and dear friend Archie Green, who had passed away on March 22 of that year. Mike's mutually productive relationship with Green had been one that both men cherished. Green had been one of Mike's strongest champions since at least 1961, when they met at the Berkeley Folk Festival, and the two had been lifelong collaborators in the campaign to document and commemorate the music of America's working people.[42]

In the early summer of 2009, Mike began to experience worsening pain and physical exhaustion, or what he, Alexia, and his doctors assumed were new symptoms of lymphoma. They soon learned, however, that he had a second type of blood cancer that was totally unrelated to the first. This condition was diagnosed as multiple myeloma, an aggressive form of cancer concentrated mostly in the bone marrow. The doctors made clear that multiple myeloma would entail more-strenuous treatment and a shortening of Mike's life expectancy, perhaps to a couple of years. Mike said to Alexia: "Things are going to be more complicated." In the first two weeks of July this certainly was true, as Mike continued to meet both his contractual obligations and some very personal ones. On July 1 he went to Owensboro, Kentucky, to conduct a lengthy interview with Hazel Dickens for an oral and visual documentary of her life to be deposited in the archives of the Bluegrass Music Hall of Fame. Pain or no pain, and like the earlier tribute to Archie Green, this was an event that Mike refused to miss. On July 11 he participated in the Third Annual Banjo Festival at the Birchmere Restaurant in Alexandria, Virginia, hosted by Cathy Fink and Marcy Marxer. There, he played four different banjos and talked about the biracial history of the instrument. On July 15 he went to the Wintergreen resort in Nelson County, Virginia, where he gave a presentation titled "An Introduction to Old-Time Country Music" as part of a larger symposium on Appalachian culture and participated with John Lohman in a conversation about the Seeger family.[43]

During this week, however, Mike's condition worsened rapidly. On July 20, at an oncology clinic appointment, his doctor admitted him to the University of Virginia hospital in Charlottesville for a further evaluation, which was then followed by chemotherapy and radiation. About a week later, Mike and Alexia received the devastating news that his multiple myeloma appeared to be unusually aggressive and that the treatment, contrary to doctors' expectations, had not induced remission. The treatment, in fact, had barely touched the cancer.

Mike's doctor explored with him the possible options for future treatment. Faced with more-severe applications of chemotherapy over a long period of time and with no assurance of success, Mike said: "I prefer to go home." By July 29 he was back home in Lexington, provided with hospice support but dependent primarily on the loving care of Alexia, his three sons (Kim, Arley, and Jeremy), and his sister Peggy, who had come to share his last days with him. During these final hours, Mike saw only his family (including his four stepchildren) and a few close friends. A short visit with Hazel Dickens was particularly poignant. Few words were spoken, but there must have been a flood of memories for these two creative people whose days of friendship and music extended back over fifty years. Mike asked Hazel to sing "Mama's Hand" and "Pretty Bird" for him someday.

Mike's life had been consumed with music, but in his last days, he wanted only quiet. He took great pleasure in the sounds of nature. If he felt pain, he did not express it. He even preserved his sense of humor: at one point when Alexia asked if he was comfortable, Mike responded that he felt "fair to middlin'."

Mike died on the afternoon of August 7, 2009, only eight days before his seventy-sixth birthday. Alexia reported that Mike's decision to reject further medical treatment and face death at home had been "totally clear and peaceful." She believed that the peace Mike experienced in that choice had evoked a responding peace in herself: "It was a great gift he gave to us. It certainly feels as though Mike died too suddenly, and way too soon. But when the time came, he did it so well. Mike truly did go in peace."[44]

7

The Mike Seeger Legacy

Alexia told me that sometime during the last few weeks before his death, Mike said, "I wonder if Bill Malone has one more question." I did, of course. In fact, there are still many questions that I would like to have asked him. Mike's life was so full and vital and his work practically unending—he was still working on instructional videos and CD anthologies within weeks of his death, including a duet album with Peggy of songs they had done in child-hood and teenhood and an audio documentary of southern banjo players (sung and unsung)[1]—that no one could ever hope to fully capture him or really have the last word on what made him distinctive. When he entered hospice care in July 2009, the news immediately evoked a touching and heartfelt display of concern, sympathy, and respect. Internet websites and blogs devoted to folk music, old-time music, bluegrass, mainstream coun-try music, and various types of roots music were filled with reminiscences and prayers for his recovery. Too soon thereafter, when Mike's death was announced, a similar host of testimonials appeared all around the world. National Public Radio, the *New York Times*, English newspapers like the *Guardian* and the *Independent*, and other leading publications abroad joined the chorus of praise and commemoration. Everywhere, Mike was remem-bered for his musical versatility, his generosity, his patience and willing-ness to help anyone who sought his counsel on a musical question, and his sense of humor. It is not surprising that many of these accounts quoted Bob Dylan. After all, Dylan's eccentric endorsements in his autobiography, *Chronicles*, had done much to reintroduce Mike's name to, and legitimize his contributions among, music fans who had grown up after the folk music revival ebbed.

The people who knew him best, though, honored his memory and shared their grief in ways that would have pleased him greatly. They held memorials filled with music, first at a gathering on September 27, 2009, at the Lime Kiln Theater in Lexington (organized by David Winston and James Leva) and then at a music-filled memorial on December 6, 2009 (hosted by Alexia at the St. Mark Presbyterian Church in Bethesda, Maryland). The Bethesda memorial consisted of family (including three wives, three children, and four stepchildren), close friends, and musicians and paid homage to every phase of Mike's life. Peggy presented a touching and humorous musical recollection of her brother that recalled their lifelong friendship and sibling rivalry. The guests and participants included Pete Seeger, Hazel Dickens, Alice Gerrard, John Cohen, Tracy Schwarz, Pete Kuykendall, David Grisman, and Bill Clifton—people who had known and played with him since his earliest days as a professional musician (or had been married to him). Younger musicians, such as Dom Flemons, Tao Rodriguez-Seeger (who played a duet with his grandfather Pete), Rafe Stefanini, David Holt, Tim O'Brien, Laurie Lewis, and fiddler Rayna Gellert, exhibited the contemporary reach of Mike's influence. More than one attendee later said that if Mike had been alive, he would have been the most active person at the celebration—and at the all-night party later that evening at the home of Marcy Marxer and Cathy Fink—moving from one group to another and playing a variety of instruments. Mike received a multitude of accolades and loving memories at these memorial services, but Clifton may have provided the most poignant assessment in a recollection that recalled his old friend's humanity and love of life. He insisted that, more than anything else, he would miss Mike's infectious laugh, which could erupt spontaneously when he was confronted with a surprising or incredulous situation.

As a child, Mike Seeger found the music he loved, became passionately committed to it, and made it his life's mission to preserve and present it to the public. Many years after that first joyous discovery, Mike said: "Old-time rural music remains at the center of my life. The words are my Shakespeare and my mysteries; the music is my Bach, my pastime, and it makes me want to dance."[2] That did not mean that he rejected other styles of music or considered them illegitimate forms of art. He never excluded modern country music, for example, from his purview. He listened to and loved such musicians as Roger Miller, Johnny Cash, Tommy Collins, Jim Nesbit, Merle Haggard, and George Jones. Pete Kuykendall insisted that Mike could have been a successful bluegrass musician, particularly as a five-string banjoist, had he chosen that genre.[3] But Mike was determined to make the world aware of the sources of modern southern music — Music from the True Vine — before they faded away.

His own music making had a twofold purpose: to entertain his audiences with the beauty and complexity of the music and to educate them about what it meant and where it came from. For over fifty years, he had also strived to make people aware of the artists, both commercial and noncommercial, who had created the music. Hence, he seldom traveled without his tape recorder, taping music in homes and at festivals, parks, and concerts. Very early in this enterprise, Mike moved away from the sole pursuit of self-education — the desire to learn the songs and styles he heard — and toward the documentation of musicians whose art deserved to be preserved and popularized. One by-product of this campaign was the bluegrass albums that he produced for Folkways in the late 1950s, which introduced this vital musical genre to the urban North and West and did much to implant the term "bluegrass" in the national consciousness. His most emotionally satisfying projects, however, came through his relationship with Libba Cotten and Dock Boggs. Mike never tired of talking about his pleasure and wonderment at seeing Cotten move from his family's house to concert stages all over America, or of bringing Boggs out of retirement and into the folk revival. Cotten and Boggs both evoked memories of his childhood homes in Chevy Chase and Silver Spring and of his family's fateful discovery of American roots music.

When Hazel Dickens said that "Mike validated my culture," her statement conveyed much more than a personal testimony. Mike's embrace of southern working-people's music and his dedicated determination to remain faithful to their styles of performance were profound democratic statements that wrought major innovations in the realm of what was then called "folk music." Earlier, folklorists and musicians had generally concentrated only on the songs themselves and on how they could be used to convey an emotion or make a particular and often ideological statement. With a very few exceptions, such as Leadbelly and Woody Guthrie, the original singers and musicians too often remained anonymous or saw their identities submerged in an amorphous entity described as "the folk." Mike and the New Lost City Ramblers did not simply perform many exciting and beautiful songs; they went beyond them to tell us also about the musicians who had originally made the music and *how* they had performed it. Roni Stoneman may have been thinking most about her father Ernest Stone-

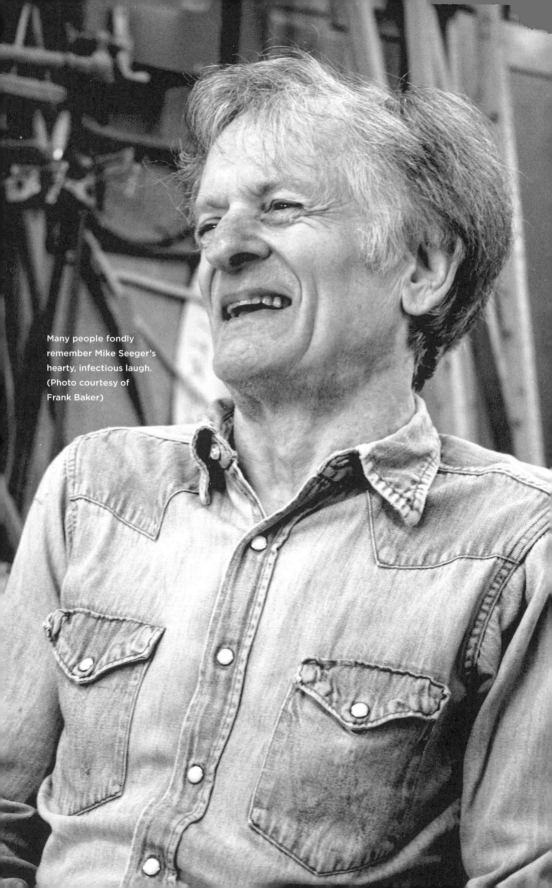

Many people fondly remember Mike Seeger's hearty, infectious laugh. (Photo courtesy of Frank Baker)

man's musical reawakening when she made this comment shortly after Mike's death, but she evoked a universal truth about Mike's art: "Everybody loved Michael because he would talk to the old people about themselves. Because of him, our legacy will probably live forever. Because of him, a lot of people will probably live forever."[4]

Mike presented musicians to the public with little or no concern for their political persuasions. He had no ideological axes to grind (even though personally he was a liberal Democrat). He did not use the music to promote a particular point of view, nor did he similarly exploit the old-time musicians that he loved. He let their music speak for itself—and for them. And, in so doing, he revealed a complex working-class culture in its broad dimensions. For all of its purported uniformity, southern working-class culture, he informed us, was remarkably rich with the diversity of individual creativity. He did not cover all the bases; both he and the Ramblers ignored some vital strains of southern rural music. But in the musical realm where he did his most passionate work—the southeastern United States—he found songs and styles of performance of remarkable diversity.

While striving to pay homage to the old-timers, Mike also inspired younger people to preserve and perform old-time music. He certainly did not work alone. His fellow Ramblers, Ralph Rinzler, David Freeman, Charles Faurot, Alan Jabbour, Ray Alden, and a host of veteran musicians like Tommy Jarrell all contributed to the revitalization of old-time music that has occurred since the 1970s. But no one worked more tirelessly or with greater patience than Mike Seeger to pass the torch of tradition on to younger generations. Since the recording in 1962 of his first solo LP, *Old Time Country Music*, he had shown them that one talented musician could successfully sample most of the basic styles and songs of traditional southern rural music. Almost until the time of his death, he continued to educate aspiring musicians through countless workshops, instructional CDs and videos, classroom presentations, concerts, and one-on-one tutorials and conversations. Largely thanks to him, a vital and constantly evolving string-band movement now flourishes in the United States.

There are many ways to measure Mike's legacy: through his impressive website; his collections at the Library of Congress and the University of North Carolina at Chapel Hill; or through the music heard on his LPs, CDs, and videos. But above all, one sees the fulfillment of his dreams in the young musicians, both famous and obscure, who keep the music alive. Fortunately, Mike lived long enough to witness the fruits of his efforts.

Alexia recalled one of the trips that she and Mike made to the Appalachian String Band Festival (held annually at Clifftop, West Virginia) just a few years before he died. Mike, she said, was very emotionally moved by what he saw and heard. As they walked through the campgrounds, witnessing a living and vital old-time string-band movement, he saw and heard the fulfillment of his lifelong dream. Everywhere, it seemed, young people were singing the old songs and joyously playing banjos, fiddles, guitars, mandolins, Dobros, and Autoharps. That kind of scene, repeated in similar settings all across the country, reveals the continued branching and flowering of Mike's True Vine.[5]

Notes

All URLs are accurate as of January 2011.

Introduction

1. Pete Seeger gave variant versions of this statement. He told me that Mike was "the best instrumentalist in the family." He said to Madelyn Rosenberg: "He is, by far, the best musician in the family." Rosenberg, "Music from the True Vine," *Roanoke Times*, http://squealermusic.com/madclips/clips/seeger.html.

2. *Pete Seeger: The Power of Song* was produced by the Jim Brown Company in New York and was first shown on the *American Masters Series* on PBS in February 2004.

3. See Neil V. Rosenberg, ed., *Transforming Tradition: Folk Music Revivals Examined* (Urbana: University of Illinois Press, 1993).

4. Archie Green, interview with David K. Dunaway, San Francisco, September 4, 1976, David Dunaway Collection of Interviews with Pete Seeger and Contemporaries, American Folklife Center, Library of Congress, Washington, D.C., December 2003. Green made similar analyses of the relationship between Mike and Pete Seeger in interviews with me by phone from San Francisco, April 13, 2006, and with Tracie Wilson, San Francisco, January 23, 2007, University of Illinois, http://www.library.illinois.edu/edx/folklore/cfc.html.

Chapter 1

1. See Ronald D. Cohen, *Rainbow Quest: The Folk Music Revival and American Society, 1940–1970* (University of Massachusetts Press, 2002).

2. Green voiced this assessment in a telephone interview with me from San Francisco on April 13, 2006; and with David Dunaway on September 4, 1976, David Dunaway Collection of Interviews with Pete Seeger and Contemporaries, American Folklife Center, Library of Congress, Washington, D.C., December 2003.

3. The biographical information found on these pages is heavily indebted to Ann M. Pescatello, *Charles Seeger: A Life in American Music* (Pittsburgh: University of Pittsburgh Press, 1992); William R. Ferris's interview of Charles Seeger, "Touching the Music: Charles Seeger," *Southern Cultures* 16, no. 3 (Fall 2010): 54–72; my two interviews with Mike Seeger in Madison, Wisconsin, on February 5 and 6, 2004; my interview with Peggy

Seeger in Madison, Wisconsin, on March 15, 2004; and my telephone interview of Pete Seeger from Beacon, New York, January 8, 2004.

4. Carole Losee, "Elizabeth Seeger: A Short Biography," http://www.passingthetontine .net/seegerbio.htm.

5. "Letters and Diary of Alan Seeger," net.lib.byu.edu/estu/wwi/memoir/seeger/alan1 .htm; www.harvardsquarelibrary.org/poets/seeger.php.

6. Pescatello, *Charles Seeger*, 33.

7. Marcus Wohlson, "Charles Seeger Inaugurates New Era of Music," *Illuminations* (April 2005), http://illuminations.berkeley.edu/archives/2005/history.php?volume=4. See also Mickey Butts, "A Hundred Years of Heavenly Singing," *Choral Music Review*, November 5, 2005, http://www.sfcv.org/arts_revs/ucbchorus_11_8_05.php.

8. See http:/music.Berkeley.edu/degree.html.

9. Charles's commitment to pacifism is discussed in Pescatello, *Charles Seeger*, 74. Her information in turn came largely from Richard Reuss, "Folk Music and Social Conscience: The Musical Odyssey of Charles Seeger," *Western Folklore* 38 (October 1979): 221–38.

10. Pete Seeger has told this story in several interviews and publications, includ-ing Alec Wilkinson, "The Protest Singer: Pete Seeger and American Folk Music," *New Yorker*, April 17, 2006, www.peteseeger.net/new_yorker041706.htm; Pete Seeger and Paul DuBois Jacobs, *Pete Seeger's Storytelling Book* (New York: Harcourt, 2000), 20; William R. Ferris and Michael K. Honey, "Pete Seeger, San Francisco, 1989," *Southern Cultures* 13 (Fall 2007): 18; and Seeger's reminiscences at the symposium, "How Can I Keep from Singing: The Seeger Family," *Folklife Center News* 28, no. 4 (Fall 2006): 3–10.

11. Ferris, "Touching the Music."

12. These topics are discussed throughout Pescatello, *Charles Seeger*; and Judith Tick, *Ruth Crawford Seeger: A Composer's Search for American Music* (New York: Oxford Univer-sity Press, 1997). Carol J. Oja provides another excellent analysis in *Making Music Modern: New York in the 1920s* (New York: Oxford University Press, 2003).

13. The best account of Ruth's life and contributions is Tick, *Ruth Crawford Seeger*. Tick graciously made much of her research available to me and consented to an interview by phone on March 22, 2010. Peggy Seeger's website (http:www.pegseeger.com) also con-tains a wealth of information about her mother and father, the Seeger family, and, of course, her own career.

14. Carl Sandburg, *The American Songbag* (New York: Harcourt Brace, 1927).

15. Judith Tick, "Ruth Crawford Seeger: A Virtual Autobiography," *ISAM Newsletter* 31, http://depthome.brooklyn.cuny.edu/isam/rcstick.html, 4.

16. Ibid.

17. Ibid.

18. See www.peggyseeger.com/topic/ruth-crawford-seeger-biography. Tick also dis-cusses this episode in *Ruth Crawford Seeger*, 134.

19. These anxieties and doubts became particularly acute in the early 1950s, not too long before she was diagnosed with her fatal disease. Mike Seeger recalled his mother's frustrations and resentments in various conversations with me, as well as in conversations

with Judith Tick in New York City on January 5, 1983, and in Lexington, Virginia, on February 10, 1984.

20. Francis James Child, *English and Scottish Popular Ballads*, 5 vols. (Boston: Houghton Mifflin, 1882–98). Child's compilation of 305 ballads and their variants have always been considered the canon of British-derived American folk music.

21. In an interview with David Dunaway, Seeger later said that the Collective members "should have sat around and sung to banjos and guitars and ukuleles, no piano in sight. Piano is a killing thing. It dominates the voice." David K. Dunaway, "Charles Seeger and Carl Sands: The Composers' Collective Years," *Ethnomusicology* 24, no. 2 (May 1980): 165.

22. Ibid.

23. Benjamin Filene, *Romancing the Folk: Public Memory and American Roots Music* (Chapel Hill: University of North Carolina Press, 2000), 69.

24. The event, though, was planned by Charles Seeger after his move to Washington. See Ronald D. Cohen, ed., *Alan Lomax: Selected Writings, 1934–1997* (New York: Routledge, 2005), 94–95. An all-encompassing history of the government cultivation of folk music in the thirties — through White House exposure and with the collecting done by the WPA and other agencies — is sorely needed.

25. Thomas Hart Benton's country music career is described in Henry Adams, "Tom Benton," on the Country Music Hall of Fame website, countrymusichalloffame.org/thomas-hart-benton; and in Justin Wolff, "The Ballad of Thomas Hart Benton," *Humanities* 28, no. 5 (September/October 2007), http://www.neh.gov/news/humanities/2007-09/Ballad.html. Benton's relationship with Jackson Pollock is related at www.warholsters.org/abstractexpressionism/timeline/abstractexpressionism30.html. David K. Dunaway tells the story of Pete Seeger's first hearing of "John Henry" in *How Can I Keep from Singing: The Ballad of Pete Seeger* (New York: Villard Books, 2008), 40; See also Marty Gallanter, "Interview with Pete Seeger," *Frets* (1979), www.peteseeger.net/frets.htm.

26. Boggs's recording was originally released in 1927 on Brunswick 132. It is now available on the CD collection of Boggs's work, *Country Blues* (Revenant 205).

27. John and Alan Lomax, *American Ballads and Folk Songs* (New York: MacMillan Publishing Company, 1934); George Pullen Jackson, *White Spirituals in the Southern Uplands* (Chapel Hill: University of North Carolina Press, 1933). The best biographical account of John Lomax and assessment of his pioneering work is Nolan Porterfield, *Last Cavalier: The Life and Times of John A. Lomax, 1867–1948* (Urbana: University of Illinois Press, 1996).

28. Aunt Molly actually had at least two "voices" — the one she used when she sang for the Library of Congress and the smooth, lilting one that she used when she recorded for Columbia Records. She was also far from being the unsophisticated backwoods woman that so captivated some of her urban champions. For example, after Professor Barnicle loaned her a copy of Francis James Child's book of ballads, she learned verbatim stanzas of some Robin Hood ballads and later recorded them for Alan Lomax as examples of songs that she had learned in childhood.

29. The best biography of Aunt Molly is Shelly Romalis, *Pistol Packin' Mama: Aunt Molly Jackson and the Politics of Folksong* (Urbana: University of Illinois Press, 1999).

30. Dunaway, "Charles Seeger and Carl Sands," 168.

31. For this phase of Charles and Ruth's life, I have relied heavily on Tick, *Ruth Crawford Seeger*, especially 253–67.

32. Stanley Baldwin, *Poverty and Politics: The Rise and Decline of the Farm Security Administration* (Chapel Hill: University of North Carolina Press, 1968), 92.

33. Paul K. Conkin, *Tomorrow a New World: The New Deal Community Program* (Ithaca, N.Y.: Cornell University Press, 1959), 153. Johnny Cash may be the most famous American who lived on a resettlement farm. His family had moved from Kingsland, Arkansas, to a government-planned community in the Delta called the Dyess Colony. Cash recalled those days in songs like "Picking Time" and "Five Feet High and Rising," as well as in his autobiography, written with Patrick Carr, *Cash: The Autobiography* (New York: Harper Collins, 1997).

34. Janelle Warren Findley, "Journal of a Field Representative: Charles Seeger and Margaret Valiant," *Ethnomusicology* 24, no. 2 (May 1980): 169–207.

35. Charles Seeger did very little collecting himself, working primarily in South Carolina and West Virginia; instead, he oversaw the work done by his assistants. Telephone conversation with Mike Seeger, February 23, 2007. On the other hand, Charles and Sidney Robertson did conduct a very important recording of the music of John L. Handcox, the African American activist who worked with the Southern Tenant Farmers Union in Arkansas. The recording was made in March 1937 for the Library of Congress Archive of American Folk Song and is described in *Rambles: A Cultural Arts Magazine*, http://www.rambles .net/handcox_stfu04.html.

36. Old-time music's indebtedness to older commercial forms of music is now well known, if not always acknowledged. See Patrick Huber, *Linthead Stomp: The Creation of Country Music in the Piedmont South* (Chapel Hill: University of North Carolina Press, 2008); Henry Sapoznik, *"You Ain't Talkin' to Me": Charlie Poole and the Roots of Country Music* (Columbia CD 2005); Karl Hagstrom Miller, *Segregating Sound: Inventing Folk and Pop Music in the Age of Jim Crow* (Durham, N.C.: Duke University Press, 2010); and Bill C. Malone and Jocelyn R. Neal, *Country Music, U.S.A.* (Austin: University of Texas Press, 2010).

37. Many of Sidney Robertson's letters are now available online, including those dealing with the valuable work she did in Wisconsin and in California with the Works Progress Administration. For Wisconsin, see http://csumc.wisc.edu/src/story.htm; and for California, see *California Gold: Northern California Folk Music from the Thirties*, American Folklife Center, Library of Congress, Washington, D.C., http://memory.loc.gov/ammem/afccchtml. Margaret Valiant's experiences in Florida have been discussed in Warren-Findley, "Journal of a Field Representative."

38. Warren-Findley, "Journal of a Field Representative," 172, 178.

39. Charles Seeger remembered an experience that Margaret Valiant had when she went to one of her first meetings in the Cherry Lake community in Florida. A farmer said to her, "You know the ways in Washington are sure strange. We need agricultural help.

We need tractors. We need all sorts of information and guess what—Washington has sent us a musician!" When the worker was reassigned a year later, however, the community bade her goodbye in tears. Described in "Reminiscences of an American Musicologist: Charles Seeger," interviewed by Adelaide G. Tusler and Ann M. Briegleb under the auspices of the Oral History Program, University of California, Los Angeles, 1972 (full text in the Internet Archive: Digital Library of Free Books, http://www.archive.org/details/reminiscencesofa00seeg). Pete Seeger also told this story to Chip Duncan on June 26, 2003, http://www.iptv.org/wallace/docs/Trans_PeteSeeger.pdf.

40. Sidney Robertson was the most prolific collector among the Resettlement Administration workers. During an eighteen-month period beginning in November 1936, she visited about twenty states. She had earlier served an apprenticeship in the use of recording machines with John Lomax in western North Carolina. She traveled with about 400 pounds of recording equipment in four large cases.

41. The song sheets were brochures that included songs along with relevant descriptive art, most of which was created by Charles Pollock. Archie Green provided an example of one, "The Farmer Is the Man," in "Commercial Graphics #33: A Resettlement Administration Song Sheet," *JEMF Quarterly* 11, pt. 2 (Summer 1975): 80–88.

42. The researcher, a man named Hampton, was a descendant of the famous South Carolina politician Wade Hampton. According to Ellen Harold and Peter Stone, who wrote an excellent "short" account of Burl Ives, Alan Lomax roused the ire of his father, John, by "leaking" material from the unfinished manuscript of *Our Singing Country* to Ives. "Wayfaring Stranger" was one of those items. Ives had been singing the song for quite awhile before he first recorded it for Okeh on October 11, 1941. See Harold and Stone, "Burl Ives (1909–1995)," http://www.culturalequity.org/alanlomax/ce_alanlomax_profile_ives.php.

43. David Whisnant, "The White Top Folk Festival: What We (Have Not) Learned" (paper presented to Virginia Highlands Festival, Southwest Virginia Higher Education, Abingdon, Virginia, August 6, 1998), http://www.h-net.org/~appalach/Whitetop3.html. Whisnant's indispensable *All That Is Native and Fine: The Politics of an American Region* (Chapel Hill: University of North Carolina Press, 1983) contains a penetrating discussion of the White Top Festival.

44. The quoted phrases come from Benjamin Filene, *Romancing the Folk: Public Memory and American Roots Music* (Chapel Hill: University of North Carolina Press, 2000), 137–39. I differ from Filene, however, in their application. Alan Lomax's impressive contributions are discussed by John Szwed in *Alan Lomax: The Man Who Recorded the World* (New York: Viking Press, 2010).

45. Alan Lomax, ed., *Check-List of Recorded Songs in the English Language in the Archive of American Folksong to July 1940*, 3 vols. (Washington, D.C.: Music Division, Library of Congress, 1942).

46. Mike maintained that he was not always aware of what his mother was listening to, but Peggy spoke of her own irritation at hearing pieces of songs repeated interminably without the fulfillment of hearing the songs completed. She recalled that this was "very

frustrating if you're six years old and want to hear the rest of the song." Quoted in Larry Polansky with Judith Tick, *Ruth Crawford Seeger: The Music of American Folk Music* (University of Rochester Press, 2001), xix.

47. Bess Lomax Hawes, "Reminiscing on Ruth," *ISAM Newsletter* 31, no. 2 (Spring 2002): 4–6. Hawes also talks about her relationship with Ruth in *Sing It Pretty: A Memoir* (Urbana: University of Illinois Press, 2008), 22–26.

48. John Lomax recalled Ruth's "meticulous listening" with a mixture of awe and frustration in *Adventures of a Ballad Hunter* (New York: The MacMillan Company, 1947), 296. The entire seventy-five-page essay was eventually published in Larry Polansky with Judith Tick, *The Music of American Folk Song and Selected Other Writings on American Folk Music* (Rochester, N.Y.: University of Rochester Press, 2001).

49. John A. Lomax and Alan Lomax, *Our Singing Country: A Second Volume of American Ballads and Folk Songs* (New York: The Macmillan Company, 1949), xviii. Ruth was listed as music editor on the front cover of the book.

50. Folklorist David Evans has criticized Ruth's "agenda" to document the complexity of American folk music. He argues that her "concern" for intricacy led her to introduce needless metrical complications. Her lack of experience as a field-worker, he maintains, caused her to underappreciate the diversity of styles in folk music. "Transcribing the Folk," *ISAM Newsletter* 21, no. 2 (Spring 2002).

Chapter 2

1. Mike Seeger's reminiscences, early July 2005 (transcribed by Charmaine Harbort, Madison, Wisc.); Judith Tick, *Ruth Crawford Seeger: A Composer's Search for American Music* (New York: Oxford University Press, 1997), 224.

2. Tick, *Ruth Crawford Seeger*, 227–28; Mike Seeger provided additional details in an interview with me on February 5, 2004, and in an e-mail to me dated October 22, 2007.

3. Tick, *Ruth Crawford Seeger*, 227–28. Tick had gotten the quotes from Pete Seeger in an interview with him on June 25, 1983.

4. Mike Seeger, e-mail, July 27, 2004.

5. Mike Seeger, e-mail, January 6, 2005.

6. Mike Seeger, "Thoughts of Silver Spring, 1938," *ISAM Newsletter* 31, no. 1 (Fall 2001): 12.

7. Peggy Seeger, interview, Madison, Wisconsin, March 15, 2004; see also http://www .peggyseeger.com/.

8. John Lomax took a particular liking to the Seeger kids and sometimes sent them postcards. For example, he sent one addressed to Michael Seeger that showed a giant horned toad sitting in a cotton field lifting a frightened African American off the ground. This attempt at humor was apparently designed to show how big things were in Texas.

9. Two of the best introductions to Henry Cowell are Michael Hicks, *Henry Cowell, Bohemian* (Urbana: University of Illinois Press, 2002); and John Sachs, *Henry Cowell: A Biography* (New York: Oxford University Press, 2007).

10. Tick, *Ruth Crawford Seeger*, 281–83, 286–87; Barbara Seeger Perfect, telephone interview, April 17, 2006.

11. Quoted in Ruth Crawford Seeger's "Virtual Autobiography," organized and annotated by Judith Tick and published in the *ISAM Newsletter* (Fall 2001).

12. Mike Seeger, interview with Karen Cardullo, August 9, 1978 (from the collection of Judith Tick).

13. See Sally Rogers, "Ruth Crawford Seeger: CMN's 2005 Magic Penny Award Recipient," a tribute to Ruth's books by the Children's Music Network, http://www.cmnonline .org/PIOArticle.aspx?ID=19.

14. The information on this phase of Ruth's life came, in part, from my interviews with Mike, Peggy, and Barbara Seeger but principally from Judith Tick's biography of Ruth Crawford Seeger and additional research that she gathered. The latter included an interview with Penny Seeger that was conducted by Matilda Gaume on October 8, 1974.

15. Peggy Seeger, interview, Madison, Wisconsin, March 15, 2004.

16. Ibid.; Ann M. Pescatello, *Charles Seeger: A Life in American Music* (Pittsburgh: University of Pittsburgh Press, 1992), 258–59; Peggy Seeger, "About Dio," *ISAM Newsletter* 31, no. 1 (Fall 2001): 13.

17. Mike Seeger, telephone conversation, May 14, 2007.

18. In addition to information supplied in various interviews, Mike also talked at length about his childhood sojourn in Florida in a telephone conversation on May 14, 2007. The letters sent to Mike by Ruth and Peggy are in Alexia Seeger's possession in Lexington, Virginia.

19. Annette C. Eshleman, "Peggy Seeger—Homeward Bound," *Dirty Linen* 108 (October-November 2003): 21.

20. Mike Seeger, "Thoughts of Silver Spring, 1938."

21. Pete Seeger, telephone interview, Beacon, New York, January 8, 2004; Peggy Seeger, interview, Madison, Wisconsin, March 15, 2004.

22. There is a voluminous library of material on Pete Seeger, but my principal source of information on him was the fine biography by David K. Dunaway, *How Can I Keep From Singing? The Ballad of Pete Seeger* (New York: McGraw-Hill, 1981; Villard, 2008). Other helpful sources included the Pete Seeger Appreciation Page, organized by Jim Capaldi, www.peteseegermusic.com/links.html; Alec Wilkinson, "The Protest Singer: Pete Seeger and American Folk Music," *New Yorker*, April 17, 2006, www.peteseeger.net/ new_yorker041706.htm; and, of course, the reminiscences and autobiography compiled by Pete himself, *The Incompleat Folksinger* (New York: Simon and Schuster, 1972).

23. Loyal Jones, *Minstrel of the Appalachians: The Story of Bascom Lamar Lunsford* (Boone, N.C.: Appalachian Consortium Press, 1984).

24. Lawrence Emery, "Young Puppeteers in Unique Tour of Rural Areas," *Daily Worker*, October 2, 1939, http://www.peteseeger.net/DW10021939.htm.

25. Pete's letters and cartoons are in the possession of Alexia Smith, Lexington, Virginia.

26. The Silver Spring years, and much more, were recounted in "Thoughts of Silver

Spring, 1938"; and "Mike's Remembrances of Family Life," written by Mike for a family re-union and sent to me by e-mail on January 6, 2005.

27. As described by Tick in *Ruth Crawford Seeger*, 292–93.

28. Peggy Seeger, interview, March 15, 2004.

29. Dyslexia was never medically diagnosed, although both Peggy and Mike surmised that he may have had the condition. Mike mentioned the possibility of vision problems in a telephone conversation on May 14, 2007. I received some insights on the problem from a short item written by Gayle Worland, "Vision Therapy Has Its Believers and Skeptics," *Wisconsin State Journal*, July 3, 2009.

30. Mike Seeger, interview, May 14, 2007.

31. The Georgetown Day School website is www.gds.org.

32. "Woodstock Country School History," http://home.gwi.net/wcs/book/chapter3_7 .htm.

33. An alumnus, James Barter, remembered Buffy: "Buffy was a blast. I found her some-body easy to talk to and confide in. A lot of kids did." Quoted in "Woodstock Country School History."

34. Letter from Ruth to Mike at Woodstock, November 26, 1950. This letter is in the possession of Alexia Smith.

35. It is not clear how closely Mike stayed in contact with his school over the years, but he did correspond at least once to an invitation to a reunion: "Wish I could come to the event this year, but I'm booked the first weekend in August. I perform southern traditional music for a living so weekends aren't generally good for me." "Alumni Updates," posted on Woodstock Country School website, May 10, 2000.

36. Judy Fisher, a former Woodstock student, provided a brief remembrance of Mounir Sa'adah on one of the school's websites. She remembered him as "the best teacher that I had." "Woodstock Country School History," http://home.gwi.net/wcs/book/chapter3_7 .htm.

37. Burl Ives's testimony, and the folk music community's reaction to it, are discussed in Ronald D. Cohen, *Rainbow Quest: The Folk Music Revival and American Society, 1940–1970* (University of Massachusetts Press, 2002), 80–81.

38. Turner's real name was William Edward Grishaw. He was from Lynchburg, Virginia, but he played music in various places around the country. He wrote and recorded a num-ber of country songs but was best known for his novelty hit of 1951, "Chew Tobacco Rag," which contains the memorable verse: "If you chew tobacco, don't spit on the floor / Expec-torate in the cuspidor."

39. Mike Seeger, interview with Ray Allen, March 15, 2002.

40. "I Remember (Song for Mike)," performed at the Bethesda Memorial event for Mike Seeger in Maryland and sent to me in an e-mail on December 16, 2009.

41. Peggy's memories of her Beacon experience were told to Ross Altman in "My Brother, Mike Seeger: Peggy Seeger Talks to *Folkworks*, Part 2," http://folkworks.org/ content/view/36226/106.

42. Dunaway, *How Can I Keep from Singing?*, 162. Hays has a few things to say about

Pete's cabin in Beacon in his biography by Doris Willens, *Lonesome Traveler* (New York: W. W. Norton & Company, 1988), but the phrase itself is not used in the book.

43. Washington Square will be discussed more fully in chapter 3.

44. Flatt and Scruggs are profiled in Neil V. Rosenberg, *Bluegrass: A History* (Urbana: University of Illinois Press, 2005); and Barry P. Willis, *America's Music: Bluegrass* (Franktown, Colorado: Pine Valley Music, 1989). Students of this phase of America's musical history should see the videos of Flatt and Scruggs's very popular television series, *The Best of the Flatt and Scruggs TV Show*, a series of DVDs spanning the years 1955 to 1962.

45. The seminal influence exerted on country music by Al Hopkins and the Hillbillies — "the band that named the music" — has been discussed by Archie Green in "Hillbilly Music: Source and Symbol," *Journal of American Folklore* 78, no. 309 (July-September 1965): 204–28. Jimmie Rodgers's principal biography is Nolan Porterfield, *Jimmie Rodgers: The Life and Times of America's Blue Yodeler* (Urbana; University of Illinois Press, 1979). Ernest Stoneman's story was told by Ivan Tribe in *The Stonemans: An Appalachian Family and the Music That Shaped Their Lives* (Urbana: University of Illinois Press, 1993); and by Henry Sapoznik in an important two-CD box set, *The Unsung Father of Country Music, 1925–1934* (New York: 5 String Productions, 2008).

46. Roy Clark, with Marc Eliot, *My Life — In Spite of Myself* (New York: Simon and Schuster, 1994).

47. An extensive interview with Connie B. Gay can be found in the Oral History Museum Collection at the Country Music Hall of Fame and Museum in Nashville. His influential role in the country music scene in both Washington and the nation as a whole is described in several published works, though probably most astutely by Diane Pecknold in *The Selling Sound: The Rise of the Country Music Industry* (Durham, N.C.: Duke University Press, 2007). Margaret Jones provides some context for the Washington country music scene in *Patsy: The Life and Times of Patsy Cline* (New York: Da Capo, 1999), as does virtually any article devoted to the life and career of Jimmy Dean.

48. Dale Miller contributed a good retrospective of Fahey in "Reinventing the Steel," originally in *Acoustic Guitar* (January-February 1992) and reprinted online at http://www.johnfahey.com/pages/ac1.html. Fahey also told a similar story in *How Bluegrass Music Destroyed My Life: Stories by John Fahey* (Chicago: Drag City, 2000).

49. Ward Boote posted a couple of items on his website about WGAY and Don Owens, including Owens's obituary from the *Washington Evening Star*, April 22, 1963: http://www.percyfaithpages.org/wqmrwgaymemories/word_boote.htm. The WSM radio announcer, musician, and country music historian Eddie Stubbs claimed that Owens booked, promoted, and emceed the first bluegrass festival at Watermelon Park in Berryville, Virginia, on August 14, 1960. See Richard D. Smith, *Can't You Hear Me Callin': The Life of Bill Monroe, Father of Bluegrass* (Boston: Little, Brown, 2000), 151–52.

50. Peggy Seeger, interview, February 2, 2004; and Richard Spottswood, interview, February 2, 2004. Peggy, however, had a vague recollection of the event and believed that Spottswood had told her about Leadbelly.

51. The Rich-R-Tone label is now located in Gallatin, Tennessee. Its website, World's

Oldest Bluegrass Record Label, is www.richrtone.com/id3.html. The Stanley Brothers' recordings for the label, made between 1947 and 1952, were first reissued on CDs on Melodeon MLP 7322.

52. Mike also used this phrase to describe two other experiences: his first encounter with the music of Libba Cotten and his visit to a Pentecostal church with Dock Boggs.

53. After Edwards died at the age of twenty-eight in an automobile accident in Australia, his collection was bequeathed to his collector friends in the United States. This material became the nucleus of the John Edwards Memorial Foundation archive, now housed in the Southern Folklife Collection at the University of North Carolina at Chapel Hill. Joseph E. Bussard Jr. was interviewed by Marshall Wyatt in the *Old-Time Herald* 6, no. 7, http://www.oldtimeherald.org/archive/back_issues/volume-6/6-7/visit-bussard.html. A few of Bussard's 25,000 78s were released on CD as *Down in the Basement: Joe Bussard's Treasure Trove of Vintage 78s* (Old Hat RCD 1004).

54. Accompanied by a ninety-six-page book, the Harry Smith collection was reissued on six CDs in 1997 by Smithsonian Folkways (SFW 40090). Exploiting the urban fascination with presumed exoticism, the principal essayist, Greil Marcus, described the recordings as "the music of the old, weird America."

55. Roy Clark talked a bit about Ralph Case in his autobiography, but Case was also the subject of occasional newspaper and magazine articles. For example, see Hamil R. Harris, "He's the Square-Dancing King: At the Age of 90, Ralph Case Is Old Man Rhythm," *Washington Post*, June 1, 2000; and Case's obituary by Bart Barnes, "Famed Area Square Dance Caller and Entertainer Ralph Case Dies," *Washington Post*, January 10, 2001.

56. Mike told Libba's story many times, but one of his best recollections came in an interview he gave to Richard Straw and Les Dotson on December 15, 1991, in Lexington, Virginia.

57. L. L. Demerle, "Remembering Elizabeth Cotten," http://www.eclectica.org/v1n1/nonfiction/demerlee.html.

58. Ed Badeaux was in the Seeger home on the evening when Mike first recorded Libba. He provided a recollection and appreciation of her in "Please Don't Tell What Train I'm On," *Sing Out!* 14, no. 4 (September 1964): 6–13.

59. *Close to Home: Old Time Music from Mike Seeger's Collection, 1952–1967* (Smithsonian Folkways CD 40097, 1997). Libba Cotten was filmed playing "Freight Train" at the Seeger home in 1957. Excerpts can be seen on the Smithsonian Folkways website.

60. Many of Mike's field recordings have been anthologized in *Close to Home*. All of the material is otherwise deposited in Mike's collection at the Southern Folklife Collection, UNC–Chapel Hill.

61. Peggy Seeger, quoted in "About Dio," *ISAM Newsletter* 31, no. 1 (Fall 2001): 13; reprinted online at http://depthome.brooklyn.cuny.edu/isam/rcspeggy.html.

62. Peggy Seeger, e-mail, July 20, 2005.

63. Peggy told this story often, including in an interview with Scott Alarik for the *Boston Globe*, April 16, 2010; reprinted at www.boston.com/. . ./folk_legend_peggy_seeger_is_leaving_boston_but_shes_not_slowing_down/.

64. Pescatello, *Charles Seeger*, 209–12,

65. Mike Seeger, e-mails, July 24, 2005, and July 27, 2005.

Chapter 3

1. I saw the letter, or a copy of it, at Mike Seeger's home in Lexington. In this letter, Charles even alluded to Mayflower ancestry.

2. Mount Wilson State Hospital and Sanitarium was established in 1925 and closed its doors in 1981. Secluded on about 200 acres, the abandoned building gained notoriety as a haunted structure. It is now the site of North Oakes Retirement Community.

3. Information on the Seeger-Dickens relationship came from interviews with Mike Seeger and Hazel Dickens. It is also mentioned in a variety of publications. I wrote about the relationship earlier in a book coauthored with Hazel Dickens, *Working Girl Blues: The Life and Music of Hazel Dickens* (Urbana: University of Illinois Press, 2005). Hillary Dickens recorded several banjo pieces for Mike Seeger that are located in Mike's collection at the Southern Folklife Collection, UNC–Chapel Hill.

4. Eddie Dean wrote a fine account of one of the most important parks, Sunset Park, near West Grove in southern Chester County, Pennsylvania. See Dean, "O Brother, Where Art the Sunsets of Yesteryear?," originally published in the *Philadelphia Weekly*, October 31, 2001; reprinted online at www.bluegrasswest.com/ideas/sunsetpark.htm.

5. Richard D. Smith provides a very useful list of country music parks in *Can't You Hear Me Callin': The Life of Bill Monroe, Father of Bluegrass* (New York: Little, Brown and Company, 2000), 135.

6. Good introductions to Ola Belle Reed and New River Ranch include Judy Marti, "A Banjo Pickin' Girl: The Life and Music of Ola Belle Reed Campbell Reed," *Old-Time Herald* 3, no. 6 (Winter 1992/93): 17–22; David Whisnant, notes to the LP *Ola Belle Reed and Family* (Rounder 0077, 1977); and Charles Camp and David E. Whisnant, "A Voice from Home: Southern Mountain Music on the Maryland-Pennsylvania Border," *Southern Exposure* 5 (1977), 80–89.

7. Probably the two best CD compilations of Ola Belle Reed's music are *Rising Sun Melodies* (Smithsonian Folkways SFW 40202) and *Ola Belle Reed* (Field Recorders' Collective FRC 203).

8. The best historical survey of bluegrass music is Neil Rosenberg, *Bluegrass: A History* (Urbana: University of Illinois Press, 1985). He also wrote a pioneering essay on the genre titled "From Sound to Style: The Emergence of Bluegrass," *Journal of American Folklore* 80 (1967), 143–50.

9. Richard Spottswood, interview, February 2, 2004.

10. Pete Kuykendall, interview, February 17, 2004; *Bluegrass Unlimited* has been an active and influential publication since 1966.

11. Mike Seeger's dub logs (a listing of the field recordings made by Mike housed in his collection at UNC–Chapel Hill, including name of performer, date, and place, with occasional brief commentary by Mike); Smith, *Can't You Hear Me Callin'*, 167.

12. Leon Kagarise, a fan from Baltimore, recorded many hours of the shows at Sunset Park on a fifty-pound Ampex 960 reel-to-reel tape recorder and took many photographs of both musicians and listeners during these halcyon days of live country entertainment. Many of his photos and slides have been publicly exhibited. See Geoffrey Himes's review of one Kagarise exhibition in Baltimore at http://www2.citypaper.com/arts/story .asp?id=20260. At least one wonderful YouTube piece (almost seven minutes long)— "The Way It Were—Leon Kagarise's Country Music Archive"—exists of musical moments at the parks documented by Kagarise. One can hear some examples of shows performed at New River Ranch on CDs by such groups as the Monroe Brothers (from the Eugene Earle Collection in the Southern Folklife Collection at UNC–Chapel Hill), the Stanley Brothers, and the Louvin Brothers (both on the Copper Creek label).

13. Ralph Lee Smith wrote a short history of the important Swarthmore festival in "If I Had a Song," *Swarthmore College Bulletin*, March 1997, 19–23, http://media.swarthmore .edu/bulletin/wp-content/archived_issues_pdf/Bulletin_1997_03.pdf. Ronald D. Cohen gives a brief account of the Swarthmore event in *A History of Folk Music Festivals in the United States: Feasts of Musical Celebration* (Lanham, Md.: Scarecrow Press, 2008), 36–37. I have had access to several interviews with Ralph Rinzler, but I am particularly indebted to his widow, Kate Hughes Rinzler, who gave me a copy of her unfinished biography of Ralph: "A Source of Wonder." Her interviews with him and Mike Seeger are located at the Smithsonian Institution. Jeff Place, curator of the Rinzler Papers, kindly made copies of them for me. Richard Straw also loaned me a copy of his interview with Rinzler, conducted in Washington, D.C., on March 10, 1987. Roger Abrahams sent me extensive e-mail recollections (January 16, 2007) of his friendship with Rinzler and his days at Swarthmore. Richard Gagne has contributed a fine summary of Rinzler's career in "Ralph Rinzler, Folklorist: A Professional Biography," *Folklore Forum* 27, no. 1 (1996), based on an interview done by Gagne on July 29, 1993, and reprinted at https://scholarworks.iu.edu/dspace/ bitstream/handle/2022/2206/27%281%29%2020-49.pdf?sequence=1.

14. Abrahams, e-mail, March 10, 1987.

15. Mike and Ralph's experiences in the New York Public Library have been described in several sources. These include various interviews; Peter D. Goldsmith, *Making People's Music: Moe Asch and Folkways Records* (Washington, D.C.: Smithsonian Institution Press, 1998), 259; and Ray Allen, *Gone to the Country: The New Lost City Ramblers and the Folk Music Revival* (Urbana: University of Illinois Press, 2010), 17–18.

16. Some sources say that Rinzler went to the New River Ranch in 1954; for example, see *Field Trip South: Exploring the Southern Folklife Collection*, http://www.lib.unc.edu/ blogs/sfc/. Mike Seeger's dub logs, though, indicate no date earlier than July 1955 for a Stanley Brothers appearance at Hillbilly Ranch. It is conceivable, but highly unlikely, that Rinzler could have been present at some show without Mike being there.

17. Ralph Rinzler, interview with Richard Straw, March 10, 1987.

18. Mike Seeger thought that the date of the reunion was July 4 and had said so in his log. Richard D. Smith described the event of May 8 and noted that it was followed up with another show on July 3, 1955, in *Can't You Hear Me Callin'*, 135.

19. Mike Seeger's tape of the event is in the Southern Folklife Collection at UNC–Chapel Hill. Another taping of the show, done by Gerald Mills, is available as *The Monroe Brothers Live at New River Ranch, 1955,* at *Field Trip South: Exploring the Southern Folklife Collection,* http://www.lib.unc.edu/blogs/sfc/index.php/2009/12/07/the-monroe-brothers-live-at-new-river-ranch-1955/.

20. Louise Scruggs was named to the International Bluegrass Music Association's Hall of Fame in 2010.

21. Rinzler made this assessment to Mike in a letter from Paris dated March 8, 1958.

22. The Monroe-Rinzler relationship is discussed in Ralph Rinzler, "Bill Monroe," in *Stars of Country Music,* ed. Bill C. Malone and Judith McCulloh (Urbana: University of Illinois Press, 1976); Rosenberg, *Bluegrass*; and Smith, *Can't You Hear Me Callin',* 167–74.

23. Baker is heard doing these songs in *Mountain Music, Bluegrass Style* (Folkways FA 2318).

24. The important bluegrass scene in Baltimore has been best described by Geoffrey Himes in "From the Hills: How Mid-Century Migrants from the Mountains Brought Bluegrass—and More—to Baltimore," *Baltimore City Paper,* http://www2.citypaper.com/news/story.asp?id=3636.

25. Hazel Dickens, interview, Chicago, November 10, 2002.

26. Forty of Dickens's best songs, along with her explanations of why they were written, are included in Malone and Dickens, *Working Girl Blues.*

27. Hazel Dickens, interview, November 10, 2002; and Mike Seeger, interview, February 6, 2004.

28. Hazel Dickens and Mike Seeger, interview with Richard Straw, Lexington, Virginia, March 18, 1984.

29. Hazel Dickens, telephone interview, April 18, 2007.

30. One of the best accounts of Washington Square, and much more, is Dave Van Ronk with Elijah Wald, *The Mayor of MacDougal Street: A Memoir* (Cambridge, Mass: Da Capo Press, 2005). Another good account is Jay Feldman, "Sunday Afternoon at Washington Square: A Nostalgic Event," *Bluegrass Unlimited* 17, no. 9 (March 1983): 21–35. A sampling of performers who attended the Sunday hootenannies can be heard on the three-disc compilation *Washington Square Memoirs: The Great Urban Folk Boom, 1950–70* (Rhino 74264).

31. Timothy Josiah Morris Pertz, "The Jewgrass Boys: Bluegrass Music's Emergence in New York City's Washington Square, 1946–1961," winner of the 2005 Hoopes Prize for Outstanding Thesis of the Senior Class at Harvard College, www.people.fas.harvard.edu/pertz.

32. Julian "Winnie" Winston, "Me and My Old Banjo," www.julianwinston.com/music/me_and_my_old_banjo.php.

33. Letter from Moe Asch to Mike Seeger, September 13, 1956. Copies are available at various places, including the Ralph Rinzler Archives at the Smithsonian Institution.

34. The best biography of Asch is Peter Goldsmith, *Making People's Music: Moe Asch and Folkways Records* (Washington, D.C.: Smithsonian Institution, 1998). Other useful accounts include Gene Bluestein, "Moses Asch, the Documentor," *American Music* 5, no. 3

(Fall 1987); and Jim Capaldi, "Conversation with Mr. Folkways: Moe Asch," *Folk Scene* (May-June 1978), reprinted online at http://www.peteseeger.net/fsmoasch.htm. Variations of the Einstein story appear in several publications, including David Kupfer, "Longtime Passing: An Interview with Pete Seeger," *Whole Earth* (Spring 2001); and on the website info@wholearthmag.com.

35. In 1987 the Smithsonian Institution Center for Folklife and Cultural Heritage acquired the Folkways Records catalog from the Asch estate. The Smithsonian agreed that virtually all 2,168 Folkways titles would remain in print forever.

36. The leading authority on Snuffy Jenkins is Pat J. Ahrens, *The Legacy of Two Legends, Snuffy Jenkins and Pappy Sherrill* (privately printed, Columbia, South Carolina, 2007). Copies of her book can be purchased through her website, Pat Ahrens — Bluegrass Historian, http://patahrens.com/Home_Page.html.

37. The original LP included twenty-seven songs. The reissued CD of 1990, *American Banjo: Three-Finger and Scruggs Style* (Smithsonian Folkways SFW 40037), included sixteen additional tracks.

38. Rosenberg, *Bluegrass*, 154.

39. *Mountain Music Bluegrass Style* was reissued on CD in 1991 (Smithsonian Folkways SFW 40038). David Grisman's comments are quoted in Jay Orr's notes to Mike Seeger's CD, *True Vine* (Smithsonian-Folkways 40136).

40. Ronald D. Cohen, ed., *Alan Lomax: Selected Writings, 1934–1997* (New York: Routledge, 2005), 187–89.

41. Cody's remark to Walt Hensley is quoted in Tina Aridas, "Walter Hensley: The Banjo Baron of Baltimore," *DC Bluegrass Union*, http://www.dcbu.org/walterhensley.htm.

42. Alan Lomax, "Bluegrass Background: Folk Music with Overdrive," *Esquire* 52, no. 4 (October 1959), 103–9. The article has since been reprinted in Cohen, *Alan Lomax*.

43. Ward did occasional odd jobs, farmed a little bit, drove his neighbors to work, and made music. It was the kind of back-to-the-land experience that many urbanites have sought. When he wrote to Mike, he signed his letters "Sincerely your Uncle Wade Ward and wife." For example, see Wade Ward to Mike Seeger, December 14, 1956.

44. See Mike Seeger's notes to Snow's recording in *Close to Home*. Snow's most important recordings are on the LP produced by Mike Seeger, *Country Songs and Tunes* (Folkways 3902). Seeger's recording of "When First unto This Country" appeared on the LP *The New Lost City Ramblers, Vol. 2* (Folkways). Good histories of the Autoharp include Ivan Stiles, "The True History of the Autoharp," www.fretlesszithers.com/ahhistory.html. A. Doyle Moore, one of the original members of the Philo Glee and Mandolin Society, spent much of his life playing the instrument and pursuing its history at the University of Illinois in Urbana-Champaign. An hour-and-a-half interview with him, conducted by Tracie Wilson, is available in the University of Illinois Campus Folksong Club Oral History Project. He is a professor emeritus of art and design at the University of Illinois.

45. Mike, however, had apparently been a good student. A. A. Richardson of the Commercial Radio Institute described him as an "above average student"; letter to the Central Scholarship Bureau, March 12, 1958.

46. Copies of the letter response that Mike made to the SSA and FBI (July 19, 1958) are in the possession of Alexia Smith.

47. The Central Scholarship Bureau had been founded by Moses Rothschild and other Baltimore leaders to support business and vocational training. See www.centralsb.org/html/history.htm.

Chapter 4

1. Letter from Charles Seeger to Mike Seeger, July 3, 1959. While it has been convincingly argued that Mike unconsciously hewed a performing path independent of his family, he nevertheless deliberately avoided any kind of controversial political involvement. He told me: "I rebelled against the whole Seeger political thing."

2. In this chapter, I have relied heavily on the work of Ray Allen, particularly *Gone to the Country: The New Lost City Ramblers and the Folk Music Revival* (Urbana: University of Illinois Press, 2010). Peter Gura wrote the best "short" account of the group: "Southern Roots and Branches: Forty Years of the New Lost City Ramblers," http://muse.jhu.edu/journals/southern_cultures/voo6/6.4gura.html.

3. Bill Clifton and his Dixie Mountain Boys, *Carter Family Memorial Album* (Starday SLP 146). These songs are now available on an eight-CD box collection of Clifton's music titled *Around the World to Poor Valley* and produced by Bear Family in Germany.

4. In an e-mail to me, Mike said that he had "wanted to record a progressive bluegrass group to balance the more traditional" bands profiled in *Mountain Music, Bluegrass Style*. He produced *Country Songs, Old and New* (Folkways FA 2409) in 1959. Pete Kuykendall produced their next two LPs: *Folk Songs and Bluegrass* (Folkways FA 2410, 1961) and *The Country Gentlemen on the Road* (Folkways FA 2411, 1963).

5. The general details of the Dildine show have been corroborated by Mike Seeger, John Cohen, and Tom Paley in various interviews. Dildine, who was a banjo player himself, produced an extensive number of folk and country shows in the Washington area, the best known of which were the Cabin John Hoots. His music collection, the John and Ginny Dildine Collection (made up largely of programs performed in Washington), is located in the American Folklife Center, Library of Congress, Washington, D.C., AFS#17511-a7538.

6. John Cohen has told his story to many people, but I first heard it in an interview with him on February 3, 2004. He also told his story to Richard Straw in Putnam Valley, New York, on May 6, 1988; and to Eli Smith, "New Lost City Ramblers 50 Years: Interview with John Cohen and Tom Paley," *Down Home Radio* (Summer 2008), available on the Web archives of the show, http://www.downhomeradioshow.com/2008/12/the-new-lost-city-ramblers-50-years-interview-with-john-cohen-tom-paley/.

7. John Cohen, notes to *There Is No Eye: Music for Photographs* (Smithsonian Folkways SF 40091, 2001); John Cohen, "Remembering the High Lonesome: Transcript," on http://www.folkstreams.net/context,92.

8. A radio sound check of this broadcast has survived: tape FT-9786, Mike Seeger Collection, Southern Folklife Collection, UNC–Chapel Hill. The songs included "Soldier's

Joy," "Weave Room Blues," "Molly and Tenbrooks," "Make Me a Pallet on Your Floor," "Colored Aristocracy," "The Boll Weevil," "Little Moses," and "Railroad Bill."

9. Izzy Young provided a short summary of his life and career in *Wasn't That a Time! Firsthand Accounts of the Folk Music Revival*, ed. Ronald D. Cohen (Metuchen, N.J., and London: Scarecrow Press, 1995). He sent a lengthy e-mail to me on September 7, 2005. "Talking Folklore Center" was published as a song sheet by the Folklore Center: http://www.bobdylanroots.com/folklore.html. For further information on Young, see Ronald D. Cohen, *Rainbow Quest: The Folk Music Revival and American Society, 1940–1970* (University of Massachusetts Press, 2002), especially 120–22; and Bob Dylan, *Chronicles: Volume One* (New York: Simon and Schuster, 2004).

10. Many years later, in a joint interview conducted by Eli Smith for *Down Home Radio*, http://www.downhomeradioshow.com/2008/12/the-new-lost-city-ramblers-50-years-interview-with-john-cohen-tom-paley/, Paley and Cohen held to their respective stories concerning the naming of the group. Mike Seeger supported Cohen's version of the story in an e-mail to me dated February 6, 2004. The best introductions to the life and music of Charlie Poole are Kinney Rorrer, *Rambling Blues: The Life and Songs of Charlie Poole* (Danville, Va.: K. Rorrer, 1992); Patrick Huber, *Linthead Stomp: The Creation of Country Music in the Piedmont South* (Chapel Hill: University of North Carolina Press, 2008); and a three-disk box collection of his music and influences produced and annotated by Henry Sapoznik, *You Ain't Talking to Me: Charlie Poole and the Roots of Country Music* (Sony BMG 2005).

11. Pete Seeger wrote to Mike on January 19, 1959, applauding the LP as "swell" and "a fine achievement": "I'd no idea you'd become such an accomplished fiddler."

12. These appearances were pieced together through conversations with Mike Seeger; his dictated notes; John Cohen's recollections in "Remembering the High Lonesome: Transcript"; and Allen, *Gone to the Country*.

13. See Joey Latimer, "Utah Phillips Interview," June 11, 1993, originally for *Folk Music Quarterly Magazine* and reprinted on the Radio Free World website, http://www.radiofreeworld.com/utahphillips/.

14. The definitive history of the folk revival has not been written, but the best book so far is Cohen, *Rainbow Quest*. Neil Rosenberg reminds us that the "big boom" of the early sixties, as he terms it, was one of many revivals that have occurred in the United States; see Rosenberg, *Transforming Tradition: Folk Music Revivals Examined* (Urbana: University of Illinois Press, 1993). The best cultural explanation of the phenomenon is Robert Cantwell, *When We Were Good: The Folk Revival* (Cambridge, Mass.: Harvard University Press, 1997).

15. Cohen, *Rainbow Quest*, 144, 145–48. The fiftieth anniversary of the festival, "Newport Folk Festival: 50 Years Later," was profiled on National Public Radio's *All Things Considered* and can be heard on the NPR website.

16. Billy Faier was a regular contributor to the little paperback folk music journal *Caravan*, the first periodical to give the Ramblers favorable reviews. His laudatory review was in no. 15 (February-March 1959). Ray Allen noted that the Ramblers also received favorable reviews in the *New York Times*, *Nation*, and *Saturday Review*. Seeing these reviews, John Cohen said that he had gotten "some perspective" on their career and felt that there

might be a larger audience for their brand of traditional music. Allen, *Gone to the Country*, 69.

17. Letters from Marge Ostrow to Mike Seeger from Yonkers, New York, July 20 and 28, 1959, and August 5, 1959.

18. Marjorie Ostrow Seeger Marash, interview, February 19, 2004 (she married Edward Kimball III on April 3, 2004); Mike Seeger's dictated notes.

19. Charles expressed his concern about Marge's trip in a letter to Mike dated February 12, 1960.

20. Recorded concerts (five seven-inch tapes) made at the Berkeley Folk Festival in 1960 are available at the American Folklife Center, Library of Congress, Washington, D.C., AFC 19, 450-17, 454; Ronald D. Cohen talks about Berkeley and other festivals in *A History of Folk Music Festivals in the United States: Feasts of Musical Celebration* (Lanham, Md.: Scarecrow Press, 2008).

21. Ruth Crawford Seeger, *American Folk Songs for Christmas* (New York: Doubleday, 1953).

22. The Ramblers actually recorded four LPs in 1959: *The New Lost City Ramblers* (Folkways FA 2396); *The New Lost City Ramblers, Vol. 2* (Folkways FA 2397); *Old Timey Songs for Children*, a ten-inch disc (Folkways FC 7064); and *Songs from the Depression* (Folkways FH 5264). Only the first two were available, however, when they made their first California jaunt.

23. *The New Lost City Ramblers Song Book* (New York: Oak Publication, 1964). The book's title was later changed to the *Old-Time Stringband Songbook* (without the authorization of the Ramblers and without their names on the cover). Hally Wood, a Texan, was also a singer of folk songs and was married for several years to author, folklorist, and radio personality John Henry Faulk.

24. Cohen's quote came from *The New Lost City Ramblers Songbook*, 10. Seeger's quote was in the liner notes of their first LP.

25. Descendants of the Gant family, a poor Mormon family who lived in the hills outside Austin, Texas, were "rediscovered" by journalist Michael Corcoran in 2010, and their story and music were profiled on a local blog. One of their songs, "When First unto This Country," collected by John and Alan Lomax, became one of Mike Seeger's favorite songs. See "Secret History of Austin Music: The Gant Family Singers," Austin360.com.

26. Quoted in Allen, *Gone to the Country*, 85.

27. Ralph Rinzler, interview with Richard Straw, March 10, 1987.

28. My original assessment of the Ramblers' vocal sound, given on pages 339–40 in the first edition of *Country Music, U.S.A.* in 1968, is still quoted. I must now confess that my judgment may have been a wee bit unnuanced.

29. Jon Pankake, "Pete's Children: The American Folk Song Revival, Pro and Con," *Little Sandy Review* (March-April 1964). Reprinted at http://www.peteseeger.net/litlesan .htm.

30. Mike wrote an essay, "Crusaders for Old-Time Music," in the 1997 *Festival of American Folk Life Program Book*.

31. Pete Seeger, *The Incompleat Folksinger* (New York: Simon and Schuster, 1972), 206. Pete also recalled that Jimmie Rodgers was one of Woody Guthrie's favorite singers (42).

32. Mike Seeger, interview with Frank Walker, 1962 (available in Mike's collections at the University of North Carolina and at the Library of Congress).

33. Cohen and Paley remembered the Jewbilly incident in an interview given to Eli Smith on Downhome Radio, September 13, 2008.

34. John Cohen, interview, February 3, 2004; John Cohen, "NLCR Reflections: The Bread Cast on the Waters Returns," *Old Time Music* 6 (Autumn 1972): 4–6.

35. "Lee Hoffman's Biography: My Folknik Days," http://cvil.wustl.edu/~gary/Lee/biography.html; Winnie Winston, "Me and Music," http://www.julianwinston.com/music/me_and_music.php; Dick Greenhaus, e-mail, July 27, 2008.

36. John Cohen, interview, February 3, 2004; Cohen's recollections in "Remembering the High Lonesome: Transcript."

37. James D. Vaughan, *Sweet Heaven* (Lawrenceburg, Tenn.: James D. Vaughan, Publisher, 1933); Uncle Tupelo, *No Depression* (Rockville Records Rock 6050–2). The magazine ceased print operations in June 2008 and has since become an online journal.

38. John Cohen recalled that the Ramblers had dressed rather "sloppily" at their first Newport gig and that the promoter who booked them into Chicago insisted that they clean up their act.

39. At the Mills College concert, for example, after the group played a fiddle breakdown, Mike said: "That breakdown is a good definition of what the New Lost City Ramblers are. We were lost most of the way through it" (Allen, *Gone to the Country*, 63). On other occasions, he might stand behind Tom Paley as he played a banjo break and turn an imaginary crank in the vicinity of his posterior. Mike also liked to say that they recorded "long play, short sales" records for Folkways. For example, see Mike Seeger, interview with Mike Storey, taped for *Folk Voice* 17 (ca. October 1960) and made available to me by Bill Clifton.

40. In a letter to Moe Asch dated April 5, 1971, Mike asked, "How about repressing *Earth Is Earth*? We can dispose of 1,000 easily. We are requested for the EP everywhere."

41. Chris Darrow, interview with Richie Unterberger, in *Urban Spacemen and Wayfaring Strangers*, excerpted online at http://www.richieunterberger.com/darrow.html.

42. Marshall Wyatt's highly instructive interviews of two of the most important collectors give us good glimpses of the world they inhabited. See "The Music Has Always Held Sway: An Interview with Bob Pinson," *Old-Time Herald* 6, no. 4, http://www.oldtimeherald.org/archive/back_issues/volume-6/6-4/pinson.html; and "Every County Has Its Own Personality: An Interview with David Freeman," *Old-Time Herald* 7, no. 2 (November 1999–January 2000): 12–20, 36, http://www.oldtimeherald.org/archive/back_issues/volume-7/7-2/david_freeman.html.

43. Several of the hillbilly folklorists contributed a series of essays to the landmark "Hillbilly Issue," *Journal of American Folklore* 78, no. 309 (July-September 1965). One of the folklorists, John Greenway, had earlier published a pioneering essay titled "Jimmie Rodgers—A Folksong Catalyst" in the *Journal of American Folklore* 70, no. 277 (July-September

1957): 231–35. Donald Knight Wilgus was one of the first scholars to show the link between commercial recordings and folk music in "A Catalogue of American Folksongs on Commercial Records" (master's thesis, Ohio State University, 1947). However, a few scholars, such as Howard Odum, had been using phonograph records as research tools since the late 1920s.

44. Robert Cantwell wrote a beautiful and insightful essay on Green titled "In Memoriam: Archie Green (1917–2009)" for the UNC Press blog, uncpressblog.com/2009/04/02/in-memoriam-archie-green. Tracie Wilson of the University of Illinois Campus Folk Song Club conducted a very long interview with Green (seventeen pages): http://www.library.illinois.edu/edx/folklore/cfc.html. I also interviewed Green by phone from San Francisco on April 13, 2006, but have known and corresponded frequently with him since at least 1965.

45. Archie Green, letter to Mike Seeger from San Francisco, January 15, 1958.

46. The best introduction to David McCarn and his music is Huber, *Linthead Stomp*; and *Gastonia Gallop: Cotton Mill Songs and Hillbilly Blues, 1927–1941* (Old Hat CD 1007), a CD anthology of cotton mill songs.

47. Archie Green, interview, April 13, 2006; Archie Green, interview with David Dunaway, David Dunaway Collection of Interviews with Pete Seeger and Contemporaries, American Folklife Center, Library of Congress, Washington, D.C., December 2003.

48. Rick March, conversation, Madison, Wisconsin, June 8, 2006.

49. Allen, *Gone to the Country*, 80.

50. *Philo Glee and Mandolin Society* (Puritan 5007, 1962). The club's second LP, *Green Fields of Illinois* (CFC-201), featured old-time musicians from Illinois. Information obtained from http://webpages.charter.net/dance/greenfields/biographies.htm and http://www.library.illinois.edu/edx/folklore/cfc.html.

51. "The Legend of Uncle Willie and the Brandy Snifters," by Lyle Lofgren as told to Liz Lofgren, in *Old-Time Herald* 8, no. 6 (Winter 2002–3); reprinted online at http://www.lizlyle.lofgrens.org/BrnSnift/BSlegend.html.

52. Jon Pankake wrote a history of *Little Sandy Review* in Cohen, *Wasn't That a Time!*, 105–14. An even longer assessment and history of the little magazine, written on July 29, 2009, is in http://newvulgate.blogspot.com/2009/07/issue-4-july-29-2009.html.

53. Ed Pearl, telephone interview, Los Angeles, June 18, 2010; Peter F. Feldmann, "Old Time Hits the Big Time in Hollywood USA," *Old-Time Herald* 5, no. 8 (1996), reprinted online at http://www.oldtimeherald.org/archive/back_issues/volume-5/5-8/hollywood.html. Kirk Silsbee, "Concerts Celebrate Ash Grove's Legacy," *Jewish Journal* (April 17, 2008), reprinted online at http://www.jewishjournal.com/music/article/concerts_celebrate_ash_groves_golden_legacy_20080418/.

54. Tom Nolan, "Ash Grove: The Other Side of Melrose," *LA Weekly*, April 16, 2008, http://www.ashgrovefilm.com/LAWeekly.pdf.

55. Ry Cooder, quoted in a review of his CD titled "Three (or Four) Chords and the Truth: The Saga of Ry Cooder and a Cat Named Buddy," *Sing Out!* 51, no. 3 (Autumn 2007): 54.

56. I had a lengthy telephone interview with Roland White (Nashville), June 4, 2010; I also profited from a book written by Roland White and Diane Bouska, with Steve Pottier and Matt Flinner, *The Essential Clarence White* (Nashville: Diane and Roland Music, 2009), 5–28. I had earlier learned the basic rudiments of Roland and Clarence White's involvement with the Ash Grove from Mike Seeger. Marge Seeger's support of the White Brothers is mentioned in Eric Von Schmidt and Jim Rooney, *Baby, Let Me Follow You Down: The Illustrated Story of the Cambridge Folk Years* (University of Massachusetts Press, 1994), 209.

57. See Matt Bowling, "The Grateful Dead: Making the Scene in Palo Alto," *The Palo Alto History Project*, http://www.paloaltohistory.com/gratefuldead.html; and Blair Jackson, *Garcia: An American Life* (New York: Penguin Books, 1999).

58. Mike Seeger's reminiscences, July 2005 (transcribed by Charmaine Harbort, Madison, Wisc.); Bill Clifton, interview, December 23, 2009.

59. The contract and letters from Ben Appel are in Alexia Seeger's possession; I obtained information on Jersey Homesteads and Roosevelt, New Jersey, from "History of Roosevelt, New Jersey," www.libraries.rutgers.edu/rul/libs/scua/roosevelt/rstory.shtml; and "Jersey Homesteads: Brief History," on Electronic New Jersey, http://www2.scc.rutgers.edu/njh/Homesteads/history.php.

60. Paul J. Stamler did an excellent interview with Peter Bartók, concentrating on his pioneering work as an audio engineer and his relationship with Moe Asch: http://scribd.com/doc/12630485/Peter-Bartok-Stamler.

61. Jon Pareles provided basic biographical information in his obituary of Robert Shelton (born Robert Shapiro) in "Robert Shelton, 69, Music Critic Who Chronicled 60's Folk Boom," *New York Times*, December 15, 1995, http://www.nytimes.com/1995/12/15/nyregion/robert-shelton-69-music-critic-who-chronicled-60-s-folk-boom.html. Ronald D. Cohen talks about Shelton throughout *Rainbow Quest*. Tom Paley's problems with the *Today Show* were discussed by him, John Cohen, and Mike Seeger in their various interviews and, of course, by Ray Allen in *Gone to the Country*, his history of the New Lost City Ramblers.

62. Tom Paley, interview with Richard Straw, October 24, 1988.

63. Lomax's putdown of the Washington Square crowd came in an essay written for "Sounds of the South" in *Alan Lomax: Selected Writings, 1934–1997*, ed. Ronald D. Cohen (New York: Routledge, 2005), 333. Many of the recordings were released in the seven-LP set *Southern Folk Heritage Series* (Atlantic) and have since been reissued on four CDs as *Sounds of the South: A Musical Journey from the Georgia Sea Islands to the Mississippi Delta* (Atlantic 82496-2).

64. Jon Pankake and Paul Nelson wrote a very full and positive review of the festival titled "The First Annual University of Chicago Folk Festival," *Little Sandy Review* 12, 3–10, 48–53. Much of the music recorded at the festival (240 tapes running 300 hours) is now deposited in the University of Chicago Folk Festival Recordings Collection in the Chicago Public Library (obtained from WFMT 98.7).

65. *Friends of Old-Time Music: The Folk Arrival, 1961–1965* (Smithsonian Folkways SFW 40160), a three-CD boxed set that includes notes by Peter Siegel and additional essays by

John Cohen and Jody Stecher. I also had a telephone interview with Peter Siegel from New York, November 9, 2007.

66. After Ralph Rinzler joined the Greenbriar Boys, the trio included Rinzler, Bob Yellin, and John Herald. They were first recorded on the anthology *New Folks* (Vanguard VRS-9096) and then on their own in *The Greenbriar Boys* (Vanguard VRS-9104) and *Ragged but Right* (Vanguard VSD 79159). Roscoe Holcomb was first heard on *Mountain Music of Kentucky* (Folkways FA 2316, 1960) and later on an anthology called *The High Lonesome Sound* (Folkways FA 2368, 1965). Cohen said that "the High Lonesome Sound" entered the terminology of bluegrass music after he gave Ralph Rinzler permission to use it on an album of Bill Monroe's music; John Cohen, telephone conversation, November 11, 2010.

67. Ashley is quoted in Philip F. Gura, "Roots and Branches: Forty Years of the New Lost City Ramblers," *Old-Time Herald* 7, no. 2 (November 1999–January 2000): 31.

68. McMichen's quote was first printed in Paul Nelson, "Newport: The Folk Spectacle Comes of Age," *Sing Out!* 14 (November 1964) and reprinted in John Bealle, *Old-Time Music and Dance: Community and Folk Revival* (Bloomington, Ind.: Quarry Books, 2005).

69. Ralph Rinzler, interview with Kate Rinzler, Folklife Archives and Collections, Center for Folklife and Cultural Heritage, Smithsonian Institution.

70. Doc Watson has elicited a voluminous library of articles and essays. Kent Gustavson, though, has written a full-scale biography titled *Blind but Now I See: The Biography of Music Legend Doc Watson* (New York: Blooming Twig Books, 2010).

71. Allen, *Gone to the Country*, 88.

72. Tom Paley, interview with Richard Straw, October 24, 1988; Allen, *Gone to the Country*, 95–96.

73. The three Ramblers gave their versions of the breakup in various interviews; Ray Allen tells the story in *Gone to the Country*, 116–17. Letters in the Moe Asch collection provide examples of the bitter nature of the feud. For example, Mark Berenson, a lawyer who represented Tom Paley, wrote to Mike on October 25, 1962, and asked Mike and John to stop using the name "New Lost City Ramblers." In a phone interview with Richard Straw from London on October 24, 1988, Paley said that he eventually got a $750 settlement and agreed to give up the use of the name. A summation of Paley's current activities is on his website, Tom Paley's Traditional Music, www.wildernessroad.net/tompaley.

74. My information on Tracy Schwarz came from a telephone interview, January 8, 2004; a letter from him, January 9, 2004; and interviews with Mike Seeger (February 5, 2004) and John Cohen (February 3, 2004). I also profited greatly from Richard Straw's interview with Schwarz (August 2, 1988).

75. Bill Clifton, interview, December 23, 2004.

76. Ibid.; Joe Ross, "Bill Clifton: Preserving the Old Songs," *Bluegrass Unlimited* 28, no. 1 (July 1993): 36–44.

77. "Rick Townend and Bill Clifton," http://www.ricktownend.co.uk/Rick-BillClifton.htm and www.ricktownend.co.uk/EMB.htm.

78. Two good websites devoted to Strachwitz and his musical contributions are Joel Selvin, "Music Man," http://articles.sfgate.com/2008-01-13/living/17150461_1_marc-

savoy-cajun-strachwitz-s-arhoolie-records (January 13, 2008); and Larry Benicewicz, "Chris Strachwitz and the Arhoolie Record Story," http://www.bluesart.at/NeueSeiten/pageA54.html.

79. Mike borrowed a small battery-powered reel-to-reel recording unit and taped much of the group's conversation and occasional music making as they traveled from place to place. He also kept a log of what he collected. I also saw a letter that John Cohen wrote to Moe Asch concerning the drinking habits of the musicians (no date given). Bear Family produced two CDs of music made on the tour but did not keep them in circulation: *American Folk and Country Festival* (Bear Family BFFM 16849, 2008).

80. Jon Pankake, "Ten Years in New Lost City," *Sing Out!* 18, no. 4 (October-November 1968): 31, 73.

81. Ray Allen says that tension between Mike and John had surfaced as early as 1965 and may have been provoked in part by John's resentment over Mike's solo career; Allen, *Gone to the Country*, 164. Mike seldom spoke of such matters to me, but his irritation with John had been expressed in letters to Moe Asch.

82. Derek Halsey, "The New Lost City Ramblers Last Ever Concert at Clifftop 2009," http://swampland.com/articles/view/title:folk_music_legend_mike_seeger_dies_at_75.

83. Craig Morrison, "Folk Revival Roots Still Evident in the 1990's: Recordings of San Francisco Veterans," *Journal of American Folklore* 114, no. 454 (Fall 2001): 478–88.

84. Cohen, notes to *On the Great Divide* (Smithsonian Folkways FW 31041, 1975).

Chapter 5

1. Jon Pankake, "Ten Years in New Lost City," *Sing Out!* 18, no. 4 (October-November 1968): 75.

2. Chris Darrow, quoted in Richie Unterberger, *Urban Spacemen and Wayfaring Strangers*, 83, http://www.richieunterberger.com/darrow.html.

3. Bob Dylan, "Blowin' in the Wind," *Hootenanny* 1, no. 1 (December 1963): 19.

4. Bob Dylan, *Chronicles: Volume One* (New York: Simon and Schuster, 2004), 70–71.

5. Ralph Rinzler, interview with Kate Rinzler, May 1990, Ralph Rinzler Collection, Smithsonian Folk Life, FP-2006-CT-0051. Transcribed to a disc by Jack Manischewitz, December 29, 2009.

6. The Swarthmore date was confirmed in an e-mail message from Mike Seeger to Ray Allen and me, February 26, 2009. Mike has expressed his reverence for Libba in several conversations and interviews.

7. Remembered by Allen Hopkins; available on the website Mandolin Café Message Board, August 8, 2009.

8. Peggy Seeger, interview, March 15, 2004.

9. Bill Clifton's recollections of and tribute to Mike Seeger are on the Bluegrass Blog, www.thebluegrassblog.com/wp-print.php?p=6309; also my interview with Clifton, December 23, 2009.

10. The album included notes written by Charles Seeger and a version of Libba Cotten's "Freight Train," sung by Peggy, under the title "Freight Train Blues."

11. Letter to Mike from Peggy Seeger, May 25, 1958 (in Alexia Seeger's possession).

12. Henry Sapoznik, e-mail, June 16, 2010.

13. D. K. Wilgus, liner notes to the LP *Mike Seeger* (Vanguard).

14. Jon Pankake and Paul Nelson, *Little Sandy Review* 30 (1965): 19.

15. Archie Green, notes to the LP *Tipple, Loom, and Rail*.

16. Peter Goldsmith, *Making People's Music: Moe Asch and Folkways Records* (Washington, D.C.: Smithsonian Institution, 1998), 339.

17. Mike's recording ventures are outlined in his logs, sometimes with brief comments about the performance or his reaction to it.

18. This music can be heard on Kilby Snow, Kenneth and Neriah Benfield, and Ernest Stoneman, *Mountain Music Played on the Autoharp* (Folkways 2365). See also Joe Riggs, "Kilby Snow and His Influential Music Style," The Field Recorders' Collective, http://www.fieldrecorder.com/docs/notes/ksnow_riggs.htm.

19. Mike's association with Maybelle Carter and her performances at the Ash Grove are discussed by Mark Zwonitzer with Charles Hirschberg in *Will You Miss Me When I'm Gone? The Carter Family and Their Legacy in American Music* (New York: Simon and Schuster, 2002), 340–45. I also learned much about Mike's relationship with Maybelle Carter through his recollections and interviews.

20. In 1966 Sara and Maybelle recorded again: *A Historic Reunion* (Columbia CS-9361). These recordings and others were reissued in 1999 on *Sara and Maybelle Carter* (Bear Family BCD 15471).

21. Eck Robertson's early recordings are discussed in Bill C. Malone, *Country Music, U.S.A.* (Austin: University of Texas Press, 2010), 35–36. A very good short biography of Robertson can be found at http://oldtimemusic.com/FHOFEck.html.

22. Robertson's recordings can be heard on two LPs: *Famous Cowboy Fiddler* (County 202), recorded in Amarillo in 1963; and *Master Fiddler* (Sonyatone STR-201), consisting of items recorded in the 1920s. His songs have also been issued on a CD titled *Old-Time Texas Fiddler* (County CD-3515, 1998).

23. The relationship between Riddle and the Carter Family is discussed by Zwonitzer and Hirshberg in *Will You Miss Me When I'm Gone?*, 128–33, 136–38, 184. Riddle can be heard doing "John Henry" on the CD compilation of over forty musicians recorded "in the field" by Mike Seeger: *Close to Home: Old Time Music from Mike Seeger's Collection, 1952–1967* (Smithsonian Folkways CD 40097, 1997). One finds a variety of material on Riddle on the Web, including "The Lesley Riddle Story," http://tvgnc.org/index.php?option=com_content&view=article&id=5:lesley-riddle-bio; and Wes Bunch, "Lesley Riddle's Music Finally Gaining Recognition," *Kingsport Times-News*, February 21, 2009, http://www.timesnews.net/article.php?id=9011949.

24. Archie Green has written the best account of Merle Travis in *Only a Miner: Studies in Recorded Coal Mining Songs* (Urbana: University of Illinois Press, 1972). Travis's Jordan

Hall concert became available in 2003 on the CD *In Boston, 1959* (Rounder 82161), with notes by Mike Seeger.

25. Some of the better accounts of Boggs and his legacy include Jack Wright, "Only Remembered for What He Has Done—Dock Boggs," *Old-Time Herald* 6, no. 5 (2005); William Hogeland, "Corn Bread When I'm Hungry," *The Atlantic*, November 1998, www .theatlantic.com/past/docs/issues/98nov/banjo.htm; Barry O'Connell, notes to *Dock Boggs: His Folkways Years, 1963–1968* (Smithsonian Folkways SF 40108); Mike Seeger, notes to *Legendary Singer and Banjo Player* (Folkways FA 2351, 1964); and Mike Seeger, Jon Pankake, Kinney Rorrer, and Willis Poyner, "Dock Boggs: Memories and Appreciations," *Old-Time Herald* 6, no. 6 (2006).

26. *Folkways, Vol. 1* (FA 2351); *Folkways, Vol. 2* (FA 2392); *Folkways, Vol. 3* (FA 3903); and excerpts from *Interviews with Dock Boggs, Legendary Singer and Banjo Player* (FA 5498). Revenant issued a CD collection of Boggs's songs titled *Complete Early Recordings, 1927–29* (Revenant RVN 205).

27. Boggs's quote is in "I Always Loved the Lonesome Songs," *Sing Out!* 14, no. 3 (July 1964): 32–37.

28. Molly Tenenbaum, review of "Country Blues," *Old-Time Herald* 6, no. 5 (Fall 1998).

29. Miltowns had only been introduced in 1955 as a tranquilizing drug. Information about Mike's anxieties and his searches for a cure came from his recollections and interviews.

30. Bill Clifton, interview, December 23, 2009.

31. Marge Seeger Ostrow, interview, February 19, 2004.

32. Ray Allen said that serious differences between Seeger and Cohen surfaced as early as 1965. Evidence of Mike's displeasure with John showed up in letters deposited in the Moe Asch Collection: letter from Mike to John, July 30, 1975; and letter from Mike to Moe Asch, also July 30, 1975.

33. The Libba Cotten, McGee Brothers, and Arthur Smith recordings are listed on Mike Seeger, Catalogue of Recordings, Books, and Videos at mikeseeger.info/catalog.html. Walt Crowley talks about the Sky River Rock Festival in *Rites of Passage: A Memoir of the Sixties in Seattle* (Seattle: University of Washington Press, 1995), quoted by Alan J. Stein on the Free Online Encyclopedia of Washington State, HistoryLink.org/essays/output.cfm?file_ id=5425.

34. There are many good sources on Reno's style and career, including his autobiography, *The Musical History of Don Reno* (privately printed in Hyattsville, Maryland, ca. 1975); Todd Callaway, "Don Reno," Mountain Grown Music: Celebrating the Traditional Mountain Music of Haywood County, North Carolina, www.mountaingrownmusic.org/don-reno .html; the website of the International Bluegrass Museum, Owensboro, Kentucky, http:// www.bluegrass-museum.org/general/zbiodonreno.php; and, of course, Neil V. Rosenberg, *Bluegrass: A History* (Urbana: University of Illinois Press, 2005).

35. Alice, on the other hand, does not remember them singing at all during their first meetings.

36. Alice does not remember the precise meeting place, but Hazel was adamant that the event occurred either in or near Alyse's apartment on Eager Street in Baltimore.

37. The basic details of the Hazel and Alice partnership are in the notes to their CDs and in Hazel Dickens and Bill C. Malone, *Working Girl Blues: The Life and Music of Hazel Dickens* (Urbana: University of Illinois Press, 2005).

38. Mike and Alice had actually been recorded on another album, *Mike and Alice Seeger in Concert* (King SKK 662), during a live concert in 1970 in Japan.

39. Alice Gerrard Foster, "Merle Haggard: I Take a Lot of Pride in What I Am," *Sing Out!* 19, no. 5 (March/April 1970): 11–17.

40. Letter to me from Tracy Schwarz, January 9, 2004. Richard Spottswood provided a good account of the group in his notes to the CD reissue of *The Strange Creek Singers* (Arhoolie 9003).

41. The lyrics of the song are included in Dickens and Malone, *Working Girl Blues*, 74–75.

42. Accounts of the Southern Folk Cultural Revival Project that have been useful to me include Gene Guerrero, "Anne Romaine," *Southern Changes* 17, nos. 3–4 (1995): 15–17; Patricia Hall, "Folk Visions and Voices," *Southern Exposure* (January-February 1986): 23–28; and Bernice Johnson Reagon, "Let the Songs and Singing Lead: The Southern Folk Festival and and Shared Music Traditions beyond Race," http://cirit.osu.edu/clustertwo/culturalcirc/abstracts/ReagonBJ.pdf.

43. Reagon, "Let the Songs and Singing Lead."

44. Dickens and Malone, *Working Girl Blues*. My conversations with Hazel Dickens have continued off and on for over ten years. They began as formal dialogues and interviews in about February 2000, when she appeared as a guest performer and lecturer in my seminars at Duke University and the University of North Carolina at Chapel Hill titled "Women in American Country and Folk Music" (Lehman Brady Visiting Joint Chair Professorship in Documentary Studies and American Studies). Videotaped copies of Dickens's presentations and performances are on file in the Southern Folklife Collection at UNC–Chapel Hill. My first formal interview with her concerning *Working Girl Blues* occurred backstage at the Old Town School of Folk Music in Chicago on November 10, 2002.

45. Information about the poster, *Mike Seeger and the New Lost City Ramblers*, came from Howard Romaine (e-mail message to me, August 8, 2006). Mike Seeger told me about Anne's love for Loretta Lynn's music.

46. Ray Allen, *Gone to the Country: The New Lost City Ramblers and the Folk Music Revival* (Urbana: University of Illinois Press, 2010), 187–88.

47. McCarn's version of "Cotton Mill Colic" and twenty-three additional textile songs can be heard on the CD *Gastonia Gallop* (Old Hat CD 1007).

48. Information about the wedding came from Mike Seeger and Hazel Dickens, as well as from Archie Green's "Reader's Report" on the manuscript copy of *Working Girl Blues* sent by Archie Green to Judith McCulloh, June 9, 2004.

49. "Upkeep" was not the only problem that contributed to Mike and Alice's problems.

The move to Pennsylvania was not universally welcomed by everyone. Alice said that she always had reservations about it. Her eldest daughter, Cory, decided to go away to school. The other kids seemed to like the countryside and the space afforded by the big house.

50. Harmony Sisters, *The Early Years* (Harmony Sound 2000), a CD compilation of Flying Fish LPs (1981 and 1983).

51. Richard Spottswood tells the story of the Strange Creek Singers in his notes to their CD collection.

52. Seeger and Rinzler detailed their personal responses to the public-sector folklorists in their interviews with Kate Rinzler; Allen gave his assessment in *Gone to the Country*, 198.

53. An explanation of the "true vine" can be found at http://calautoharp.com/2006/MikeSeeger.html.

54. Gene Bluestein (1928–2002) was an English professor, musician, folklorist, and social activist. With NEA funding, he established a semester-long folk-artist-in-residence program that brought musicians like Mike Seeger to the Fresno campus.

55. Information on the Fresno residency was provided by Mike Seeger. Tommy Collins and the Bakersfield country music scene are well covered in two books: Gerald Haslam, *Workin' Man Blues: Country Music in California* (Berkeley: University of California Press, 1999); and Peter La Chapelle, *Proud to Be an Okie: Cultural Politics, Country Music, and Migration to Southern California* (Berkeley: University of California Press, 2007).

56. The string-band resurgence of the late sixties and early seventies is discussed by Norm Cohen, "The Folk Revival: Revisited, Revived, and Revised," *Journal of American Folklore* 103, no. 410 (October-December 1990): 514–25; John Cohen, "The Folksong Revival—A Historical Perspective, Part II," *Old-Time Herald* 3, no. 4 (Summer 1992): 34–40; and R. Raymond Allen, "Old-Time Music and the Urban Folk Revival" (master's thesis, Western Kentucky University, April 1981).

57. For further information on Freeman, see Marshall Wyatt, "Every County Has Its Own Personality: An Interview with David Freeman," *Old-Time Herald* 7, no. 2 (November 1999–January 2000): 12–20, 36. John Cohen also interviewed Freeman in "County Records Reissues," *Sing Out!* 19, no. 2 (July-August 1969): 49, 51. Charles Faurot had been in communication with Mike Seeger since at least 1957. In a letter dated October 20, 1957, he had asked Mike about the construction of fretless banjos. The County LPs produced by Faurot were rereleased on a CD in 2006. They were remembered and praised by Paul Brown in a story titled "Historic Recordings Tell Clawhammer Banjo History" on *All Things Considered*, National Public Radio, March 21, 2006. Charles Wolfe discussed the important role played by County Records in "County Records and Blue Ridge Music," *Appalachian Journal* 7 (Spring 1980): 234–38. Another useful account is Robert Cochran, "Rise and Bloom Again: County Records and the Legacy of Tommy Jarrell," *Gadfly* (January/February 2000), http://www.gadflyonline.com/archive/JanFeb00/archive-riseandbloom.html.

58. Ray Alden, "Music from the Round Peak," *Old-Time Music* 19 (1975–76): 8–16; Paul Brown, interview, February 7, 2004. See also Mark Rubin's interview with Henry Sapoznik, originally in the *Banjo Newsletter* and available at www.markrubin.com/sapoznik.html.

59. Richard Straw interviewed Alan Jabbour at the Library of Congress in Washington, D.C., on March 11, 1987. I interviewed Jabbour by telephone from Washington, D.C., on December 3, 2004. Jabbour talked about his mentor in "The Art and Influence of Henry Reed," *Folklife Center News* 22, no. 3 (Summer 2000): 10–12. One of the best items on Tommy Jarrell that I have seen is Ray Alden, "Tommy Jarrell," The Field Recorders' Collective (FRC 211 and FRC 212), http://www.fieldrecorder.com/docs/notes/jarrell_alden .htm. Alden talks about the discovery of Jarrell in his notes to *Tommy and Fred* (County CD 2702). Another good description of Jarrell and Round Peak music is "Tommy Jarrell and Fred Cockerham: North Carolina Fiddle and Fretless Banjo," *Musical Traditions*, no. 11 (1993), http://mustrad.org.uk/articles/jarrell.httm. One of the earliest examples of the string-band resurgence came with the recording of *The Hollow Rock String Band* (Kanawha 311). The Highwoods String Band first recorded in 1973. Their early recordings have been reissued on *Feed Your Babies Onions* (Rounder 11569).

60. Interview with Alice Gerrard, December 17, 2009; Mike Seeger's reminiscences, March, 2007 (transcribed by Charmaine Harbort, Madison, Wisc.).

61. *Sing Out!* 21, no. 6 (1972): 18.

62. Alice Gerrard, telephone interview, December 17, 2009. Mike's remarks came from both telephone conversations (especially the one on June 28, 2009) and e-mail exchanges. Hazel Dickens provided her recollections of Mike and Alice's relationship in a phone conversation on November 23, 2009.

63. See Bess Lomax Hawes, *Sing It Pretty: A Memoir* (Urbana: University of Illinois Press, 2008).

64. Da Costa Woltz and his Southern Broadcasters recorded eighteen songs for Gennett in 1927. They are now available on CD on the Document label (DOCD-8023). Tony Russell provides a discussion of the group in *Country Music Originals: The Legends and the Lost* (New York: Oxford University Press, 2007). *Sprout Wings and Fly* is available from Flower Films, 10341 San Pablo Avenue, El Cerrito, California. A brief segment of the film can be viewed on YouTube. Tommy Jarrell's LP, *Sail Away Ladies* (County 756), with descriptive notes by Barry Poss, is a fine introduction to his music. He typically introduces each song with an explanation of where and from whom he first heard it.

65. Yasha Aginsky, telephone interview, December 15, 2009. The forty-minute film can be viewed online at Folkstreams.net/film,153.

66. Mike's Grammy nominations and other awards are outlined on his website.

67. Letter from Charles Seeger to Mike Seeger, April 19, 1964.

68. Ann M. Pescatello, *Charles Seeger: A Life in American Music* (Pittsburgh: University of Pittsburgh Press, 1992), 286. In their edited book *Understanding Charles Seeger: Pioneer in American Musicology* (Urbana: University of Illinois Press, 1999), Bell Yung and Helen Rees noted that the wide-ranging influence of Seeger's scholarship could be discerned from the obituaries that he received in such journals as *Ethnomusicology, Journal of American Folklore, Musical Quarterly*, and *Yearbook of the International Folk Music Council*.

69. Charles had used some of Mike's documentary LPs in his ethnomusicology classes.

He described the Scruggs-style LP as a "grand record" (letter to Mike, August 22, 1957) and asked for a copy of the first New Lost City Ramblers' LP (letter to Mike, May 24, 1959).

70. John McCutcheon is a Wisconsin-born singer and musician who has long lived in Georgia. He recorded his first album, *How Can I Keep from Singing?*, in 1974. With over thirty albums and at least six Grammy nominations, he has carved out one of the most successful and influential careers in the folk music revival. "Christmas in the Trenches" is probably his best-known song.

71. Letter from Mike Seeger to Moe Asch, April 28, 1983. The other details of Mike's career came from interviews and his recollections.

72. Alice Gerrard, interview, December 17, 2009; Hazel Dickens, phone conversation, November 23, 2009.

73. Mike Seeger, phone conversation, March 1, 2007; Mike Seeger, various e-mails.

Chapter 6

1. These concerns were voiced to me in telephone calls made by Mike Seeger on March 1, 2007, and July 17, 2009. Mike's fascination with Virginia probably began as early as 1941, when he traveled to Galax with his father. Visits with Wade Ward much later in Independence, Virginia, confirmed his attachment to the rural flavor of the state.

2. Brad Leftwich, Al Tharp, and Odell McGuire, "The Complete History of the Plank Road String Band and the Lexington, Va., Music Scene," The Field Recorders' Collective, http://www.fieldrecorder.com/docs/notes/plankroad.htm; Tad Dickens, "Geologist McGuire Championed Old Music," *Roanoke Times*, December 17, 2008, www.roanoke.com/news/roanoke/wb/187921.

3. Mike Seeger, telephone conversations and e-mail messages.

4. I talked to David Winston by phone on November 13, 2010, and he sent me a copy of the talk that he gave at the memorial celebration in Lexington, Virginia, on September 27, 2009. The talk was also quoted by reporter Tad Dickens in "A Memorial in Music for Scholar, Performer Mike Seeger," *Roanoke Times*, September 28, 2009, http://roanoke.com/news/roanoke/wb/220522.

5. See www.rockbridgefestival.org.

6. The varied programs promoted by the Virginia Commission for the Arts are outlined on its website: http://www.arts.state.va.us/. The exhibition on Virginia roots music stressed the contributions made by commercial recording companies and folklorists in collecting and documenting the impressive body of grassroots music forms found in the state. Mike's role in environmental protection and conservation were remembered by reporter Kit Huffman at a memorial in Lexington and quoted by Tad Dickens in "A Memorial in Music for Scholar."

7. Stefanini's official website is www.rafestefanini.com. At Mike Seeger's memorial service in Bethesda, Stefanini recalled that the Stefanini Brothers had dressed in black clothes and vests because the New Lost City Ramblers did.

8. Information on Ralph Epperson and WPAQ were obtained from an interview made with him by Paul Brown for National Public Radio's *All Things Considered* on June 1, 2006. It was called "Ralph Epperson: Beloved Voice of the Blue Ridge" and can be found online at http://www.npr.org/templates/story/story.php?storyId=5444800. See also the liner notes by Paul Brown for the CD *WPAQ: The Voice of the Blue Ridge Mountains* (Rounder CD 0404).

9. Dick Hulan told me about this event many years ago. I have since seen a microfilm copy of the advertisement for the festival in the *Virginia Gazette*. The event is often mentioned by students of the fiddle. For example, see Chris Goertzen, "Balancing Local and National Approaches at American Fiddle Contests," *American Music* 14, no. 3 (Fall 1996): 352–81. For a discussion of the importance of dancing in southern working-class culture and country music, see the chapter on "dancing" in Bill C. Malone, *Don't Get above Your Raisin': Country Music and the Southern Working Class* (Urbana: University of Illinois Press, 2002).

10. The *Talking Feet* documentary can be seen online at http://www.folkstreams.net/film,121. The origins, production, and bibliography of the film are also outlined on the Folkstreams website.

11. Tim Jones review, *William and Mary News*, August 13, 2003.

12. Mike Seeger, "Catalog," http://mikeseeger.info/catalog.html.

13. One of the best short discussions of the origins of the Muhlenberg guitar style, and a modification of the Kennedy Jones story, is Erika Brady, "That Muhlenberg Sound: Western Kentucky's Unique Guitar Style," Kentucky Folklife Program, Western Kentucky University, http://www.wku.edu/kentuckyfolkweb/KYFolklife_Muhlenburg.html. For an introduction to the style itself, see Tommy Flint, *Mel Bay Presents the Merle Travis Guitar Style* (Pacific, Mo.: Mel Bay Publications, 1995).

14. "Where Things Are Beautiful: Time Spent with Nimrod Workman," October 14, 2008, http://roothogordie.wordpress.com/category/kentucky. Appalshop in Whitesburg, Kentucky, produced a video documentary of Workman called *Nimrod Workman: To Fit My Own Category* (AF 6022). Also worth seeing is the show devoted to Workman produced on the Down Home Radio Show website, http://www.downhomeradioshow.com/2007/05/nimrod-workman-feature-episode/.

15. *Retrograss* was released on Grisman's Acoustic Disc label. In his review in *No Depression*, Jon Weisberger said that not every experiment on the CD worked, but that "at its best . . . the album more than justifies Seeger's liner notes' claim that 'it won't be boring—at least not for long.'" *No Depression*, no. 24 (December 1999).

16. Much of my information on the Berkeley–San Francisco scene came from a phone interview with Hank Bradley in Seattle on December 9, 2009, and a lengthy e-mail from Bradley on December 14, 2009. Molly Tenenbaum and Kerry Blech were also very informative in "Hank Bradley: A Fiddler from the Villages," *Old-Time Herald* 1, no. 2 (Winter 1987–88): 28–34. For information on Mac Benford's bands and career, see his website, "My Musical Life," http://macbenford.com/id2.html. I also had a helpful phone interview

with him on January 26, 2004. Alice Gerrard wrote a very cogent article titled "Colby Street to New York and Points South: The Highwoods String Band," *Old-Time Herald* 3, no. 4 (Summer 1992): 26–32.

17. Mike Seeger, quoted in Emily Friedman, "The Prospects for Traditional Music: A Talk with Mike Seeger and Tony Barrand," *Come for to Sing: Folk Music in Chicago and the Midwest* 10, no. 1 (Winter 1884). Mike also spoke often to me about the young musicians' indifference to singing. It should be noted, however, that singing has revived since the 1980s among such string-band enthusiasts as Carol Elizabeth Jones, Norman Blake, Tim O'Brien, Robin and Linda Williams, Uncle Earl, and Jim Watson.

18. Rita Weill wrote the tongue-in-cheek liner notes for the Berkeley Farms recording. They are excerpted in The Berkeley Old Time Music Convention, www.berkeleyoldtime music.org/history.html. Mayne Smith also talks about this scene in "Redwood Canyon Ramblers," www.maynesmith.com/redwood.htm. John Cohen also recorded the Berkeley scene, but this music was not released until 2007, when it appeared on a CD called *Berkeley in the 1960s* (Field Recorders Collective FRC 609).

19. These recordings are all available on Mike's website. I had a short telephone interview with Tim O'Brien from Nashville on December 14, 2009, and a lengthy e-mail response from Carol Elizabeth Jones dated January 16, 2007.

20. Alexia Smith, telephone interview, July 17, 2007.

21. Ibid.

22. Although both Mike and Alexia told me about their wedding, I learned additional information from Hazel Dickens. Peter Gott was a graduate of Cornell who, with his wife, made a home in Shelton Laurel, North Carolina. He was a singer of traditional songs, a banjo player, and a master builder of log cabins. He is given much credit for reinvigorating the performance of traditional balladry in western North Carolina.

23. David Winston, memorial celebration for Mike Seeger, Lexington, Virginia, September 27, 2009.

24. There are several explanations of the disease on the Web. The one I have relied on is by the Leukemia and Lymphoma Society, http://www.leukemia-lymphoma.org/hm_lls. John Hartford died of lymphoma on June 4, 2001, after a twenty-one-year battle. Mike Seeger reminisced about him in *Old-Time Herald* 8, no. 1 (2001). Mike used the phrase "a very full and happy life" in his taped reminiscences.

25. *Frets* magazine concentrated on all kinds of acoustic roots music. It is now defunct. Elderly Instruments of Lansing, Michigan, advertised online that it had complete runs of the issues of *Frets* published between 1979 and 1989 (www.elderly.com/vintage/items/300U-1777.htm).

26. A great introduction to Smith's music and personality is the series of recordings made in Chicago by a local collector and folklorist, *In Sacred Trust: The 1963 Fleming Brown Tapes* (Smithsonian Folkways). Flemons tells the story of his relationship with Mike Seeger on YouTube (Don Flemons at Jammin Java, December 7, 2009) and at www.myspace.com/donflemonsmusic.

27. One of the most fascinating aspects of the widespread vogue of the five-string banjo

in our time is the renewed recognition of the role played by African American musicians in its history and styles. See Cecelia Conway, *African Banjo Echoes in Appalachia: A Study of Folk Traditions* (Knoxville: University of Tennessee Press, 1995). The first Black Banjo Gathering Then and Now met at Appalachian State University in Boone, North Carolina, April 7–10, 2005, and has convened annually since that time.

28. Todd Cambio, e-mail, December 9, 2009. Cambio also discussed his relationship with Mike Seeger in "A Guitar for Mike Seeger," http://fraulini.blogspot.com/2009/03/guitar-for-mike-seeger.html.

29. See Mike's website. To cite one example of Mike's use of the lecture/concert format: at the Festival of the Rivers in Hinton, West Virginia, he gave four separate concerts featuring "Tipple, Loom, and Rail" and other educational topics advertised on his website.

30. The Oberlin Folk Festival (May 2003) can be heard on an MP3 on the Down Home Radio Show site. Tom Martin-Erickson was the host of the long-running folk music show *Simply Folk*, broadcast on Sundays on Wisconsin Public Radio in Madison. He typically records the Sugar Maple Festival each year.

31. Student evaluations were printed on Professor Pen's website, http://pen-points .blogspot.com.

32. Material collected by Collins is in the Fletcher Collins Jr. Collection of the Library of Congress, AFC 1939/003, which includes thirty-four twelve-inch discs recorded under the auspices of the WPA Joint Committee on Folk Arts and the Library of Congress from 1935 to 1942. Some information about Fletcher Collins appears in an article about his son, Francis S. Collins, who was director of the National Human Genome Research Institute and the National Institutes of Health, in Peter J. Boyer, "The Covenant," *New Yorker*, September 6, 2010, 60–67. Dawn Medley discussed Fletcher Collins in "He Led with Love," *MBC News* (Mary Baldwin College), http://www.mbc.edu/news/r_detail.php?id=1665.

33. Colonial Faire is described on the Hesperus website, http://hesperus.org/schedule .php. Julie Powell discusses the relationship between Hesperus and Mike Seeger in "Celtic Roots," http://www.onlineathens.com/stories/042999/mar_celtics.shtml; and Dan Willging adds to that discussion with "Hesperus: 8 Centuries & 4 Continents of Music," *Dirty Linen*, no. 85 (December 1999–January 2000).

34. Mike emulated various forms of traditional country hollering at festivals and workshops. He seems to have become fascinated with the phenomenon because of the contests held at Spivey's Corner, North Carolina, which have gone on for over forty years.

35. The event at Stanford featuring the Ying Quartet and Mike Seeger ("No Boundaries") on November 30, 2005, is described online at http://events.stanford.edu/events/64/6468. Announcements and descriptions of similar events are at http://blog.syracuse.com/critics/2007/08/skaneateles_festival_opening_n.html; and http://www.esm.rochester .edu/faculty/?id=19. Alexia Smith also discussed her recollections of these classical events in her conversations with me.

36. The composer of "John Hardy's Dream" is discussed in "Romeo Named Interim Director of the Crooked Road," in *A! Magazine for the Arts* 17, no. 1 (October 26, 2008), http://www.artsmagazine.info/articles.php?view=detail&id=2008102618533768867.

37. "Aaron Copland and His World" (Bard College press release for Bard Music Festival), http://www.bard.edu/news/releases/pr/fstory.php?id=877. See also "Special Selections in Honor of Aaron Copland's Centennial," Janus Museum, http://www.janusmuseum.org/.

38. Judith Tick, telephone interview, March 22, 2010.

39. Ruth Crawford Seeger Conference Schedule of Events, Brooklyn College, City University of New York, October 26–27, 2001, http://depthome.brooklyn.cuny.edu/isam/rcsout.html.

40. The schedule for the musical phase of the event was printed as "Seeger Family Concert" in "How Can I Keep From Singing? A Seeger Family Tribute," http://www.loc.gov/folklife/Seegersymposium/concertlog.html. Mike Joyce wrote the review "No Bruce, but Plenty of Seegers to Go around, Thank You," *Washington Post*, March 18, 2007, http://www.washingtonpost.com/wp-dyn/content/article/2007/03/17/AR2007031701299.html.

41. Some of Mike's awards are listed on his website at http://mikeseeger.info/about.html. The Bess Lomax Hawes National Endowment Fellowship is described at http://www.nea.gov/news/news09/2009-NEA-Heritage-Fellows-Announced.html.

42. Tribute to Archie Green, April 23, 2009,, posted on http://kmunson-mac.blogspot.com/2009/04/tribute-to-archie-green.html. Hazel Dickens, telephone conversation, August 27, 2009.

43. Juli Thanki, "At Birchmere, Banjos, and Bonhomie," *Washington Post*, July 13, 2009, http://www.washingtonpost.com/wp-dyn/content/article/2009/07/12/AR2009071202036.html. John Lohman reminisced about Mike and the Wintergreen event, as well as about receiving the news of Mike's fatal illness, in http://blog.encyclopediavirginia.org/2009/08/10/remembering-mike-seeger.

44. Alexia Smith described Mike's last few days in her welcoming address at his memorial — held at the St. Mark Presbyterian Church on December 6, 2009, in Bethesda, Maryland — and in "Remembering Mike," the brochure prepared for the gathering. She also shared these memories in conversations with me and in various e-mails. Hazel Dickens, in a telephone conversation on August 5, 2009, told me about her last meeting with Mike.

Chapter 7

1. Alexia Smith, e-mail, December 2, 2010.

2. Quoted in the notes to the New Lost City Ramblers, *There Ain't No Way Out* (Smithsonian Folkways CD SF 40098, 1997).

3. Mike Seeger, "A Contemporary Folk Esthetic," *Sing Out!* 16, no. 1 (February/March 1966): 59–61; Mike Seeger, interview with Richard Straw, Lexington, Kentucky, March 18, 1984; Pete Kuykendall, telephone interview, February 17, 2004.

4. Quoted in Madelyn Rosenberg, "Music from the True Vine," *Roanoke Times*, http://squealermusic.com/madclips/clips/seeger.html. More information on Stoneman is available in Roni Stoneman, as told to Ellen Wright, *Pressing On: The Roni Stoneman Story* (Urbana: University of Illinois Press, 2007).

5. The Appalachian String Band Music Festival, which is generally referred to as Clifftop, began in 1990 under the auspices of the West Virginia Division of Culture and History. John Lilly provided a tribute and twenty-year retrospective of the event in "Open Arms at Clifftop: Appalachian String Band Music Festival at 20," *Goldenseal*, www.wvculture.org/goldenseal/summer09/clifftop.html.

Note on Sources

My research on Mike Seeger began as early as 1959, when I started buying records made by him and the New Lost City Ramblers. Not too long after that, I also obtained the important anthology that he produced for Folkways, *Mountain Music Bluegrass Style*, and his first solo album, *Old Time Country Music*. These were my introductions to the Folkways catalogue and to the eccentric but useful liner notes that the record jackets contained. Songs and information learned from these recordings, and from *The New Lost City Ramblers Song Book* (New York: Oak Publications, 1964), became significant ingredients of my first book, *Country Music, U.S.A.* (1968). I renewed my immersion in that material when I began working on this biography.

After our first real meeting in London in 2003, when we agreed that I would write his biography, Mike began providing contact information for his relatives and people who had been instrumental in his career. Only a couple of years later, he also began dictating reminiscences and detailed data about his life and career into a recording unit, which in turn were transcribed by Charmaine Harbort in Madison, Wisconsin. Mike typically filled up the tapes he was using and then taped over them after Charmaine had finished her transcriptions. Mike spent an enormous amount of time making these details of his life and career available. The reader can assume that when material is supplied in this manuscript without attribution, the information came from these dictated notes. This material, along with the taped interviews that I compiled, will be deposited in the Southern Folklife Collection at the University of North Carolina at Chapel Hill.

I also interviewed Mike Seeger extensively on February 5, 6, and 19, 2004. Since that time, I enjoyed contact with him quite often through phone calls, conversations, and e-mails. He even appeared at least a couple of times (September 2, 2002, and April 13, 2005) as a guest and cohost on my radio show, *Back to the Country*, on WORT-FM in Madison. These programs were also taped. He made available his recording logs, which detailed the performances that he recorded at his home in Maryland, at the country music parks in Pennsylvania and Maryland, and in other venues throughout the United States. I visited his home in Lexington, Virginia, for several days in April 2008 and was able to see an extensive number of personal letters, business records, brochures, flyers, promotional material, and other data that helped to clarify his career and personal relationships. I found other letters and similar data at the Ralph Rinzler Collection at the Smithsonian Institution (including the Moe Asch Collection) that were immensely helpful. Judith Tick also provided some letters and interviews that she had used in her biography of Mike's mother,

Ruth Crawford Seeger: A Composer's Search for American Music (New York: Oxford University Press, 1997). This material also included transcripts of interviews done with various members of the Seeger family by Matilda Gaume for her doctoral dissertation at Indiana University on Ruth Crawford Seeger in 1973 (published as *Ruth Crawford Seeger: Memories, Memoirs, Music* in 1986) and by Karen Cardullo for her master's thesis on Ruth Seeger at George Washington University in 1980.

Other interviews and conversations that proved very helpful to me were with Pete Seeger, Peggy Seeger, Barbara Seeger Perfect, Marjorie Seeger Marash, Alice Gerrard, Alexia Smith, Kim Seeger, John Cohen, Tracy Schwarz, Hazel Dickens, Richard Spottswood, Pete Kuykendall, Bill Clifton, Archie Green, Judith Tick, Alan Jabbour, Paul Brown, Dom Flemons, Ed Pearl, Roland White, Kate Hughes Rinzler, David Grisman, Yasha Aginsky, Tao Rodriguez-Seeger, David Winston, Tom Piazza, Hank Bradley, Mac Benford, Todd Cambio, Tim O'Brien, Phil Jamison, Rick March, and Peter K. Siegel. I did not interview Roger Abrahams, Carol Elizabeth Jones, Howard Romaine, Henry Sapoznik, or Israel Young, but I received lengthy and highly informative e-mails from each of them. Henry Sapoznik also read chapter 5 of my manuscript.

I also profited greatly from interviews conducted by other people who were gracious enough to make the transcripts or disc copies available to me. Richard Straw, of Radford College in Virginia, was extremely helpful to me. He did extensive interviews with Mike Seeger, Ralph Rinzler, John Cohen, Tom Paley, Tracy Schwarz, and Hazel Dickens. William Ferris sent me a copy of his published interviews with Charles Seeger (*Southern Cultures* 16, no. 3 [Fall 2010]: 54–72) as well as the original unedited interview on which the article was based. Michael F. Scully (Austin, Texas), who has written a fine study of the folk music revival titled *The Never-Ending Revival: Rounder Records and the Folk Alliance* (Urbana: University of Illinois Press, 2008), provided disc copies of some very insightful interviews that he did with Seeger, Cohen, and Schwarz in September 1993. Jeff Place, archivist for the Ralph Rinzler Folklife Archives and Collections at the Smithsonian Institution, provided me disc copies of interviews done by Kate Rinzler with Mike Seeger and Ralph Rinzler. Kate also consented to an interview and loaned me a copy of "A Source of Wonder," an unfinished biography of her husband, Ralph Rinzler, that she had worked on during the mid-1990s. The David Dunaway Collection of Interviews with Pete Seeger and Contemporaries at the American Folklife Center (AFC2000/019) is an invaluable resource based on the information that Dunaway compiled for his biography of Pete Seeger, *How Can I Keep from Singing? The Ballad of Pete Seeger* (New York: McGraw-Hill, 1981). Ronald D. Cohen, who has been extremely helpful in many ways, first made me aware of this collection and gave me transcripts of interviews done by Dunaway with Pete and Mike Seeger. The Dunaway Collection and other indispensable sources located at the American Folklife Center at the Library of Congress are listed in the Seeger Family Material in the Archive of Folk Culture, compiled by Todd Harvey on March 16, 2007, for the website How Can I Keep From Singing? A Seeger Family Tribute (http://www.loc.gov/folklife/Seegersymposium/).

Interviews with Mike Seeger, Peggy Seeger, Charles Seeger, and Pete Seeger abound on the Internet and in scattered journals. One source that I learned about too late to fully absorb, but which appears to be comprehensive in scope, is Adelaide G. Tusler and Ann M. Brieglet, *Reminiscences of an American Musicologist: Charles Seeger*, completed under the auspices of the Oral History Program at UCLA (Internet Archive: Digital Library of Free Books, 1972). John Cohen has also been interviewed extensively on the Internet (or in formats that later appeared there) and has also been prolific in telling his own story and that of the New Lost City Ramblers. Although much of this material is listed in my endnotes, I want to make special mention of the interviews done by Eli Smith for his great online folk music show, *Down Home Radio*. His interviews with Tom Paley and John Cohen were particularly insightful. Special note should be made of a lengthy (three and a half hours) online interview done by Tracie Wilson with Archie Green for the Campus Folk Song Club at the University of Illinois in Urbana-Champaign. The interview can be both read and heard, at www.library.illinois.edu. Richard Gagne also conducted a highly detailed interview with Ralph Rinzler, originally published as "Ralph Rinzler, Folklorist: Professional Biography" in *Folklore Forum* 27, no. 1 (1996) (https://scholarworks.iu.edu/dspace/bitstream/handle/2022/2206/27%281%29%2020-49.pdf?sequence=1).

Ray Allen's work, both published and unpublished, has been indispensable to me. He has been a constant informant and guide through conversations, e-mail messages, and published work. He and Ron Cohen also read the manuscript while it was being considered for publication. His support will be noted throughout my endnotes, but his book on the New Lost City Ramblers, *Gone to the Country: The New Lost City Ramblers and the Folk Music Revival* (Urbana: University of Illinois Press, 2010), merits special attention and praise. This book is one of the finest contributions yet made to the literature of the American folk music revival. I feel very fortunate that Allen made the uncorrected proofs of the book available to me.

I also feel lucky that I collected over the years an extensive amount of ephemera associated with the folk revival. Beginning in the early 1960s, I purchased copies of any folk and country music periodicals that I could find. These include numerous copies of *Sing Out!* magazine, the *Little Sandy Review*, *Caravan*, *Bluegrass Unlimited*, and assorted editions of various short-lived folkie publications. The *Little Sandy Review*, above all, proved immensely useful to me because its editors, Paul Nelson and Jon Pankake, were staunch but critical supporters of Mike Seeger and the New Lost City Ramblers. More recently, I have learned much from such publications as the *Old-Time Herald* and *No Depression* magazine (now an online journal).

Published books and articles dealing with Mike and the Seeger family and various aspects of American roots music appear frequently in my endnotes. I will list a few of them here. Judith Tick, *Ruth Crawford Seeger: A Composer's Search for American Music*, and Ann M. Pescatello, *Charles Seeger: A Life in American Music* (Pittsburgh: University of Pittsburgh Press, 1992), are the principal sources for my knowledge of Mike's parents. Other published contributions made by Tick have been utilized in my book, including "Ruth Crawford Seeger's Different Tunes," *ISAM Newsletter* 30, no. 2 (Spring 2001); and her collaboration with Larry Polansky, *Ruth Crawford Seeger: The Music of American Folk Song, and Selected Other Writings on American Folk Music* (Rochester: University of Rochester Press, 2001).

Philip F. Gura made the first serious study of the New Lost City Ramblers in "Southern Roots and Branches: Forty Years of the New Lost City Ramblers," *Southern Cultures* 6, no. 4 (2000): 58–81. A longer version, in two parts, first appeared in the *Old-Time Herald* (1999–2000), muse.jhu.edu/journals/southern_cultures/v006/6.4gura_fig06.html. Jon Weisberger wrote the finest short biography and critique of Mike Seeger: "Mike Seeger: True Stories," *No Depression*, no. 47 (September-October 2003), archives.nodepression. com/author/jon-weisberger/page/7/.

Ronald D. Cohen has been a prolific student of the folk revival, and I found most helpful his *Rainbow Quest: The Folk Music Revival and American Society, 1940–1970* (Boston: University of Massachusetts Press, 2002); *Wasn't That a Time! Firsthand Accounts of the Folk Music Revival* (Metuchen, N.J., 1995); and *Alan Lomax: Selected Writings, 1934–1997* (New York: Routledge, 2005). David K. Dunaway, *How Can I Keep from Singing? The Ballad of Pete Seeger* (New York: McGraw-Hill, 1981), is the best account of that iconic singer. Pete Seeger has also told his own story, including *The Incompleat Folk Singer* (New York: Simon and Schuster, 1972).

Other useful studies that relate to my work include John Bealle, *Old-Time Music and Dance: Community and Folk Revival* (Bloomington, Ind.: Quarry Books, 2004); Archie Green, *Only a Miner: Studies in Recorded Coal-Mining Songs* (Urbana: University of Illinois Press, 1972); Tony Russell, *Country Music Records: A Discography, 1921–1942* (New York: Oxford University Press, 2004), and *Country Music Originals: The Legends and the Lost* (New York: Oxford University Press, 2007); David Whisnant, *All That Is Native and Fine: The Politics of Culture in an American Region* (Chapel Hill: University of North Carolina Press, 1983); Bob Dylan, *Chronicles: Volume One* (New York: Simon and Schuster, 2004); Bess Lomax Hawes, *Sing It Pretty: A Memoir* (Urbana: University of Illinois Press, 2008); Benjamin Filene, *Romancing the Folk: Public Memory and American Roots Music* (Chapel Hill: University of North Carolina Press, 2000); Shelly Romalis, *Pistol Packin' Mama: Aunt Molly Jackson and the Politics of Folksong* (Urbana: University of Illinois Press, 1999); Loyal Jones, *Minstrel of the Appalachians: The Story of Bascom Lamar Lunsford* (Boone, N.C.: Appalachian Consortium Press, 1984); Dave Van Ronk with Elijah Wald, *The Mayor of MacDougal Street: A Memoir* (New York: Da Capo Press, 2005); Peter D. Goldsmith, *Making People's Music: Moe Asch and Folkways Records* (Washington, D.C.: Smithsonian Institution Press, 1998); Neil V. Rosenberg, *Bluegrass: A History* (Urbana: University of Illinois Press, 1985), and *Transforming Tradition: Folk Music Revivals Examined* (Urbana: University of Illinois Press, 1993); Nolan Porterfield, *The Last Cavalier: The Life and Times of John A. Lomax, 1867–1948* (Urbana: University of Illinois Press, 1996); Richard D. Smith, *Can't You Hear Me Callin': The Life of Bill Monroe, the Father of Bluegrass* (New York: Da Capo Press, 2000); Thomas Goldstein, ed., *The Bluegrass Reader* (Urbana: University of Illinois Press, 2004); Tom Ewing, ed., *The Bill Monroe Reader* (Urbana: University of Illinois Press, 2000); Mark Zwonitzer with Charles Hirshberg, *Will You Miss Me When I'm Gone? The Carter Family and*

Their Legacy in American Music (New York: Simon and Schuster, 2002); Karl Hagstrom Miller, *Segregating Sound: Inventing Folk and Pop Music in the Age of Jim Crow* (Durham, N.C.: Duke University Press, 2010); Patrick Huber, *Linthead Stomp: The Creation of Country Music in the Piedmont South* (Chapel Hill: University of North Carolina Press, 2008); Hazel Dickens and Bill C. Malone, *Working Girl Blues: The Life and Music of Hazel Dickens* (Urbana: University of Illinois Press, 2008); and Robert S. Cantwell, *When We Were Good: The Folk Revival* (Harvard University Press, 1996), the most insightful account yet written of the revival.

The Web is a new resource for me, but it will be noted that I have utilized it often in this manuscript. It was a delightful revelation to find that I could actually hear Mike Seeger in concert at such venues as Oberlin College—and of course on YouTube, MP3, and other music sites. I was also able to hear and see the documentaries *Talking Feet* and *Homemade American Music*. Of course, I also found enormously helpful websites such as those maintained by Peggy Seeger (which included the virtual autobiography of Ruth Seeger assembled by Judith Tick) and Mike Seeger. Mike's and the New Lost City Ramblers discographies appear on their websites, the Smithsonian-Folkways website, and also on those devoted to the Grateful Dead and Bob Dylan. Numerous journal articles, book excerpts, advertisements of shows, concerts, recordings, reviews, biographies of musicians, and other assorted data appear all over the Web.

Selected Works by Mike Seeger

These and other works made or produced by Mike Seeger,
along with the LPs that he made with the New Lost City Ramblers,
are listed on his website or on the Smithsonian Folkways website.

Recordings and DVDs

Always Been a Rambler—The New Lost City Ramblers. A film by Yasha Aginsky. Arhoolie
Foundation, 2009. DVD.

American Folksongs for Children. With Peggy Seeger. Rounder, 1977. Two-CD set.

Animal Folksongs for Children—And Other People. With Penny, Barbara, and Peggy Seeger
and others. Rounder, 1992.

Early Southern Guitar Sounds. Smithsonian Folkways, 2007.

50 Years: Where Do You Come From? Where Do You Go? With the New Lost City Ramblers.
Smithsonian Folkways, 2009. Three-CD set.

40 Years of Concert Recordings. With the New Lost City Ramblers. Rounder, 2001.
Two-CD set.

Retrograss. With David Grisman and John Hartford. Acoustic Disc, 1999.

Solo: Oldtime Country Music. Rounder, 1991.

Southern Banjo Sounds. Smithsonian Folkways, 1998.

There Ain't No Way Out. With the New Lost City Ramblers. Smithsonian Folkways, 1997.

Third Annual Farewell Reunion. With twenty-three assorted musicians and bands.
Rounder, 1994.

True Vine. Smithsonian Folkways, 2003.

Way Down in North Carolina. With Paul Brown. Rounder, 1996.

Music and Dance Documentation

Close to Home: Old Time Music from Mike Seeger's Collection, 1952–1967. Smithsonian
Folkways, 1997.

Talking Feet: Solo Southern Dance: Flatfoot, Buck and Tap. Smithsonian Folkways,
1984/2006. DVD.

Instructional DVDs

Early Southern Guitar Styles. Homespun Tapes, 2008. Two-DVD set.

Guitar Styles of the Carter Family. With Janette Carter. Homespun Tapes, 2000.

Old-Time Banjo Styles. With Etta Baker, Greg Hooven, Kirk Sutphin, and Joe and Odell Thompson. Homespun Tapes, 1994.

Southern Banjo Styles. Homespun Tapes, 2000, 2001, 2002. Three-volume set of DVDs with tabs and detailed notes.

Index

hood of, 12, 14; on Composers' Collective, 19; Thomas Hart Benton and, 20; influence on Ralph Rinzler, 60; on Jimmie Rodgers, 89, 192 (n. 31); Archie Green and, 96; *American Industrial Ballads*, 120; Alexia Smith and, 155–56; Library of Congress tribute to Seeger family and, 165; Ruth Seeger and, 165; performs with Mike and Peggy Seeger, 165–66; on Woody Guthrie, 192 (n. 31)

Seeger, Ruth Crawford, 21, 49, 59; folk music and, 9, 18–19, 25–26, 85–86, 90, 124; childhood and early life of, 15–17; career of, 16–17, 25–26, 164–65, 165, 179–80 (n. 46), 180 (nn. 48, 49, 50); Mike and, 27–33, 36, 37, 41, 162; illness and death of, 50–51, 144

Seeger, Sally Parsons, 10

Seeger, Toshi, 85, 100

"Serves Them Fine," 91–92, 95

Sevenoaks School, 116

Shahn, Ben, 91, 101

Shanklin, Bob, 62–64

Shanty Boys, 67

Sharp, Cecil, 9, 24, 86

Shelton, Robert, 101–2

Sherrill, Homer "Pappy," 71

Shines, Johnny, 132, 137

Short Sisters, 165

Shuffler, George, 109, 128

Shultz, Arnold, 152

Siegmeister, Elie, 18–19, 29

Silver Spring, Md., 29–36

Sing Out! (magazine), 62, 80, 113–14, 142

"Sittin' on the Dock of the Bay," 153

"Sixteen Tons," 124

Skaneateles Festival, 163

Skiffle, 64

Skillet Lickers, 81, 88, 105

Sky River Rock Festival and Lighter than Air Fair, 127–28

Smiley, Red, 58, 59

Smith, Alexia, 155–57, 156–57, 160, 163–64, 167, 168, 169, 174

Smith, Arthur, 66, 75

Smith, Curly, 45, 46

Smith, Harry, 47. See also *Anthology of American Folk Music*

Smith, Hobart, 157–58

Smith, Slim, 92

Smithsonian Folk-Life Company, 135

Smithsonian National Folklife Festival, 113, 123, 135–36, 140, 151

Snow, Hank, 3, 57

Snow, Kilby, 74–75, 103, 122, 188 (n. 44), 197 (n. 18)

"Snow Dove," 64

Socialism, 13

Society for American Music, 165, 166

"Soldier's Joy," 80, 189–90 (n. 8)

Solo—Oldtime Country Music (CD), 157–58

Song Catcher, 162–63

Songs from the Depression (LP), 91–92, 191 (n. 22)

Sounds of the South: A Musical Journey from the Georgia Sea Islands to the Mississippi Delta (CD), 194 (n. 63)

South, the: popularity of old-time music in, 102–3; *Tipple, Loom, and Rail: Songs of the Industrialization of the South* and, 119–20; Southern Folklore Project and, 131–34; the "True Vine" and, 137; dancing in, 151

Southern Banjo Sounds (CD), 159

Southern Broadcasters, 143, 201 (n. 65)

Southern Folk Cultural Revival Project, 113, 131–34

Southern Folk Festival, 131–34

Southern Folk Heritage Series (LP), 194 (n. 63)

Southern Student Organizing Committee, 131

Southern Tenant Farmers Union, 178 (n. 35)

Spottswood, Richard, 43, 45, 46–47, 58, 59, 71, 94

Sprout Wings and Fly (film), 143

Sprung, Roger, 43, 67, 69

St. Marie, Buffy, 115

Stanford University, 101, 163